CATHOLIC ART AND CULTURE

RHEIMS, WEST DOOR, A.D. 1250

The figures include Solomon and the Queen of Sheba, and St. Nicaise,
Bishop of Rheims, beheaded by the Vandals between two angels.

CATHOLIC ART
AND CULTURE

By

E. I. WATKIN

REVISED EDITION

WITH 41 ILLUSTRATIONS

LONDON
HOLLIS & CARTER
1947

First published . . *1942*
New illustrated edition . *1947*

THIS BOOK IS PRODUCED IN COMPLETE CONFORMITY WITH
AUTHORIZED ECONOMY STANDARDS AND MADE
AND PRINTED IN GREAT BRITAIN FOR
HOLLIS AND CARTER LTD.

TO
MY DEAR DAUGHTER
MAGDALEN

NOTE

This study of Catholic Culture is deeply indebted to the work of Christopher Dawson, in particular to his "Making of Europe" and "Medieval Religion." To the Rev. Cuthbert King, S.J., I am indebted for valuable information relative to the art of the catacombs, among other things, the reference to Kaufmann's textbook.

E. I. W.

CONTENTS

LIST OF ILLUSTRATIONS

THE CLASSICAL AUTUMN
THE CHRISTIAN SPRING

" SEEK ye first the Kingdom of God . . . and all these things
shall be added unto you." The Gospel did not propose
to create a new culture or regenerate an old. Its purpose
was to set up a Kingdom of redeemed souls to share the
supernatural life of God, on earth by grace, hereafter in glory.
With the exception of St. Paul, the Apostles were uncultivated
men, uneducated fishermen or men little above them in
social position, and, though St. Paul was educated in the
rabbinical schools, he wished to know nothing save Christ
crucified, counting all else loss for Him and disprizing the
wisdom of secular philosophy. The primitive Christians
were convinced that their " citizenship was in heaven " and
that " here they had no abiding city," no roots therefore in
the city of classical antiquity, in its life, its culture, its buildings
and its works of art. " As the servants of God," wrote Hermas
in his *Shepherd*, " you are living in a strange country, for
your city is far from this city. If then you know your city,
in which you are going to dwell, why do you here prepare
lands and costly establishments and buildings and vain
dwellings ? Do you not understand that all these things
are foreign to you and are under the power of another ? "
Such spiritual aliens will care as little for the thought, the
literature and the art, in short the culture, of the earthly city.

Moreover, the culture and art of the ancient world seemed
indelibly stamped with the pagan religion which had inspired
them and which they served. For a purely secular culture
is a portent reserved for the modern world. Every culture
of antiquity was a religion-culture, a culture, that is to say,
dominated and inspired by a religion. And the religion
which had created the classical culture into which Christianity
was born was the idolatrous polytheism which the early
Christians hated as warmly and as indiscriminately as had

I

the Jews before them. It is the destruction, not the re-
generation, of the classical order with all its cultural and
artistic achievements to which the Apocalypse looks forward
with such longing. As for creating a new religion-culture,
a Christian religion-culture, to replace the pagan, what time
was there for this when at any moment Christ might return
and bring the present world to a close ? When Tertullian
rejected with scorn the wisdom of Greek philosophy, the Stoa
and the Academy, his angry rhetoric voiced the attitude still
most common in the Church. The language, whether Greek
or Latin, of the inscriptions in the catacombs is uneducated
and ungrammatical. The oldest Latin version of scripture
and the earliest Latin liturgical texts are written not in the
polished and grammatical language of the classical masters
but in a rough popular Latin that would have disgusted them
as much as it did those Renaissance purists who asked leave
to say their office in Greek lest the bad Latin might injure
their style. Though the Church contained members of every
class, even before the first century closed of the Imperial
family, it was chiefly composed of the lower middle class,
superior slaves and freedmen, petty artisans, and small shop-
keepers. The social status of Pope Callistus, a former slave
whose master had put him in charge of a bank, was that of
the majority of Christians. The members of the primitive
Church belonged in the main to the same class, from which
in England and Wales the Nonconformist sects have drawn
their membership. And this lower middle class has always
and everywhere been more distinguished for propriety of
conduct than for culture.

Moreover, as a spiritual and a supernatural religion,
Christianity did not embody the horizontal movement of
the human mind which finds expression in secular knowledge,
in culture and in art, a movement in harmony with the
deification by the pagan nature religions of natural forces
and human powers. It embodied the vertical movement
upward to God, downward to the depths of the soul, the
movement that would find classical utterance in Augustine's
dictum that he wished to know God and the soul and if he
knew them would gain nothing by knowing anything besides.
This more or less exclusive and always unbalanced vertical
direction of thought and interest was inevitable and therefore

beneficial, if supernatural religion were to assert itself against pagan naturalism and humanism. But while Christianity was at death-grips with the latter, battling for victory even at the cost of martyrdom, it could not do justice to the abiding value and truth of the horizontal movement, to nature, philosophy, culture, science, and art. And its stern rejection of all save the unum necessarium reinforced with a religious Puritanism the temperamental Puritanism of a class which is the least open to the appeal of beauty, the least interested in the things of the mind.

The Theatre was condemned indiscriminately. The *Apostolic Tradition* of Hippolytus forbids an actor converted to Christianity to continue such, and what is even more significant it permits a convert to remain a teacher, to " teach children worldly " (secular) " knowledge " only if he can earn his living in no other way. This proscription proves that at any rate influential circles in the Church, represented here by a leading Roman teacher and antipope, regarded secular learning and literature as irredeemably idolatrous. And centuries later Pope Gregory the Great was of the same mind when he condemned a bishop for teaching " grammar," that is to say classical literature.

Nevertheless the principle of a new culture and art was implicit from the first in the New Religion. However supernatural and other-worldly it may be, every religion is the religion of men living in a human society and therefore in some degree of contact with a cultural and artistic environment, and containing in their own human nature the potentialities whence culture and art arise. Nor can a world religion be confined to hermits. It was the Christian mission to mix with the world, to leaven and convert it. This made it necessary to address possible converts in language intelligible to them, through ideas and images bearing the stamp of the culture to which they owed their origin. And these concepts and images in turn must influence the presentation and understanding of the new religion. St. Paul might reject the wisdom of worldly philosophy and find the simple preaching of Christ crucified more fruitful in Corinth than his attempt to connect Christianity with the noblest Hellenic thought had proved at Athens. Nevertheless he was " a debtor to the Gentile as well as the Jew " and " made himself all things to all men." And he wrote the charter of Christian humanism, when he wrote " all that is true, all that is seemly, all that is just, all that is pure, all that is loveable, all that is winning, whatever is virtuous or praiseworthy—let such things fill your thoughts." [1]

Moreover, the religion of the Incarnation, the religion which taught the deification of humanity in Christ and the resurrection of the body could not be confined to the vertical movement, however it might predominate. In principle everything human save sin had been sanctified by God made Man, who might truly have said of Himself the famous words of the Latin dramatist, " Homo sum et nihil humanum a me alienum puto." " I am a Man and nothing human is alien to Me." Obviously the immediate interest of the apostolic and subapostolic Christians and their understanding and application of Christianity, necessarily restricted to the essential message of their faith, could not exhaust its significance or be its only mode of operation. The belief that the end of the world was at hand, so that the entire fashion of this world was passing away, could not long survive the refutation of the event. Even so the New Testament, in spite, or was it not because ? of its writers' carelessness of literary effect, represented a high and a novel literary achievement. If St. Luke was not the artist of the brush that later legend depicted him, he was a consummate artist of the pen. Though St. Paul's style is difficult, often confused and scarcely grammatical, it attained a torrential force as of the flow of burning lava and contains passages of sublime eloquence, the sublimer because unstudied, such as his hymn of charity and his paean over defeated death.

And the future wedlock between Greek philosophy and Christian theology was already begun by St. John's Prologue of the Logos. Everything in fact that the evangelist says of the Word unincarnate would be accepted later by a Neoplatonic thinker—a Hellenist to the backbone, as stating his own philosophy.

Most of the scanty subapostolic literature is, it is true, mediocre in quality. But St. Ignatius' letter to the Romans rises to a noble eloquence in its praise of martyrdom for Christ's love. It is far more moving than Tacitus' accounts of the political martyrdoms of those Stoics who, inspired by belated

[1] Philippians, 4. 8, trs. Westminster Version.

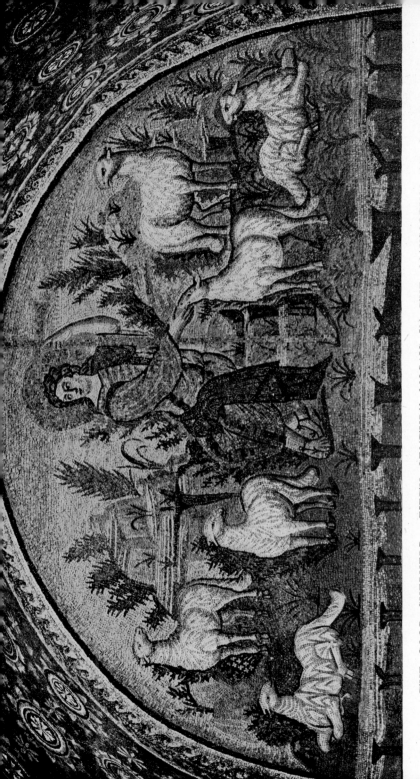

THE GOOD SHEPHERD: FIFTH CENTURY MOSAIC IN THE MAUSOLEUM OF GALLA
PLACIDIA, RAVENNA; A DAUGHTER OF THEODORUS THE GREAT

"The beginnings of Christian art are dominated by the figure of the Good Shepherd."

CHURCH OF ST. PRASSEDE, ROME

Built upon the site of a small oratory founded by Pope Pius (A.D. 150) as a place of security for early Christians in times of persecution.

regrets for a vanished republic, opposed the Emperor to their destruction.

The exaggerated estimate which bore the Shepherd of Hermas to the threshold of the Canon has been succeeded by an unjust depreciation. The visions of this second-century Roman prophet of Divine Pardon have the beauty of a fine day in early spring when we are aware even sensibly of the life rising again in the veins of plants, when the crocus foretells the rose, and a few early buds are the pledge of summer's future luxury. In these visions of Hermas we discern the rising sap of a future Christian culture to be inspired by the new life of this supernatural spring. There is an austere joy in the Shepherd, a purity warm with the love of God, a child's confidence in the Divine mercy that predict the abundant harvest of a Catholic holiness. As Hermas walks along a country road " glorifying the creation of God for its greatness and splendour and might," or sits alone on a hillside keeping his fast, he looks forward to St. Francis walking among these fields of Italy with his gospel of nature redeemed and sanctified. " The God of the powers by His mighty power and by His great wisdom created the world and by His glorious counsel surrounded His creation with beauty. . . . Lo, He changes the heavens and the mountains and the hills and the seas and all things are becoming smooth for His chosen." These words of promise read to Hermas by the Lady who represents the Church were no doubt understood too literally of an approaching physical transformation of the earth. But they convey a sense of that rising sap of which I have just spoken, the sap of a spiritual renovation with its fulfilled promise of a new world of culture and art, of thought and poetry, the religion-culture of Catholic Christendom. The same joy of new life and nature rejuvenated in Christ is sensible in the scene where the Maidens around the Tower, another symbol of the Church, who themselves represent the Christian virtues, receive Hermas into their merry company. They " began to lead me round the Tower and to play with me. I too had as it were become young again and began to play with them myself. For some were dancing, others were gavotting, others were singing and I walked in silence with them round the Tower and was merry with them." It is Fra Angelico's picture of Paradise painted in words more than a millennium earlier. "Every joyful man does good deeds and has good thoughts and despises grief. But the mournful man grieves the Holy Spirit which is given to man in joyfulness. For the intercession of the mournful man has nowhere power to ascend to the altar of God . . . the grief which is mixed with his intercession does not permit the intercession to ascend in purity to the altar. Therefore purify yourself from this wicked grief and you shall live to God and all shall live to God who cast away from themselves grief and put on all joyfulness." [1] This is the world renewing joy of a spiritual spring pregnant with cultural and artistic promise. If there was Puritanism in the primitive Church, it was a joyful austerity, not the sourness that kills joy and hates life. Christian wisdom will not always be so joyful. For Christendom will prove a disillusionment, as well as a fulfilment of this hope of a new world.

Willow shoots severed from the parent tree and apparently dry revive when watered. They are souls severed by sin from the Divine Law, the new Christian law, "God's Son preached to the ends of the earth," but revived by pardoning grace. "This tree is a willow and is a species tenacious of life. If then the sticks be planted and receive a little moisture, many of them will live." Here once more we are aware of the new life potent and therefore patient, strong to survive and overcome the assaults of evil, and now rising in the world as the sap in branches seemingly dead, to make its presence felt in the swelling and opening buds.

The Shepherd of Hermas is in truth a prophecy, the prophecy of the Christian spring to an "unawakened earth," of a culture to be created by the life-giving Spirit. The renewal is in fact symbolised, though unintentionally, by the progressive rejuvenation of the Church as she appears to Hermas in successive visions.

Hermas' Shepherd was the Angel of repentance. But the Shepherd is normally Divine, as for example in a vision of St. Perpetua the martyr, Our Lord, the Good Shepherd. And this brings us to the first beginnings of Christian art. For they are dominated by the figure of the Good Shepherd. Not as in Byzantine art Christ reigning in glory, nor as in medieval art the Crucified, but the Good Shepherd presides

[1] These translations from the *Shepherd* are by Pr. Kirsopp Lake (Loeb edition of the Apostolic Fathers).

over the catacombs where, beneath the earth, Christian art put out its first tender growth. He is no reminiscence of the actual figure of Our Lord, as He walked the earth, a figure which faded at once from the memory of a Church that with St. Paul would no longer "know Him after the flesh." He is an idealised figure of classic type, young and beardless, deliberately conceived after the pattern of Hermes Kriophoros or Orpheus. The latter indeed will even be depicted as His representative. The motive was no doubt concealment, as when the persecuted Japanese Christians disguised the Madonna under the lineaments of Kwanon, the Buddhist Mother of mercy. But the choice witnesses to at least a subconscious sense of affinity, a perception that the Shepherd Hermes and Orpheus were prototypes of the Divine Shepherd and Orpheus moreover of Him who by the music of His Gospel was taming the savage hearts of men and laying the world beneath His spell.[1]

Here already, be it with an intention at first of mere prudence, Christianity had made the contact with classical art, which would end in its baptism. The Catacomb artists worked in the convention of contemporary classical painting. They simplified outlines and reduced accessories to bring out the teaching they sought to convey. For, as Dom Leclerc shows,[2] the aim of their art was not aesthetic, not therefore strictly artistic, but religious and moral, to instruct and to edify. In execution accordingly, they fall short of contemporary pagan art. But whereas the latter was dilettante, the amusement of cultured wealth, the new truth which Christian art sought to convey brought with it a new life. It is no doubt true, as Dom Leclerc points out, that the figure of the Shepherd sacrifices the proportions of the human form, by overbalancing with the sheep on his shoulders the upper, as opposed to the lower, portion of the body. But in spite of this justifiable criticism he cannot withhold his admiration of a third-century statue of the Good Shepherd in the Lateran museum. Unfortunately the head of the sheep has been badly restored so that it no longer returns the look of love on the Shepherd's face. But that love is not the weak sentimentality which has been mistaken for divine love

[1] Compare the etymological connection between ' Pan ' and ' pastor '—each of which means the feeder, the Shepherd.

[2] *Dictionaire d'Archéologie Chrétienne.*

by those responsible for the modern equivalent of the Good Shepherd, the statue of the Sacred Heart.

The Shepherd has a dignity, a restraint, a physical comeliness which look back to the Hellenic divinity, forward to the great achievements of Christian art. As a result probably of technical incompetence many, perhaps most, representations in the Catacombs of the Good Shepherd are of mediocre quality. But there emerges the typical figure of a youth more frequently beardless and slim. And on occasion, though more often on sarcophagi of later date, the artist has presented the ideal Shepherd of Christian devotion, " the comely youth, tall and refined, graceful and slender " . . . the " divine ephebus " whom Dom Leclerc with enthusiastic exaggeration regards as normal.[1] It is still widely believed by neopagans that " the pale Galilean " banished from a " world grown grey " the radiant Apollo. In fact, it is as a youth, a Hermes refined and spiritualised that the Galilean makes His first appearance in the field of art.

The Classical dislike for scenes of horror was reinforced among the early Christians by their sense of redemption and rebirth to a new life immortal and divine. Throughout these first centuries of savage persecution, representations of torment are banished from Christian art. Save for a solitary picture of the Crowning with thorns the Passion is not represented.[2] The Crucifixion is depicted only on two or three gems, of purely individual choice and possibly Gnostic. The public art of the Church was even more averse to representing the suffering of her Lord than modern Catholic art to representing His risen glory. There are a number of symbolic scenes from the Gospel, scenes of healing or resurrection from the dead, and always and everywhere the Good Shepherd, youthful and strong, bearing home in triumph His sheep, the soul He has saved. " Rejoice with Me for I have found the sheep that was lost." But there is no Passion. Even Good Friday was kept only as a fast in preparation for the Easter festival.[3]

---

[1] *Dictionaire d'Archéologie Chrétienne*, ii. 291.

[2] Another possible exception is the cross (?) of a domestic shrine excavated at Herculaneum.

[3] Hippolytus however prescribes hours of prayer in honour of the Passion. (Apostolic Tradition xxxvi.) And the sign of the cross was in constant use.

As the centuries advance and persecution is succeeded by external triumph, it will be very different. Gradually the Crucified and the torments of Martyrdom will occupy the field of Christian iconography, scenes also of torment in hell or in purgatory. For the world will have entered the Church and will have proved itself the old unregenerate world. No longer will the Church identify herself so confidently with the new world of the Resurrection in which her members are risen with Christ. Rather will she see with Pascal " Christ in agony until the end of the world " suffering in His sinful and suffering body. When some Dominican postulants giggled nervously during Compline and a friar rebuked them, Blessed Jordan of Saxony said to the young men, " Laugh on. You may well laugh for you have escaped from the devil who formerly held you in bondage. Laugh away, dear sons." In a baptised world, only those who had escaped to a religious order could laugh with this sense of redeemed security. When the world persecuted the Church the entire Church was felt as a refuge from it, where men could laugh, because in Christ they had been redeemed and reborn to a life of fellowship with Him.

The peaceful happy art of the catacombs reflects the austere happiness and the spiritual joy that would later be almost reserved for religious communities observant and fervent. The *Tradition* of Hippolytus expects from the ordinary Christian married and unmarried daily prayers at the canonical hours, among them midnight and cockcrow, the observance to-day only of the most austere religious houses. And Wednesday and Friday were observed until sunset as rigid fasts from liquid as well as from solid food. But in and through the austerity there was serenity and joy. " Thanks be to God," says Perpetua in a vision, " as I was merry in the flesh, so am I now still merrier here." " Laugh on, dear sons and daughters." In this spring of a new world all things were made new. It was indeed this conception of the Church as a religious order of truly regenerate souls that made the subapostolic Church so loath to admit the possibility of mortal sins after baptism and apply the power of the keys to their pardon. It was an impracticable severity and an untenable reluctance But this view of the Church as a holy society redeemed from the world makes it intelligible. To conquer the world the Church must stoop to the world. But she has never ceased to look back wistfully to the days when as a persecuted minority she could stand erect with head unbowed.

There is, it is true, in the art of the catacombs a monotonous repetition of the same subjects, a few scenes of deliverance from the Old Testament, a few scenes from the New, a few symbols and a few decorative motifs derived from contemporary art. But Christian art of every period, indeed the art of every religion-culture, tends to the monotonous repetition of a few themes. Of the host of vegetable forms which the illuminator could have depicted, only a few appear in fifteenth-century manuscripts from many countries. The strawberry, the pink, the daisy, the rose, and three or four conventional blossoms hard to identify botanically, these wellnigh exhaust the flora of a book of hours. The law of inertia operating in a society of conservative temper tends to confine artists to a few subjects, motifs and methods of treatment.

Moreover, an educational art intended for simple and uneducated people must employ that constant repetition which is the "secret" of successful propaganda, a secret not discovered for the first time by the modern advertiser and political propagandist.

Side by side with the Shepherd is a female figure, the Orante. Standing upright she raises her hands in prayer. It is the gesture of classical prayer, pagan and Christian, the sole attitude of prayer the Nicene Council will permit during Paschaltide, and which still survives for the Priest in the Canon of the Mass. It is indeed a noble gesture, the gesture befitting a man restored in Christ to the dignity of God's adopted son addressing a son's prayer to His Heavenly Father.[1] The Orante has been mistaken for a symbol of the Church.[1] And, in truth, before devotion to Our Lady could safely develop, the Church, as we may gather from Hermas, the Second Epistle of Clement and the Apocalypse, took an analogous place in Christian imagination as Christ's mystical Mother and Bride [2] and the Mother of His Christian brethren.

[1] In the opinion of C. M. Kaufman (Handbuch der Chr. Archaeologie) the Church is in some instances possibly intended. But this was not the normal significance of the symbol.

[2] Mother because the Church was envisaged as continuous with the Jewish Church she succeeded.

It is not easy to determine exactly the meaning of the Orante. In the opinion of recent archaeologists she represents the departed soul in the bliss of heaven. The hands are raised in prayer either to adore or more probably to intercede for the faithful, relatives in particular and friends, left behind on earth.

We could wish that both the Good Shepherd and the Orante might be restored to Catholic art, that is, if we could be certain they would not be sentimentalised.

As Dom Leclerc has pointed out, the themes of catacomb art, like the Christian liturgy itself, were largely determined by the formulas employed by the synagogue, which moreover did not then ban pictorial decoration so rigidly as it has banished it later. But the artistic treatment was never Jewish. At first, indeed, there was nothing but mere decoration, the decorative motifs of contemporary pagan art in the contemporary pagan style, and probably the work of pagan artists. There is nothing Jewish in the figures depicted in catacomb frescoes. The Apocalypse whose imagery betrays the oriental love of gold and precious stones had no influence on early Christian art. In art, in poetry, and in liturgical formulas, and in the vision of St. Satyrus, St. Perpetua's companion, which of course derived its imagery from his environment, heaven is depicted not as by John, as a city of gold and gems, but as " a garden having rose trees and all kinds of flowers. . . . The height of the trees was like the height of a cypress whose leaves sang without ceasing. We crossed a place strewn with violets." [1] Heaven is the garden of a Roman villa, or the green pasture " amoena virentia " where the Shepherd feeds His flock.

This tradition of a heavenly pleasaunce will survive into the sterner religion of the Dark Ages. It is the theme of the lovely hymn ' Ad perennis vitae fontem ' in which the austere Peter Damiani pictures a delight in spring flowers he would hardly have permitted himself on earth.

The contact, made for practical or precautionary reasons with classical art, was deliberately effected with classical thought in Alexandria by a group of Christians who, under the influence of that melting pot of cultures where Judaism had already Hellenised, rejected the normal Christian attitude to heathen wisdom. Towards the close of the second century

[1] Acts of Perpetua and Felicitas, XII.

the catechetical school of Alexandria produced in Clement a teacher who saw in Greek philosophy the counterpart of Jewish prophecy as a preparation for the Gospel. What Moses was for the Jews, Plato was for the Gentiles. " Perchance philosophy was given to the Greeks till the Lord should call the Greeks. For it was a schoolmaster to bring the Hellenic mind, as the law the Hebrews, to Christ. Philosophy was paving the way for him who is perfected in Christ." [1] The belief, already held by hellenising Judaism, that Plato had borrowed from Moses made this attitude easier to adopt. But it was in fact determined by Clement's appreciation of the profound spiritual truth contained in Platonism. Henceforward Christianity and Platonism would never be put asunder. Clement was also attracted by the Stoic philosophy, excessively indeed, for, strangely forgetful of Our Lord's agony in the garden, he held up its impossible and inhuman lack of feeling, " apatheia," as the mark of the Christian sage.

The austerity recommended by Clement is the austerity of the Greek philosopher rather than the Christian ascetic. Though he condemns the wearing of garlands he allows us to enjoy the scent and beauty of flowers. " Do not encircle my head with a crown, for in the springtime it is delightful to wile away the time on the dewy meads, while soft and many coloured flowers are in bloom, and like the bees, enjoy a natural and pure fragrance." This is not the language of an Antony or a Peter Damiani. " As beauty, so also the flower delights when looked at ; and it is meet to glorify the Creator by the enjoyment of the sight of beautiful objects." [2] This is aesthetic delight in beauty for its own sake, its enjoyment regarded as praise of the Creator. The principle here enunciated is the title deed of Christian art. In the autumn of Christian culture we shall meet again, in Yves de Paris, a worthy son of St. Francis, this frank enjoyment of natural beauty and in particular the scent of flowers which Clement, following his Master's praise of the lilies, was the first to express in its early spring.

Clement's attitude and work were continued by his successor, a thinker of far greater genius, Origen. Origen lets

---

[1] *Stromata,* 7. 5, trs. Wilson.
[2] *Paedagogus,* I, II, 8, trs. Wilson.

BASILICA OF SAN LORENZO FUORI LE MURA, FOUNDED BY CONSTANTINE ABOUT A.D. 330 AND ENLARGED IN THE FIFTH AND SIXTH CENTURIES

One of the seven foundation churches of Constantine and one of the seven pilgrimage churches. The classical pillars in the Ionic style were taken from earlier Roman buildings.

THE REDEEMER :

CHURCH OF S. APOLLINARE NUOVO, RAVENNA. SIXTH CENTURY MOSAIC

" Enthroned aloft, to receive the adoration of His earthly in unison with His heavenly courtiers, was the Majestic Figure of Christ, Emperor of the World, as He was depicted in the mosaic of apse or dome."

his dissatisfaction with the narrow and unintellectual religion of the average Christian plainly appear. Indeed I think it possible that it even led to a temporary alienation from the faith, for which as a boy he longed to suffer martyrdom. This at least is the obvious implication of a passage in his *Periarchon* which has been surprisingly overlooked. " There are many among Greeks and barbarians alike who promise us the truth and yet we gave up seeking for it from all who claimed it for false opinions AFTER WE HAD COME TO *Believe* that Christ was the Son of God and had become convinced that we must learn the truth from Him." [1]

However this may be, he certainly sat under Ammonius Saccas, the philosopher who, whether or not he had already abandoned Christianity, was later the teacher of Plotinus and presumably therefore the father of Neoplatonism. Pagans such as Porphyry were surprised and perhaps disconcerted to remark in Origen the combination of a wide and sympathetic knowledge of Greek philosophy and a Hellenic intellectual temper with a devout Christianity. It was Origen who first attempted a systematic exposition of Christian doctrine making use, for that purpose, of Greek philosophy. His *Periarchon* anticipates by a millennium the *Summa Theologica*. A pioneer in a field so difficult had no prospect of success. Christian theology was far too undeveloped to employ with safety the double-edged weapons of pagan wisdom.

For Origen, as for Clement before him, Christ is rather the Teacher than the Redeemer. And their ideal identifies too closely the saint and the sage. Indeed Origen's picture of heavenly bliss was largely the satisfaction of his desire for astronomical knowledge, Virgil's desire " rerum cognoscere causas . . . caeli vias et sidera . . . defectus solis varios lunaeque labores," " To understand the causes of phenomena . . . the ways of heaven and the stars—the eclipses of the sun and the moon's changing phases." " When

---

[1] Origen appears to use the first person singular and plural interchangeably in reference to himself. It is difficult to see to whom the latter can otherwise refer in this passage. When I first called attention to it in my *Men and Tendencies* (p. 171), I supported my interpretation by a dubious identification of the Christian Origen with the Origen who was Plotinus' fellow-student under Ammonius Saccas. But, however that may be, Origen's words retain their force. What else can they mean when used by the son of Christian parents ?

the saints have reached the heavenly places they will
see clearly the nature of the stars one by one . . . For
God will show to them as to sons the causes of things . . .
teaching them why one star is placed in its particular
position in the sky and why it is separated from another
by so great an interval of space ; what would happen
if it were nearer or farther away ; or if this star had
been greater than that." [1]   Though we cannot think of the
Astronomer Royal as enjoying the bliss of the saints, the
passage is a striking proof of Origen's enthusiasm for knowledge, whose religious value moreover he perceives. It is
a moie Catholic attitude than Saint Augustine's when he said
that the man who knew God and his own soul would be no
better off if he knew other things, such things, for example, as
the astronomy Origen prized so dearly.

Though Origen leant heavily towards what would soon be
Neoplatonism he never knowingly rejected any portion of
Christian belief. He would not have approved the attitude
adopted by the fifth-century Christian Neoplatonist Synesius,
who, when a bishopric was thrust upon him by his fellow-
citizens, frankly informed his future metropolitan, Theophilus
of Alexandria, that on certain matters he would teach the
orthodox doctrine only for the benefit of his ignorant flock,
reserving the right to hold privately the more intelligent
doctrine of Neoplatonism. Therefore until his formal condemnation some three centuries later Origen did not lack a
school of devoted followers. And through the Cappadocians
he permanently influenced Greek theology, imparting to its
best representatives a philosophic temper and imbuing them
with a Christian humanism. Deified humanity has always been
a leitmotiv of Greek theological thought. And already in the
second century the Greek Irenaeus, teaching the recapitulation
of humanity in the new Adam and the restoration of all things
in Him, had introduced the theme to Western Christendom.

Deified humanity—it combines the utmost height and the
utmost breadth, the farthest reach of the vertical and the
farthest reach of the horizontal movement. Deification is
the highest flight of the spirit above the world and the merely
human. Humanity, the subject of deification, is the utmost
scope of human interest, comprising every aspect of human

[1] *Periarchon*, ii, ch. xi, trs. G. W. Butterworth.

life and thought. The deification of humanity is the sum of Christianity, the meaning and fulfilment of the Incarnation. In principle accomplished when the Word was made flesh its accomplishment in the Church is the history of Catholic culture and art ; but also its lack of accomplishment.

Human limitation has involved a tension between the two factors and movements which have determined the history of Christendom. The vertical movement towards God has too often conflicted with the horizontal movement of human interests and natural knowledge. And the latter in turn has reacted by weakening, even denying the former. The former demands detachment from the things of earth, the latter involves us in them. Baron Von Hugel sought a solution of the conflict which may be summarised by the formula : " A maximum of detachment, a maximum of attachment." His meaning is true, profoundly true. But his formula is misstated. For detachment and attachment are contradictions which cannot coexist. I would therefore suggest an amendment. The formula should, I suggest, be this : " A maximum of detachment, a maximum of appreciation." Far from excluding detachment, appreciation alone makes a fruitful detachment possible. There can be little spiritual profit in detachment from what we do not value. But to put the formula into practice is so difficult, that it requires the entire Church in her entire history to carry it out perfectly. Meantime the tension remains with excesses in either direction and excessive reactions against them. Detachment becomes blindness, hostility or contempt. Appreciation becomes attachment, and blindness of the other eye.

Many collects ask for grace " terrena despicere." In their author's intention " despicere " meant despise, surely an undue depreciation of God's creatures. But nothing prevents us from understanding the word " despicere " literally, in accordance with its etymology, " to look down upon." To look down on earthly things from the height of God to whom we are supernaturally united. This is Christian detachment. And for this we must pray. But what we thus see from above, need and should not therefore be undervalued. The value of earthly things is most clearly discerned from above, as contours hitherto invisible have been discovered and photographed from the air. It is from the aerial perspective of the supernature to which we are raised by Christian grace and truth, that we shall most clearly perceive the contours of culture and art spread out in the panorama of history viewed thus *sub specie eternitatis.* Christians occupied with the cultural task are apt to lose sight of the heavenly vision, and those who keep that vision in view are apt to disprize the cultural task. Hence the excesses in either direction and the abiding tension throughout the history of Christian culture.

In this pre-Nicene springtime the tension still lay in embryo. For the horizontal movement of appreciation was checked by the conditions of Christian life in a hostile world and under threat of persecution. But we descry it already in the opposition between the hellenising Alexandrines and the believers who resented any philosophising that disturbed their simple faith, and in Tertullian's vehemence against any compromise with the world and its wisdom.

The third century was distinguished by the greatest achievement of Greek philosophy since Aristotle, the work of the first and the greatest Neoplatonist, Plotinus. His philosophy was a synthesis of Platonism and Aristotelianism and in this respect akin to the later Scholasticism. But unlike the latter, it was a synthesis in which the Platonic factor was predominant. Otherwise the century was barren. Culture declined, art deteriorated and pagan literature sank almost to zero.

Christian literature also, after the fiery rhetoric of Tertullian, whose legal training impressed a legal temper and mould on Latin theology and the official dignity of Cyprian's prose, shared the decline. This retrogression of civilisation which paved the way for the final collapse of the Roman order was due to the anarchy of constant civil wars between legions pushing each the claim of its commander to the imperial throne. When the administrative genius of Diocletian restored internal order and buttressed the Empire against barbarian assaults, the cultural revival of the fourth century followed.

The failure of the last and most systematic persecution was succeeded by the conversion of Constantine and the triumph of Christianity. Henceforward Christianity would be the official creed of the Empire. The price paid was indeed heavy :

*SIXTH CENTURY
APSE MOSAIC:
CHURCH OF
S. COSMAS AND
S. DAMIAN,
ROME*

*The Saviour, with St.
Peter and St. Paul in
white togas presenting
S. Cosmas and S.
Damian. Below, the
Lamb and twelve sheep,
emblems of the Saviour
and the Apostles.*

A ROMANESQUE CHURCH: THE CLOISTERS, ST. TROPHIS-MUS, ARLES

St. Trophismus was one of the founders of the Gallic Church and this church, with its lovely cloisters and highly-decorated porch, is a product of the religious revival in Southern France, and particularly the Auvergne, which coincided with the monastic reforms of Cluny and the revival of Papal authority under the leadership of Pope Gregory the Seventh.

Erastian usurpation, imperial patronage of heresies, the unregenerate world ensconced firmly in the Church. But it is not easy to see how the Church could otherwise have won the entire Greco-Roman world and the order and the religion-culture of Catholic Europe have come into existence.

The world's invasion of the Church was answered by a powerful movement of uncompromising renunciation of the world. Contemporaneously with the conversion of the Empire, the deserts of Egypt and Syria were peopled by an army of solitaries and cenobites. They pushed asceticism to its extreme. Their labour was manual, their food the bare minimum necessary to maintain existence, their sole literature the Scriptures and spiritual writers. They represented the vertical movement as exclusively as it can be represented by men living in the flesh. The revival and subsequent fall of the Empire left them unmoved. Arsenius, once tutor to the sons of the Emperor Theodosius, refused even to administer the imperial alms. It might seem as though such men, whose citizenship was not in the earthly city, had no place in the history of culture. And in fact, the survivors of pagan Hellenism, Rutilianus for example, could see in the monks only fanatics and barbarians, the sworn foes of every grace and decency of human life.

In reality these men were the saviours of culture. For every organic, that is every living, culture, must be inspired by a religion which exercises in it a function analogous to that exercised by the soul in the living body. Without a living religion a culture perishes and disintegrates like the human body when the soul has departed. However majestic its monuments, the pagan religion was moribund. Imperial persecution did but hasten its inevitable demise. It could not therefore inspire a religion-culture.

For this the Greco-Roman world must look to Christianity. But the Christian salt was in danger of losing its savour. A Church so largely composed of worldlings, and oppressed by governments that demanded control in return for their favour, and whose episcopate included many bishops whose sole qualification was influence at court or at best capacity for the tasks of secular administration henceforward entrusted to them, could not unaided breathe into the vast body of the converted empire the breath of spiritual life. For that a spiritual power-house was needed. It was provided. It was monasticism.

If the monks fled from the world, the world pursued the monks. Emperors corresponded with ascetics of the desert. Arab tribes thronged the foot of St. Simeon's column to hear the Stylite's preaching. Many of the greatest rulers and teachers of the Church were trained by monasticism. Augustine, Chrysostom, Basil, Jerome, Martin, Gregory were monks. Monastic action extended even to social service and justice. The monks' intervention shielded Antioch from imperial vengeance and the Stylite told an Egyptian village community which sent envoys to consult him to divide fairly among its members the supply of water for irrigation. The ascent of monasticism to God raised the Church with it. Christian spirituality, ascetic and mystical, was and would continue a monastic product impregnated with the asceticism and the other-worldliness of the cloister. And the influence could not be purely one-sided. When, throughout a large portion of the Empire, civilisation foundered in the anarchy and savagery of successive barbarian invasions, culture sought and found refuge in the peaceful oases of monasticism. Art and literature were given asylum by the monks, who had rejected them for God. No doubt the balance leant heavily to the vertical and world renouncing movement. It was but the remnant of a culture which the cloister sheltered. But this also was in the interest of the Christian religion culture. Otherwise the paste of classical culture would have been too much for the Christian yeast.

Post-Nicene religious literature was heavily burdened by the necessities of doctrinal controversy. Since the number of religious truths is necessarily limited, whereas the impulse to proclaim and defend them is powerful, these writings are not free from the besetting sin of religious literature, monotonous repetition of the same themes. But they are alive with a vigorous life, pregnant with future possibilities. Moreover, precisely because it represented the vertical movement, this Christian literature explored the soul as it had not been explored in the past. Augustine's exploration of the depths of the soul in her commerce with God was the discovery of terra incognita and his *Confessions* the pioneer of a new genre of literature, the spiritual autobiography. Since the study of literature is man, the exploration of the human soul at a depth unexplored hitherto was an event of capital importance for literature, its renewal and enrichment.

The vertical movement which in its search for God had opened up the recesses of the human heart, rising aloft to the Eternal, achieved a deeper and more comprehensive vision of human history. A genuine philosophy of human history, that is a view of its course and meaning in the light of ultimate truth, was not indeed altogether new. It had been attempted by Plato, who by his spiritual and religious metaphysic was a forerunner of Christianity. But it was now attempted on a wider scale and in greater detail. Orosius composed a history of the world in the light of revelation. The detailed execution of his design was indeed crude and inadequate. What else could it be, when the material of history was so scanty, and historical criticism in its infancy? But his work inspired his friend Augustine to write his *City of God* in which he presented the history of mankind as a struggle between two societies, the City of God, the communion of souls inspired by charity who love God even to contempt of self, and the city of the devil, the society of fallen men who remain unregenerate or fall from grace and are inspired by a concupiscence which issues in love of self even to contempt of God. Whatever the excessive simplifications imposed by his polemical ardour and lack of detailed knowledge, St. Augustine's vision of history saw it not as an insignificant chaos of haphazard events, but as the product and battlefield of spiritual principles which invest every historical character and event with a lasting significance for good or evil, give each a place in the drama of human will that must choose between love and self-seeking lust, between God and the devil. In this field, also, literature was enriched with a new genre and novel perspectives were opened up to it.

And it was Christian thinkers of this age, and moreover monastic thinkers, who baptised the final achievement of Greek philosophy. Augustine, whose mind ruled Western theology for the following millennium and who had travelled to Christianity by way of Plotinus,[1] borrowed extensively from Neoplatonism in constructing his edifice of Christian thought. And Neoplatonism was incorporated even more whole-heartedly by the anonymous Eastern monk who, under

[1] As translated and interpreted by Victorinus.

the pseudonym of the Areopagite, about the year 500 gave the world a Christian version of Proclus. Even the last of the pagans, such men as the Emperor Julian and later Proclus, in their attempt to save the letter of classical religion reversed its spirit. For they hoped to save the dying religion by artificial respiration. They sought to breathe into a religion which was essentially naturalist, the worship of natural forces, the spirituality, asceticism and other-worldliness of Neoplatonism and Christianity. The ascetic Julian and the philosopher who at the university of Athens lived the " religious life " of a pagan monk were, as Professor Gilbert Murray has observed,[1] far closer to their Christian opponents than to the pagans of antiquity. Proclus did not labour in vain. For he laboured unwittingly for " Dionysius " and through him for Christian mysticism. The Cappadocian fathers, heirs as we have seen of the hellenising Origen, were more humanist than Augustine. But they too were monastic and their Hellenism material for the spiritual and transcendental religion of the cloister. Nevertheless they allowed more to the humanist factor of Christian humanism. It is surely no accident that in the cosmogony of this Cappadocian school we meet with an anticipation of transformist evolution.

Thus the religious and the religious-philosophic literature of this first period of Christendom, by which I mean a Christian society and culture, displays a vigorous and fruitful life. It takes over the latest and most synthetic achievement of Greek philosophy and explores new ground, the philosophy or rather the theology of history and the profound life of the human soul, human nature where it is supernaturalised and deified by grace. For all its unreliabilities and excesses psychoanalysis has thrown much light on the manifestations of concupiscence both as the lust for pleasure (Freud) and as the lust for power (Adler). But the psychoanalysts have not, like Augustine, penetrated to its root or seen its metaphysical, still less its theological, significance. The psychoanalyst can but cure the symptoms of concupiscence, libido as he terms it, by sublimating its manifestations. Augustine pointed out its radical cure, supernaturalisation that is sublimation above nature by the charity which replaces its direction towards self by direction towards God. Much

[1] *Four Stages of Greek Religion.*

no doubt can be learned from psychoanalytic technique and discoveries of detail. But it must be placed in the metaphysical and theological setting Augustine derived from his Christianity.

Indeed the very limitations of horizontal perspective, a scientific ignorance and lack of scientific curiosity, a view of the world narrowly restricted in time and space, concentrated the powers of the human spirit upon the vertical movement and its discoveries in the human depth and Divine height and thereby saved the human mind, limited as it is, from being prematurely overpowered by the contemplation of a space-time and magnitudes imaginatively infinite. Man was enabled to find God and himself as an immortal spirit before he was confronted with a universe and a time series which seemed to reduce him to the insignificance of his superficial position in them.

Thus Christian thought and the literature which embodied it flourished with a new vigour and sowed the seed from which the harvest of Christian thought and culture would spring hereafter.

When we turn to what we may term roughly belles lettres our impression is very different. A literary revival there certainly was during the fourth and fifth centuries. But for the barbarian conquests a permanent literary culture and tradition would doubtless have established themselves.

But would it have been Christian ? And would it have been living ? It would of course have been Christian in the sense that the writers would have been Christians. But its Christian inspiration would have been more dubious. For in fact the literary tradition of the period between the peace of the Church and the final collapse of the Roman order in the West was not Christian. It was but a revival of the old classical tradition, frankly pagan or veneered with Christianity. Nor was it living. The old and hackneyed themes are repeated and the stereotyped treatment of them.

The burden of a classical dictionary erudition, which weighed heavy even on the minor Augustans, covers and almost chokes a thinner stream of genuine inspiration. Moreover, we are, I think, conscious in this literature of the autumnal character we shall meet twelve centuries later in the baroque culture which closed the cycle of the Christian cultural year. When the spring of Christian thought was advancing towards the future summer, for literature it was late autumn. It was not the fruitful autumn of the true baroque which garnered the achievement of Christendom and lived with the Christian life of the Catholic religion-culture. But the analogy remains. This late Latin culture was baroque in its equipment of conventional learning. It was in a better sense baroque in its love for the decorations of civilised life, whatever is precious in stuff and texture, gems, furniture, the work of the goldsmith and the silversmith, marble, tapestries, embroidered robes, pictures and statues. The philosopher Boethius will look back regretfully to the ivory and glass furnishings of his library. Like the men of baroque these legatees of classical culture delighted in formal gardens laid out in squares, such as that described by Ausonius, in luxurious villas and in the milder natural beauty of a landscape tamed to man's use and subordinate to his buildings.

The Gallic poet Ausonius, raised by his pupil Gratian to the dignity of consul, was a typical representative of this baroque culture. The sincerity of the poet's Christianity has often been questioned, largely because in a poem recounting his daily occupations, he said " Satis precum datum Deo," " Enough of prayer to God." His critics forget that he continues by observing that sinners can never say enough prayers for their need. And the prayer itself is both long and unexceptionable in its sentiments. Ausonius, however, represents that vast mass of converts of sincere faith and decent living whose interests were nevertheless worldly, the baptised world of which I spoke. He simply could not understand his pupil St. Paulinus when he sold his vast estates and retired from the world where he might have played a brilliant part to live a practically, though not formally, " Religious " life at Nola. Their correspondence states the issue between the baptised world and the mighty movement of ascetic Christianity. Ausonius' heart is with the world, in his work as a writer and a teacher of literature, in his political ambitions.

The flavour of his poetry is " baroque." " You would doubt," he says, " whether the dawn stole her red from the roses or bestowed it on them and the new daylight painted the blossoms." The conceit might have been taken from any of those " baroque " poets of the seventeenth century in England, termed by Johnson, oddly enough, metaphysical.

" Cupid tormented, 'affixus cruci,' by the shades of un-
happy lovers : " the theme and treatment are those of a minor
baroque poet. Ausonius has the baroque observation of
fine shades and particularly effects of colour, the baroque
love of the picturesque. He watches the opening roses from
the first appearance of the petal through the sheaf of the
bud to their fall. In his account of the Moselle he observes
the play of light in the water and its effects on the weed, pebbles
and fishes. He speaks of the weed trembling in the current, the
pebble which shines out as a ray of light strikes it and then
is hid in darkness " lucetque latetque." His fancy toys with
the shadows in the water, shadows of men and boats, shadows
of hill and villa. Nor is the mythological machinery of nymphs
and satyrs forgotten.

It is the artificial world of a culture mature, indeed over-
ripe. How are we to account for this unexpected autumn
in the advancing spring of the Christian religion-culture ?
It does not belong to that culture, has no part in its cycle.
It is the last revival of the old classical culture, the flicker of
a candle about to expire.   In the field of culture and particularly in the field of letters the classical tradition was too
strong for the Christian spirit to master and mould.   There
was too much of the classical dough for the Christian leaven.
The matter of the Christian religion-culture would always
be in the main the classical culture inherited from Greece and
Rome.   But the Christian form could inspire and refashion
it only when its strength and volume had been reduced by the
barbarian conquests. In the sphere of philosophy annexed
by the great Christian thinkers and in ecclesiastical art [1] the
Christian spirit was sufficiently powerful and alert to subject
from the outset the classical material to its purpose, to inspire
and renew. With literature and general culture it was otherwise.
Here the classical tradition persisted substantially unchanged.
The Indian summer of the prechristian religion-culture was
contemporary with the spring of the Christian.   The worldly
Christians, even if they were bishops, represented the former,
the ascetics the latter.

The life of the Gallic nobility in fifth-century Gaul described by Sidonius Apollinaris, himself one of them, is

[1] In architecture, however, the vertical aspiration of Christianity did
not overcome the classical horizontalism of the Roman basilica.

strikingly similar to the lives of the nobility during the *ancien régime*, the baroque culture of Christian Europe. Wealthy and of literary tastes, they passed their time between sport and an artificial and dilettante culture. The luxurious villas of these millionaires were equipped with elaborate baths and embellished with gardens equally elaborate. They also possessed well-stocked libraries. But the culture of these noblemen was wholly of the past. They had no part in the active life of their age. If, however, like Sidonius, they became bishops their entire life was altered. They became the leaders of their people, and exchanged their dilettante classicism for a living theology and such philosophy as it already implied. In his introduction to a translation of Sidonius' letters Mr. Dalton notes the contrast. " There was," he writes, " no scope for active brains among the nobles except in literature. . . . But there was now within the Roman Empire an organism which drew to itself new blood and amid the general enfeeblement of old institutions grew daily in vitality. . . . The Church had a future and a present; the state had only a past." That is to say the secular society like its literature was autumnal, indeed on the verge of winter, the Church and her literature were vernal. The autumn of decaying antiquity was the springtime of Catholic Christendom.

The writings of Sidonius, both his poems and his letters, are as autumnal and as baroque as were those of Ausonius in the previous century. Even when episcopal consecration brought his life and active work into the ecclesiastical spring, his literary taste and style which he could hardly have changed in middle age remained autumnal, the precious and highly rhetorical taste and style of the classical baroque.

Even in his letters and still more in his poems Sidonius retails at length the stock repertory of classical myth and history. He employs all the mannerisms, tricks and clichés of the rhetorical schools. Mr. Dalton calls attention to his verbal conceits. And there are also conceits of the imagination. For example, he describes a tapestry representing " wild beasts . . . driven to madness by wounds skilfully feigned in red from which a blood which is no blood seems to issue " (IX, 13). P. R. Anderson, the translator of his works for the Loeb series, says of his style, " So many recherché effects had never before been found concentrated in such small space.

If he took liberties with the meaning of words that only increased the dazzling glamour of it all." And he speaks of his "forced antithesis, over-elaboration and far-fetched conceits." And Mr. Dalton calls attention to "similitudes . . . like the 'mysticus adeps' and 'spiritalis arvina'" (mystical fat and spiritual lard) which recall the startling similes of a Crashaw and a Donne. And he applies to Sidonius Johnson's criticism of the English baroque poets of the seventeenth century. In this he is as unfair to the latter as was the uncomprehending Johnson. Sidonius' baroque is seldom the living baroque they represented, but the dead baroque of later third-rate poets. But he has observed truly the baroque character of his writing. Sidonius himself praises "great opulence of words" and the "long drawn beauty of ornate diction" (IV, 3), just what the later baroque would admire. He also praises verse "All fluent and ductile . . . as when the finger glides lightly over a surface of polished crystal or onyx where there is not the slightest crack or fissure to stay its passage" (IX, 7). Here we may observe the baroque love of polish and the baroque feeling for precious stones. The same love of precious stones finds expression in his *Epithalamium for Ruricius and Hiberia*. He imagines a temple built by Vulcan. " Here is stone from five regions giving forth five hues, Aethiopian, Phrygian, Parian, Punic, Spartan-purple, green, mottled, ivory, white. The yellow glow of topaz flashes through the door-post. Porcelain, sardonyx, Caucasian amethyst, Indian jasper, Chalcidian and Scythian stones, beryl and agate, form the double doors that rise upon silver pivots and through these doors the shadowy recess beyond pours out the sheen of the emeralds that are within. Onyx thickly encrusts the threshold and hard by the blue colour of amethyst casts upon the lagoon a harmonious hue." [1] Describing a basilica built by Bishop Patiens at Lyons he speaks of it as " Bright with diverse marbles, floor, vaulting and windows all adorned with figures of most various colour and mosaic green as a blooming mead " that " shows its design of sapphire cubes through the ground of verdant glass." This delight in rich colours reminds us of the glowing tints of autumn leaves before they are stripped from the boughs by the storm or frost of winter.

[1] Trs. W. B. Anderson.

And Sidonius' baroque appreciation of effects of light, shared with Ausonius before and Fortunatus after him, is as the light of a sunny autumn day kindling this brilliant foliage. Of Patiens's basilica he writes : " Within is shining light and the gilding of the coffered ceiling allures the sunbeams golden as itself" (II, 10). In these descriptions of colour and light Sidonius is not, as too often, a poetaster and lifeless rhetorician but a genuine literary artist in the manner of the greater baroque. Describing a lake at his country villa he writes : " On the south-west the shallows along the banks look green ; overarching boughs lend the water their own hue and the water transmits it to the pebbles at the bottom " (II, 2). Of the river Gardon he says : " It looks red through its tawny gravels and glows still and pellucid over its pebbly bed " (II, 8). And in the *Epithalamium* he dwells on the sunlight in sea-water. " There emerges . . . a bay enclosed by wings of piled rocks . . . in which retreat, just as if the whole radiance of the sky were concentrated there, the daylight is gathered into a narrow space and penetrating the quivering waters it searches out the secluded depths and so the ripples pass on, bathed in deep shining brightness and, wondrous to tell, the water drinks in the sun, and the light, pushed into the limpid stream, bores unwetted through the wet with arid ray." He closes with a baroque conceit.

We observe the baroque delight in the picturesque. These descriptions are in fact verbal pictures in the essentially pictorial media of colour and light. They call for translation into painting, the art to which they strictly belong. Just such a pictorial, literally picturesque character will also be found in the later literature of baroque, the culture moreover that will give birth to landscape painting. The sunlit bay described above suggests a landscape by Claude. Indeed he has surely depicted that bay, a scene of rocky sea coast where rocks and water are bathed in rich glowing sunlight. Sidonius at best, as at worst, is an autumnal and a baroque writer.

The old autumn and the new spring could meet in the same individual. They met in the life of Sidonius Apollinaris —his writing is wholly of the autumn—and in the writing as well as in the life of Venantius Fortunatus a century later. Like Sidonius, Fortunatus was a man of letters who ended his life a bishop. He was of the classical autumn when he wrote his complimentary and secular verse, of the Christian spring when he wrote his paeans of the Risen Lord and the Triumphant Cross.

Though apart from these hymns and the magnificent poem on the Resurrection, " Salve festa dies," Fortunatus is but a mediocre poet, his work is significant for this mingling of the baroque autumn of antiquity and the Catholic spring. His poetry repeats the well-worn themes. He celebrates with a tedious colloquy between Venus and Cupid the marriage of King Sigebert with the notorious Brunhilde. He delights in conceits, even in his prose letters, for example in his letter to Bishop Felix of Nantes. He twisted verses into anagrammatic designs such as we find in George Herbert and other poets of the Christian baroque. With this he has the interest in observing picturesque detail that we have remarked in Ausonius. He celebrates the Egircius after the fashion in which Ausonius had celebrated the Moselle. And he notes in detail the effects of drought and flood.

Like Ausonius he has an eye for effects of light. He sings of the light reflected from a church ceiling. " If the passing traveller looks into the church at night he will believe the earth has her constellations . . . truly may I say, when the darkness of night returns, the world is wrapped in night, this hall holds the day." It is the language of the seventeenth century. He displays the baroque delight in costly material, marble, gems and precious metals.

When Fortunatus turns to Christian themes the spring breaks in upon autumn. In the " Salve festa dies " he hymns Christ's resurrection, when the life of spring rises from the grave of winter. The natural and the supernatural spring blend and reinforce each other to inspire an unconscious prophecy of the renovation of Europe by the Christian religion culture.

" Lo, the beauty of the world reborn witnesses that all her gifts have returned with their Lord." The good gifts of culture would return in a civilisation reborn in Christ.

Moreover, here and there Fortunatus strikes a note to be seldom heard during the six centuries ensuing, a note of devotion to the Human Jesus. " Vagit infans inter arcta conditus presepia, membra pannis involuta Virgo mater alligat et pedes manusque, crura stricta stringit fascia."

" The Babe cries in His narrow crib.   And His Virgin Mother
binds in close swaddling bonds the feet, hands and legs of
God."   " Flecte ramos arbor alta . . . ut superni membra
regis miti tendas stipite."   " Mite corpus perforatur."   " Bend
your boughs, tall tree, and with gentle embrace support the
limbs of Heaven's King.   The tender body is pierced."   This
loving contemplation of the newborn babe tended by his
mother's care and the suffering Body on whose behalf the
poet appeals to the cross itself for tenderness must wait for
Bernard and Francis before it finds utterance once more.
And the same note is heard when he exclaims " Serge sepulte
MEUS " : " Arise MY Buried One."   As literally with trees and
shrubs, beneath the autumnal foliage of the classical culture
we can see the buds of the Christian culture already formed.
It is the law of culture, as of nature, that autumn contains
the promise of spring.

The concluding phases of the classical and of the Christian
culture, these two baroque cultures, resemble each other
because the latter was a classical as well as a Christian culture.
When the hour of Christian baroque came the classical inheritance had been restored.   The matter, that is to say, ol
both baroque cultures was substantially identical.   But in
the former Christianity, culturally still immature, had not
mastered it, and stood aside protesting.   In the latter, culturally
mature, its mastery was sufficient to produce a living culture.

Therefore the collapse of the classical culture, when it
foundered in the storm of barbarism, proved the indispensable
condition of a complete and unified Christian culture.   Though
the summer was delayed by many centuries, when it came
it redeemed the pledge of spring.   It was the summer of a
Christian religion-culture.   Enough and no more survived
of the classical inheritance to provide the Christian spirit
with the cultural matter on which to impress its form.   More
would have been too much.

Moreover, the human material of the Christian culture was
renewed by the infusion of new blood, by the entrance of
young peoples fresh from the life of primitives in the midst
of an untamed nature.   The modicum of classical culture
surviving in these Dark Ages which was transmitted to them
by the Christian clergy educated without overwhelming
them.   It was not a burden but a stimulus.

Art meanwhile had taken another road. Released from the imprisonment of the catacombs and furnished with the technical resources and wealth of the Empire it went forward on new paths. Of Eastern inspiration, Byzantine art and Romanesque, which developed in the West under Byzantine influence, bridged the gulf between classical and Gothic art. The architectural forms and decorations of Romanesque were partly Byzantine. Such were the rounded apse and the mosaic. And if, as we should, we classify art not by the forms employed, but by the spirit which employs them, Romanesque must be regarded as the Western continuation of Byzantine. It is in fact related to Byzantine much as baroque is related to Gothic. The external relation is even closer. Many buildings, for example, the Basilicas of Ravenna, and at Rome, Sancta Maria in Cosmedin, and later the basilica erected by Charlemagne at Aachen are intermediate between Byzantine and Romanesque, indeed more Byzantine than Romanesque. Purely Byzantine are the Ravenna mosaics and, at a later period, St. Mark's, Venice.

The dome and the round arch mediated between the horizontal forms of the purest Hellenic and Greco-Roman art, the artistic embodiment of the horizontal and humanist movement which they expressed and the pointed arch of Gothic aspiration which, though adopted as a piece of practical engineering, would soar heavenward as the architectural expression of the vertical movement to God.

*   *   *

The predominant note of Byzantine architecture is majesty. The architecture of an autocratic court in which moreover Byzantine Caesaropapism had half deified the Emperor, it conceived of Christ as the heavenly despot, the Saints and Angels as His court. The plebeian Shepherd gave place to the heavenly Monarch. In an age when the fabric of civilisation was threatened, indeed largely demolished, by anarchy the primary need was a strong ruler, and a ruler whose sway would extend over Christendom. For such a monarch the papacy never ceased to look, in Byzantium first, later in France, later still in Germany, and usually in vain. At such a time it was well to emphasise the Divine

Monarchy, exemplar and sanction of earthly kingship, and impose it on the popular imagination.

A Church composed so largely of ignorant and rude converts was wholesomely impressed by the awe of the King who held his court with the solemn ceremonial of Catholic worship. It was at this period that the celebration of the liturgy was invested with the ornate ritual, befitting such a view of it. Sacred vestments were set apart for it, the gestures of worship were multiplied and elaborated, ceremonial lights were burned, incense offered. The supreme achievement of Christian art and poetry at this period was in fact the liturgy whether in its more elaborate oriental and Gallican forms or in the comparative sobriety of the Roman rite. Enthroned aloft to receive the adoration of His earthly in unison with His heavenly courtiers was the Majestic Figure of Christ, Emperor of the world, as He was depicted in the mosaic of apse or dome.

Though this insistence on the awful aspect of Godhead was necessary and salutary, the disappearance of the loving Shepherd behind the terrifying features of the " King of dread Majesty " entailed losses, not the less regrettable because inevitable. Christianity became a religion in which fear and law were more prominent than love and free grace. It was all very well to overawe barbarians like Clovis with fear of the Divine Monarch. But even the sane and generous wisdom of St. Benedict's rule is at times overcast by a conception of wrathful Deity for which there should have been little place in a school of Christian perfection. " The twelfth step of humility is reached when a monk not only has humility in his heart but even shows it exteriorly to all who behold him. Wheresoever he be sitting, standing or walking always let him with head bent and eyes fixed on the ground bethink himself of his sins and imagine that he is arraigned before the dread judgement of God." [1] Not all the reverence and gratitude due to the patriarch and legislator of western monasticism should make us regard this constant terror of an angry judge as the fitting attitude of an adopted son to his Father, and moreover of a son who has advanced so far in his Father's service and in the intimacy of communion with Him. But it reflects faithfully the dominant note of contemporary religion as understood by those who practised it most fer-

[1] Rule, trs. Gasquet.

vently and as it found expression in this art of majesty and awe.

If the note of fear is not thus prominent in the Roman liturgy, though it was mainly the work of this period, it is probably due, under Divine Providence, to the fact that its formulas were in the main composed by the secular clergy whose view of God was presumably less austere than that entertained by the practitioners of austerity. To the monk's eyes fixed on the ground I prefer Clement's enjoyment of the flowery meadows in spring.

The monks, however, will not long keep their eyes on the ground. They will soon employ them in artistic creation and cultural work for the glory of God. And in the person of Pope Gregory, the monk will employ his ears to bring plain chant to perfection.

Plain chant, the creation of this epoch, was a superb achievement of the new Christian culture. Its sublime aspiration and exultant worship are restrained, even austere in their expression. The majesty of Christian Rome found utterance in the chant over whose birth it presided. Throughout the western world order was crashing and the discord of savage war prevailed almost everywhere. At this very time Pope Gregory brought to perfection the harmony [1] of a music which, in the body of musical forms inherited through Rome from Hellas, incorporated the soul of Christian religion. Ascending with the sacred chant to the Divine harmony of God's heavenly Kingdom, " the Jerusalem that is above," the soul escaped from the disharmony of the earthly kingdom in disintegration and collapse. And from that vantage-ground it could derive, as did the undaunted spirit of the musical pontiff, the strength to grapple bravely with the anarchy below and lay the foundations of a new order. Never has any Pope better realised the meaning of his title than Pope Gregory. To be the Pontifex maximus, the supreme bridge builder, such was indeed St. Gregory's office. Intent on strengthening the bridge of faith and worship between earth and heaven, unconsciously, for he believed the end of all things was at hand, he built a bridge between the dying

[1] I am not, of course, speaking of harmony in the technical sense, which is absent from plain chant, but of harmony in the wider sense of an accordant and melodious arrangement of sounds. The word was used by the Greeks of their unharmonised music.

civilisation of antiquity and the Catholic culture that would take its place.   Tasks of secular administration which the feeble government of the Eastern Emperor could not fulfil, he shouldered from a sickbed.   He fed the Romans from the Sicilian estates of the Church.   He defended Rome against the Lombards.   Thereby he laid the foundation of the temporal government of the Papacy, at the outset neither asked by the Popes nor even given, but thrust upon them by the situation itself.   And his mission to England restored a lost province to Christendom.   And these foundations of a Catholic Europe were laid to music, music that utters and sanctifies the need and the aspiration of man, individual and social.

To-day the corpse of a deceased culture, the religion-culture of Catholic Christendom, is in process of dissolution and must give place to a civilisation whose lineaments we can scarce foresee.   But we can sing Gregory's melodies of the heavenly kingdom and with him derive from the Divine order to which they lift us courage to face the unknown future and the determination that however lengthy the process, however stern the struggle, however painful the wounds, we shall work undaunted for the new order that shall finally come to birth, an order inspired and moulded by the timeless truth of God as He has revealed it to man which shall thus be wrought into a religion-culture better than the old, inasmuch as it will not be imposed from above on multitudes too barbarous to receive it otherwise but will proceed wholly from within, from the charity and the spiritual understanding of God's people.

For in fact an interior and profound Christianity was to be confined in the main to the clergy and professed religious during the centuries that witnessed the slow formation of Christian Europe.   There were of course many individual exceptions, some like Charlemagne, Alfred the Great, Wenceslas, Stephen of Hungary, and Canute, men of outstanding achievement.   And in Italy learning never became so exclusive a clerical monopoly as elsewhere.   But we cannot contest the substantial truth of St. Gregory's observation : " The priest must be among the lay people as a lump of salt among brute beasts "—" bruta animalia."   " Bruta animalia," the words described only too accurately the laity of these dark ages, indeed even the clergy, when and where they were the nominees of unworthy lay rulers.

THE CRUCIFIXION:
BYZANTINE MOSAIC OF THE 11th CENTURY, DAPHNI.

"Gradually the Risen Lord was eclipsed by the Crucified. The advent of
the Judge is no longer awaited as in the primitive church with longing but
with dread."

A ROMANESQUE
CHURCH :
CHURCH OF THE
TRINITY, CAEN.
BUILT BY
MATILDA, WIFE
OF WILLIAM THE
CONQUEROR.

"Massive, a veritable
fortress of the Christian
army and dark with
its narrow windows.
But it was brightly,
even garishly painted.
The effect must, I think,
have been oriental."

How ignorant the laity were is shown by the fact that St. Augustine found it necessary to explain to his congregation that when Our Lord called His Apostles the salt of the earth He did not mean the soil, " the earth trodden by the feet of the body," and that when He called them the light of the world He did not mean " the earth and sky." From men so ignorant and stupid an intelligent understanding of their religion could not be expected. " Bruta animalia " indeed.

Those who complain of papal and clerical usurpation have no notion of the civilising work which the clergy performed and which they alone could perform.

No priestly power and no papal power, no civilised Europe : that is the historical fact, as the word clerk witnesses to this day.

Even less than St. Gregory had St. Benedict any thought of salvaging civilisation. His more modest purpose was but to secure monasticism from anarchy and extravagance and legislate for the Christian life of small monastic families engaged in praising God, saving their souls and supporting themselves by their labour. The Benedictine order fulfilled once again Christ's promise. Seeking God and His kingdom it played an outstanding part in saving the classical inheritance of European humanity.

Nevertheless, one of the greatest among those who between the old world and the new handed on to the latter the intellectual heritage of the former was an eminent layman, Boethius. He, however, came of the old Roman stock, not yet swamped out of existence by the barbarian deluge.

Boethius was a scientist and a philosopher with the comprehensive interest of Greek philosophy at its best. He experimented with sundials and waterclocks, wrote on geometry and the technique of music. He was as interested in astronomy as Origen had been and no doubt appreciated his astronomical vision of heavenly bliss.

His philosophic ambition extended to the scope of St. Thomas. For he set about translating into Latin the works of Plato and Aristotle and sought to reconcile them. That is to say, he wished to secure for the Latin west the philosophic achievement of antiquity and to perform the work that Scholasticism would accomplish almost a millennium later. Unfortunately he was also a statesman and political enmities cut short his career and life.

But it was amid the suffering and anxiety of his prison that he wrote his great original work, the *Consolation of Philosophy*. Though his philosophy is Platonic he seeks from it what the Stoics and Epicureans had sought, a happiness within man himself of which no external misfortune can deprive him. But it is not, as with them, a human self-sufficiency. It is communion with God, nothing less in fact than deification here, and hereafter the vision of God.

That Boethius thus turned in the hour of testing to Platonic philosophy for consolation rather than to Christian faith has led many to question his Christianity and contest his authorship of the theological tracts which pass under his name. It must, I think, be admitted that we cannot affirm his authorship positively on the strength of a single manuscript of a letter by Cassiodorus which may have been interpolated. But since the Gothic ruler of Italy was an Arian, his Latin subjects Catholics, a pagan would hardly have been raised to high political office. That such a lover of truth dissembled his unbelief is incredible. If the *Consolation of Philosophy* is a pagan work it is strange that it was welcomed warmly by Christians of later times, by King Alfred, for example, who translated it. An allusion to humble prayer for grace is a distinctively Christian note. And although deification is mentioned once in the *Phaedo* the emphasis placed upon it by Boethius is Christian. On the other hand, two Platonic doctrines incompatible with Christian orthodoxy are distinctly taught, the pre-existence of souls before their descent into the body and the everlastingness—not the eternity—of the world. But these are precisely two Platonic doctrines taught by Origen. It would seem therefore that Boethius was a Christian of Origen's Alexandrine school. His asceticism is the philosophic asceticism of Clement's Gnostic freely enjoying natural beauty. And as we have seen, he shared Origen's devotion to astronomy. That Origenism was still a powerful force is proved by the fact that Justinian thought it necessary to have it formally condemned a few years later. If Boethius departed, as it seems he did, from Origen in accepting hell as well as purgatory it was perhaps in deference to Plato. He was a Christian Platonist, whose Platonism on certain points interfered with a Christianity undoubtedly genuine.

The poetry which alternates with the prose of the *Consolation* belongs to the baroque autumn of which I have spoken above. It is heavily laden with the conventional erudition that will still be adorning the literature of Christian baroque. The auriferous sands of the Tagus, for example, appear both in Boethius' *Consolation* and in Crashaw's *Weeper*. Even in his philosophy, though he enriched it with his memorable definition of eternity—" the perfect and simultaneous possession of boundless life "—Boethius does not belong, like Augustine or " Dionysius " among the Christian Platonists, to the new Christian spring. He is the last of the ancients collecting and handing on their philosophic heritage, understood, however, as they had understood it, not as Christian thought understands it. The sole effect of Boethius' sincere personal Christianity visible in the *Consolation* is his accent, the emphasis he places on communion with God and the deification it brings. To re-emphasise is hardly to re-mould. Nevertheless, since we cannot, like Ficino, repay Plato's work of preparation for Christ by giving him the honours of a Christian saint, we are glad to pay this tribute to his prophetic achievement in the person of his disciple. For Boethius has been accorded a local cultus as a Christian martyr.

We have remarked the predominance in the art and piety of this epoch of the Divine Monarchy. The sense of majesty was strengthened by the genius of Benedict and Gregory as monastic and ecclesiastical rulers and by the extensive scope of government secular as well as religious committed to the hierarchy. And Boethius' philosophy also is dominated by the Divine Ruler and the inflexible law of His Governance displayed in the evident order of nature and traceable by the philosopher's vision amid the apparent disorder of human affairs. Indeed, the *Consolation* is the spirit's cry for order and its satisfaction by Wisdom.

And it was at this period of earthly disorder, when the Divine Office took shape, that Psalm 118, the Psalm of law, bringing the soul into obedient conformity with the Divine law of nature and grace, the order of God's universal government, was appointed for daily recitation, to fashion in its mould the countless souls who would be saying it day by day throughout the centuries to come.

Thus in every sphere the challenge of anarchy was met by the affirmation of an order established by the Divine Ruler, perfect above, to be wrought out below, the order of Church government, the ecclesiastical hierarchy reflecting, as Dionysius saw it, the hierarchy of heaven, of Roman law, codified at this epoch by Justinian, of religious obedience, of the Liturgy, now fixed in detail, of an art hieratic, formal, courtly and majestic and of the disciplined Gregorian music. It was an historical necessity metaphysically grounded. The Creation of a world is the imposition of order, of form which is order, upon the chaos of matter. The creation of a religion-culture is the imposition of an order, the order whose form that religion supplies, upon the chaos of human lusts warring in the darkness of human ignorance.

Over all this work of saving and restoring order, work carried on in every sphere against such desperate odds of rising anarchy, sat enthroned the Christus Pantocrator of the Byzantine apse, Christ, Monarch and Teacher of the World, the Creative Word Who directly or by His human delegates imposes on all things the law of their forms, creates by ruling and instructing. Imposing the law of Christ, His Church created Christendom.

THE VISION OF ST. BERNARD, BY FILIPPINO LIPPI, IN THE
CHURCH OF THE BADIA, FLORENCE

" St. Bernard is generally regarded as the founder of the new devotion to
the sacred Humanity.   In fact, he regards it as subordinate and preparatory
to an ascending devotion to the Divine Word."

THE NORTH DOOR, CHARTRES CATHEDRAL

" *Let us contemplate the mediaeval cathedral as the epitome and embodiment of the Catholic religious culture in its mediaeval summer. It has been aptly styled a Summa in stone.*"

SUMMER : MEDIEVAL CHRISTENDOM

In our English spring, even in late spring, spells of storm or frost are only too common which destroy the blossom in our orchards and blight their rich promise of fruit. The spring of the Catholic religion-culture of Latin Europe witnessed a series of blizzards which destroyed many promising hopes of a new civilisation and prolonged the winter of barbarism.

In Gaul the milder and half Latinised rule of the Visigoths and Burgundians was overthrown by the more barbarous Franks. Theodoric's attempt to continue Roman culture under the aegis of his Ostrogoths was ruined by the jealousies and hostility between conquerors and conquered—they cost Boethius his life—by the war of Byzantine reconquest and the Lombard invasion which with a symbolic appropriateness laid in ruins St. Benedict's foundation at Monte Cassino. Visigothic Spain had not long entered the full communion of Christendom by the conversion of her rulers from Arianism when the country was almost completely conquered by the Arab invaders. Their conquest, it is true, produced a culture more brilliant than anything Western Christendom would possess for centuries. And this Arab culture would finally fertilise medieval Christendom. But it was a Moslem culture apart from the Christian religion-culture. France and Rhineland Germany that went with it were ravaged by endless strife between Merovingian princelings. The heathen Angles and Saxons drove British Christianity to the far west of the island. And when they had been converted and were developing a Christian culture the tempest of Viking invasion fell furiously upon them. In Ireland the successive missions of the " elder " and " younger " Patrick[1] converted to the

[1] Patrick-Palladius d.c. 461. See Pr. O'Rahilly *The Two St. Patricks.*

Catholic Church, and therefore in a measure to Latin culture, a people hitherto outside the Roman orbit. The result was a vigorous and original religion-culture that filled the island with monastic schools, produced the art, strangely oriental in character, of which the Book of Kells is an example, and sent out swarms of scholar missionaries to barbarised or pagan continental lands.

It was distinguished by a love and a poetry of natural beauty such as we associate with St. Francis and the literature influenced by his spirit. With this it combined the austerity of oriental asceticism. And it was marked by a roving spirit which drove Irish monks abroad over the Continent and far overseas to the discovery of Iceland. But Irish paganism had submitted too easily to be inwardly vanquished. Even the Irish Saint inherited its bellicose spirit. He cursed as the pagan priest had cursed before him. St. Columba could stir up a bloody war to avenge a judicial decision he regarded as unjust. And fasting was abused as a weapon against enemies. Even the old gods survived as fairies.

The consequent disorder and constant strife, completed by the Viking invasion, blighted the promise of the Irish religion-culture. In the days of St. Bernard the religion of Ireland, once a school of sanctity for Western Europe, was regarded on the Continent as little better than a veneered paganism. The description which prefaces St. Bernard's life of St. Malachy, and which is repeated a few years later by the biographer of St. Lawrence O'Toole, was doubtless exaggerated and coloured by the prejudice of the foreigner. Nevertheless it was the impression left with St. Bernard by the holy Irish bishop who died in his abbey.

The eighth century witnessed the first flowering of a Latin religion-culture, under the protection of a Latin Empire embracing the greater part of Western Europe. It was the Carolingian Renaissance patronised by the Frankish ruler whom the Pope crowned as the first Holy Roman Emperor. Though Charlemagne himself could only read, not write, he encouraged learning and the monasteries which were its centres. Under his aegis the Roman liturgy, enriched by Gallican additions, spread over the West and along with it its chant. Silent since Boethius philosophy revived in the work of an original, if eccentric and puzzling thinker, the

Irish scholar Scotus Eriugena. For a moment it might have seemed that the culture which had broken off under Theodoric would now go forward on the wider arena of an international European Empire. But the new Empire lacked foundations sufficiently strong. The Imperial administration reposed not on disciplined legions loyal to the Empire but on barbarous and self-seeking nobles, ripe for revolt and engaging in private warfare. Dynastic disputes finally severed the lands to the west and the east of the Rhine thus producing the division and hostility between France and Germany, whose bitter fruit we are still tasting to-day. As the reins of power fell from the hands of puppet Emperors the Empire and its culture foundered in the anarchy of warring princelets and nobles. And the anarchy was multiplied by Viking invasions in the North, Saracen inroads in the South and attacks by Slav and Magyar in the East. Meantime the Byzantine Empire and culture whose very tongue was almost unknown in the West drifted apart from the religion of Latin Europe until the rift between the Eastern and Western Churches finally became an impassable gulf. Rome herself gradually decayed. When the strife of the dark ages had done its worst the capital city of Christendom could show little save the ruins of her former splendour and the fortresses her warring nobles had built from them. When we contemplate these successive tempests and the ravage they left behind we are surprised that culture did not wholly perish.

Nevertheless the traditional culture was alive. If it was trampled underfoot in one region, it sought refuge in another. And at the first promise of peace, the least modicum of security, it revived. Frostbitten and storm-tossed the tree never died, and with the first spell of finer weather its stubborn life put out fresh leaves. Barbarian invasion had so depopulated a coastal district of Gaul that St. Patrick's shipmates, driven on to its shore by a storm, were reduced to the verge of starvation in a region as uninhabited as Crusoe's island. Yet Palladius could learn at Lerins the Christian doctrine and the Latin culture with which he would evangelise Ireland and establish the Irish outpost of Latin Christianity and its religion-culture.

And other regions of Gaul appear to have suffered little from the progressive Teutonic conquests. In their luxurious villas Sidonius Apollinaris and his fellow-nobles pursued their lives of cultured leisure as though Gaul were still enjoying the Antonine peace.[1]

The Anglo-Saxons had not completed their conquest before they received Christianity and England became the seat of a Christian culture in intimate touch both with Ireland and with Rome, the culture of Monk Wearmouth and its Codex Amiatinus, of the great Abbesses, of the Venerable Bede, of Alfred and of Dunstan. And the son of the barbarous Viking Sweyn became the devout Canute, zealous for the good government of his people and the patron of monks.

" Sweetly sang the monks of Ely when Canute the King passed by." " Row closer, boatmen," said the King, " and let us hear these sweet monks sing."[2] The well-known story is typical. Over and over again throughout these dark ages the chant of the monks, and the religion-culture it expressed, softened and made Christians and civilised men of rulers great and small who had been or would otherwise have been barbarians. The greatest of these Christianised and civilised chiefs was of course Charlemagne, of whom I have already spoken. But he is but the most eminent of many like him. In the West the Magyars threatened Germany. It would not be long before St. Stephen founded a Catholic Hungary. The Slavs produced their " good King " Wenceslas, so Christian that when an aggressor made war upon him he risked his life in single combat to spare the blood of his people. For all our boast of progress, that is not the way of modern rulers. For many a sad year the Papacy was basely enslaved to unscrupulous women of the local nobility. But it could produce a Nicholas denouncing judicial torture and a Leo IX. And the end of its servitude would be the achievement of Hildebrand vindicating the freedom and purity of the clergy against their oppression and pollution by nobles and monarchs. His friend and ally, the Countess Matilda,

---

[1] The conflicting evidence of St. Patrick's letter and the letters of Sidonius is not altogether easy to reconcile. We may, however, conclude that the coastal region had been devastated by raiders, presumably the savage Saxons whose sudden attacks are graphically described by Sidonius (Letters 8, 6) who had slaughtered the inhabitants or carried them into slavery or had driven them inland.

[2] " Sweetly " rather than " merrily " translates the original Latin and is a more suitable description of the monastic chant : " DULCE cantabant monachi in Eli."

was a learned woman, who superintended an edition of Justinian's Pandects and received from St. Anselm the gift of his Meditations. Contemporary with Hildebrand the literary and medical school of Salerno flourished. For the stubborn life of this ever-reviving culture was the religion that inspired it. Where Latin Christianity was present Latin and therefore Hellenic culture could not be wholly absent. The very definitions of Christian doctrine brought with them the Greek philosophy in whose terms they were stated. The chant of the Church brought the inheritance of classical music. The liturgy enshrined the Latin majesty in the homilies of a Leo or Gregory, in the lapidary formulas of the collect. The Canon law of the Church continued the tradition, and to a large extent embodied the decisions, of Roman law. In her hierarchy, international government survived. Gregory had indeed frowned on the pagan poets, and Jerome attempted unsuccessfully to repent of his devotion to Cicero. Nevertheless the monk and the missionary, most commonly the missionary monk, brought with him the selection of classical authors that would be the literary education of the new Europe. It was as impossible to sever Latin culture from Latin Christianity as to sever a living body from its soul.

The library of classical writers which thus accompanied the Christian teacher was, it is true, small. Inasmuch as they were regarded as educational they were predominantly ethical. There were Persius, Juvenal and Terence. Hroswitha, a nun of Gandersheim, in the tenth century wrote a series of miracle plays modelled on Terence and taken from the legends of Saints. There was of course Virgil and there were Ovid and Lucan and the Satires of Horace. His Odes were little known. There were Caesar and Cicero who handed on the Greek philosophy he had popularised and simplified.

There was Seneca also and a number of late Latin writers down to the widely read Boethius. There was Orosius' Christian theology of history, and Christian poets. There were Latin fathers and above all the man who exercised an undisputed sway over the mind of Latin Christendom, St. Augustine. When we exclude the Christian writers there are left but a small number of writers to represent the inheritance of antiquity. But the comparative scantiness of the material made it easy to incorporate into a definitely Christian education and culture. Though such scholars as Gerbert in the tenth century display a literary humanism as ardent as that of any Renaissance scholar there was no danger that humanism might contest with theology the intelligence of Europe. The horizontal movement, the direction of interest to man and nature, was so restricted in the material at its disposal and in its opportunities of peaceful satisfaction—for it had no cities of refuge save those monastic or capitular citadels which were centres of the vertical and supernatural movement towards God—that it could not rebel against the latter and dispute its supremacy. Gerbert became Pope Sylvester.

In face of these successive floods of barbarian invasion the first and the supreme need throughout the Dark Ages was government, the establishment of law and order. The Herculean task was begun again and yet again as each new attempt at a Christian civilisation was made on the ruins of a former. The indomitable courage to undertake it was drawn from faith in a Divine Ruler and from the support of the sole society and the only Government which had survived the collapse of the old order, the Church He had founded and ruled through His earthly representative. The organisers and rulers during these centuries were predominantly ecclesiastics or laymen such as Charlemagne and Alfred working in close collaboration with them. Scrutiny of the Roman martyrology, to which must be added those less official Saints whose popular cultus has been permitted, shows that a very large proportion of the men and women who played a leading part in the public life of Christendom during these centuries were Saints or Beati. It is true that before official canonisation was introduced at the close of the tenth century access to the calendar was far easier than it has since become. The Celts, Saxons and Francs accorded a local cultus to any missionary or ascetic of reasonably decent conduct who founded a church or monastery, or ruled as bishop or abbot. But when every allowance has been made, the fact remains that the Christian leaders of Europe were men of profound religion, men who sought the glory of God and wished to make human society serve His glory. Amid Merovingian barbarism a host of saintly bishops struggled for religion and civilisation assisted by saintly princes, ministers of state, queens and princesses. St. Radegund, escaping from a court as savage as that of a Zulu chief, founded at Poitiers an asylum of religion and culture. St. Bathildis, raised like Cophetuas' beggar maid from a kitchen slave to the French throne, was regent for her three royal sons before retiring to a convent. The ancestor of the Carolingian dynasty, Pepin of Landen, Mayor of the Palace, that is the virtual monarch, was the husband and father of Saints and has himself received the honours of a beatus. Charlemagne himself, though his life was not altogether that of a Saint, has been rewarded for his services to the Church and Christendom by a cultus continued to this day. The Anglo-Saxon kingdoms produced a galaxy of Saintly kings such as Ethelbert, Edwin and Oswald, queens and princesses who left the world for the cloister to influence and civilise the world from it. And it was the Saint and monk Dunstan who, not content with reforming monasticism and the clergy and practising the arts, as Edgar's minister reconciled the Danes and the English with greater success than any modern statesman confronted by national antagonisms. Norway produced the missionary monarch Olaf, Denmark two saintly Canutes from the same stock as the holy, if uncanonised, Canute of our history. On the Eastern border of Latin Christendom we have already observed the Hungarian Stephen and the Czech Wenceslas. And Germany, evangelised by English monks, produced the sainted Emperor and Empress Henry and Cunegund and the holy, though uncanonised Otto III. If in Italy the Saints do not seem to have played as prominent a part in public life, it was probably due to the reluctance of Roman conservatism to admit confessors so easily to the honours of sanctity, also perhaps to a survival of the imperial tradition of lay administration. But the secular government of the Popes was developing at Rome which had produced perhaps the most influential of these saintly statesmen, Gregory the Great.

Equipped with a baggage of culture sufficient to educate, insufficient to distract their vision, the makers of Latin Christendom had their eyes fixed on heaven, as in face of odds seemingly overwhelming and undismayed by constant defeats they strove against barbarian anarchy and violence and laboured for the kingdom of God. If the vertical movement predominated, even to excess, a vision thus sustained above the storm-tossed earth in the calm sunlight of eternal truth enabled them to move so surely amidst the storm and push their way steadily through the mist. It was the contemplation and praise of the cloister that trained the men who evangelised and civilised heathen hordes and brought waste places under cultivation. It is true these centuries of heroic struggle against human and natural disorder imbued Latin Christianity with the legal spirit that has often degenerated into legalism and with which the Orientals reproach it. And it produced a powerful hierarchical government, which inevitably fostered an ecclesiastical bureaucracy. But the germ and principle of both these developments and therefore the occasion of their corresponding abuses was the Divine Constitution of a visible Church. And the foundations of Christian Europe could not have been laid otherwise.

Ecclesiastical art, as was equally inevitable, continued to express predominantly the Power of the Divine Monarch. But as the centuries advanced, the King was depicted as Crucified, reigning, robed and crowned from the tree. In the members, as in the Head, the victory of God's Kingdom could be achieved only by suffering and apparent defeat. Saracens massacred the monks of Lerins and capturing Rome pillaged the tombs of the Apostles. The Apostle of Germany and the royal Apostle of Norway died a martyr's death. The Northmen all but drowned English Christianity in the blood of the slain, monasteries being the favourite victims of their fury. And hosts of nominal Christians, not least monarchs and nobles, were no less savage and vicious than these avowed pagans. It is not therefore surprising that piety assumed a sombre hue. Gradually, despite the witness of the liturgy, the Risen Lord was eclipsed by the Crucified. And the advent of the Judge is no longer awaited as in the primitive Church with longing but with dread. " Come quickly, Lord Jesus." " Dies irae," " calamitatis et miseriae—dies amara valde." And between this hope and fear is the expectation of a Bernard of Cluny, longing indeed for the advent of the Judge, but that He may take vengeance on a world of sin and the righteous escape from it. It was during these centuries that the belief became general that the vast majority even of Catholics would be damned. Their behaviour seemed to prove it. The gloom with which the Catholic religion is so often charged by her pagan detractors and which

THE SIGNS OF THE ZODIAC AND THE LABOURS OF THE MONTHS (JANUARY AND FEBRUARY) FROM AMIENS CATHEDRAL

"The cathedral embodied the same lifegiving order of Catholic wisdom in a representative material of encyclopaedic extent. The sciences and the arts, legend and history, every department of human activity and the forms of vegetable and animal life, were drawn upon to provide symbols and expressions of Catholic truth, notes of praise made permanent in paint and stone."

THE
CATHEDRAL,
SIENA, ARCHI-
TECT GIOVANNI
OF PISA, A.D. 1284

A centre of conservative
and aristocratic influ-
ences in Italy, as op-
posed to democratic and
progressive Florence.
At Siena the building
material was alternate
courses of black and
white marble. This
emphasis upon the hori-
zontal lines of the building is in sharp contrast
to the emphasis upon the
uprising lines of French
and true Gothic.

has indeed darkened at times the countenance of devotion did not descend from the light it brings from heaven. It arose from the darkness of earth which that light did but make blacker.

We must not, however, forget that a Romanesque Church —in England we call the style Norman—was not as severe, when first erected, as we now see it. True, it was massive, a veritable fortress of the Christian army and dark with its narrow windows. But it was brightly, even garishly, painted. The effect must, I think, have been oriental. Even without its paint the many arched crypt of Worcester is distinctly reminiscent of the many arched Mosque of Cordova. The Chapter House at Bristol and the Galilee at Durham wear an oriental aspect. The gulf between the art of Islam and the art of Christendom was not so wide as is often believed. Anglo-Saxon and Norman carving which do not differ essentially from the contemporary sculpture of the Continent strike us as decidedly eastern in style and spirit.

For Byzantine form and feeling, the offspring of an Orient intermediate between Islam and Latin Christendom, survive in this Norman Romanesque. Examples are the three semi-circular apses which terminated the Norman cathedral at Norwich and such a typical carving as the Byzantine Christ in glory which fills the tympanum of a door at Castor, Northamptonshire. But they were fading and giving place to the novel inspiration of Gothic and the new forms in which it would shortly be expressed. And the difference between the Byzantine spirit on its deathbed and the Gothic coming to birth was, in brief, this. The former was a vertical movement away from the world and humanity to God. The latter combined with this vertical movement a horizontal, a movement towards creatures. It therefore embraced and appreciated nature and man as creatures of God, and as such, reflecting His glory. To estimate the artistic effect of this novel direction of interest, we have but to compare a Byzantine with a Gothic madonna, the Byzantine monarch reigning robed and crowned from the Tree with the sufferer of a Gothic Crucifix.[1]

In the realm of pure thought one great figure stands out in an age whose utmost achievement was a fragmentary

[1] Spengler's distinction between the " Magic " Byzantine and the " Faustian " Gothic and post-Gothic cultures exaggerates and distorts the genuine difference between them.

preservation of the classical philosophic inheritance, the Christianised platonism of Augustine and Boethius. He was the Irish Carolingian philosopher, John Scotus Eriugena. Stimulated by the writings of the Areopagite, lately sent to France from Byzantium and other Greek Christian thinkers, which, moreover, he could read in the original Greek, he re-thought Christian Neoplatonism. Was he a pantheist who substituted for creation as the origin of creatures their emanation from God ? His language, as Pr. Wulf says, is obscure and hard to reconcile. It would, however, seem that he was so impressed by the comparative unreality of created being and the fact that its positive being is a communication of God that he was betrayed into language which appears to assert the sheer unreality of creatures, the language of acosmism, leaving no room for created being. I believe, that in fact it was the intention of his *De Divisione Naturae* to convey a vision of the Divine Nature as the sole perfect reality overflowing by a free communication of Itself and thus producing beings intermediate between God and nothingness. He cannot, however, be acquitted of misusing the term creation to describe the generation of the creative exemplars in the Divine Mind and even of confusing the Holy Spirit with the creation He inspires and moves. And he seems to have taught a final return of creatures to God which would destroy their distinct being and would involve the final end of all evil. But he mitigates this view by affirming what is apparently a survival of creatures, even of demons and impenitent sinners, on the phenomenal plane though on the noumenal they have been absorbed into their Divine Source. In short, Scotus was poised uneasily on the boundary between Christian theism and an acosmism such as was being taught by his Indian contemporary,[1] the Vedantist Sankara. He has curious affinities with the sophiological school of modern Russian thinkers, with men such as Berdyaev, Bulgakov and Soloviev. Like them he views the universe and the Church that crowns it as a theophany—the term is Scotus'—of the Divine Wisdom. This Irish sage, is in fact, a Russian Christian before the conversion of Russia. It is not surprising that he inclined to the Eastern as against the Western Church on the question of

[1] Sankara died about 55 years before Eriugena. But we may regard them as roughly contemporary.

the Double Procession and that his influence on the later development of Western thought was slight. His philosophy represents, however, an excess of the vertical movement, tending as it does to annul creatures in God, and to deny their distinct value and existence. As such it belonged to the prevailing direction of human interest.

The eleventh century at the close of the Dark Ages gave Europe another original thinker, St. Anselm. He sought a rational understanding of Christian truth, thought out by himself, not simply repeated from past thinkers. But he had neither the rashness nor the comprehensiveness of Eriugena. He was content to study individual problems and with a careful regard to orthodoxy. He worked out a proof of God's existence which, even if, as St. Thomas thought, unsound, displayed great acumen, and he carried forward the theology of the Atonement.

As Dom. David Knowles in his study of Benedictine monachism in England and Dr. Clement Webb in his monograph on John of Salisbury have shown, though the twelfth century did not reach the philosophic and theological achievement of the thirteenth, it was more humanist than its successor. Interest in classical literature and in cognate studies was keener and more widespread than in the age of the great metaphysical syntheses. Bernard of Chartres led " a humanistic movement, anticipating in its Platonism and its love of ancient literature some of the characteristic tendencies of the Renaissance "[1] King Stephen's brother, Bishop Henry of Winchester, had the tastes of an Italian prelate of the Quattrocento. He took advantage of a visit to Rome to purchase ancient and pagan statuary.[2] John of Salisbury was a polymath and a didactic poet, a classical scholar, acquainted with Greek and Hebrew, the enthusiastic encomiast of Cicero,[3] using a text of Petronius fuller than any known until the seventeenth century and of Macrobius more complete than we possess to-day.[4] William of Malmesbury displays the mentality, if he lacked the equipment, of the scientific and critical historian. Meteor of the intellectual firmament, in temper though not intent, a rationalist, Abelard asked but did not answer or unsatisfactorily

---

[1] Clement Webb, *John of Salisbury*, p. 6.
[2] *Ibid.* pp. 135-6.
[3] *Ibid.* p. 32.
[4] *Ibid.* pp. 63-4.

answered questions to which the scholastic syntheses would return more satisfactory replies.

The twelfth century was a period of monastic revival, the age of the Cistercians and St. Bernard. But the focus and seminary of knowledge will no longer be the monastery or the cathedral school. It will be the University. For the University alone can embody and sustain the medieval ideal of a universal education open to students of every provenance.

So we have passed on to the summer of the Catholic religion-culture, to the May of the twelfth and the June of the thirteenth century.

It was indeed a summer such as ours in England. Cold and stormy weather did not cease. Beneath the medieval order at its greatest achievement lay a disorder of war, insecurity, plague, and famine. Those who like Kenelm Digby or Pugin had eyes only for the positive aspect of the Middle Ages, could see nothing save the ideal it saw and sought to realise, a Divine human order conforming the kingdom of earth to the kingdom of heaven. Those who have eyes only for its negative aspect see nothing but the gulf which divided the ideal from the reality, the lamentable failure to give effect to the splendid vision. It is high time to see the Middle Ages as a whole, the positive and the negative, the light and the darkness.

The high Middle Ages, if I may so term these great centuries, differ from the Dark Ages that travailed so painfully to give them birth, not by the cessation of disorder, but its impotence to check the progressive achievement of a superincumbent order.

Whatever the violence and suffering of men's lives and whatever the strife of nobles and kings, whatever the tyranny of Johns and Ezzelinos, whatever the squalor, ignorance and disease prevalent among the masses, above them the vast and lofty cathedral of a Catholic order, an order of culture, speculation and art crowned by a religious order rose steadily heavenward, as the cathedral which embodied it in stone rose above the squalid hovels at its foot.

At this point I expect an indignant protest. Did not the hovel belie the Cathedral? Of what value is a culture which is but the refuge of a small minority from the misery of their fellows? What is the worth of a religion-culture which

TRIUMPH OF ST. THOMAS AQUINAS: FRESCO BY FILIPPINO LIPPI, IN THE DOMINICAN CHURCH OF SANTA MARIA SOPRA MINERVA, ROME

Painted in 1487 for the Caraffa Chapel. The Saint is expounding the Scriptures in the presence of the leaders of the Church.

THE PATH TO PARADISE (DOMINICAN ART) ANDREA DI FIRENZE (1358–1371); SANTA MARIA NOVELLA, FLORENCE

In the lower tier is seen the Duomo of Florence, with Giotto's Tower, and around the heroes of the Church Militant, headed by the Pope and the Emperor, and attended by the black and white Hounds of the Dominican Order, this being a subtle pun, "Domini canes" meaning the dogs of the Lord, Cardinals, archbishops, bishops and other Estates of Mediaeval society are shown. In the upper tiers are the Faithful attached by the snares of heresy to worldly vanities, but still protected by the Dominicans. At the top are shown the joys of the Heavenly Places, the whole composition being crowned with the figure of Christ in Glory.

must blossom in the seclusion of the monastery, anchorage and cathedral close, and leave the world outside in the thraldom of oppression, violence and ignorance ? This, I think, is the attitude of such a critic as Dr. Coulton who sees the Middle Ages against the contrasted background of the secure and decent world inhabited by the respectable Victorian, and therefore finds them so much more unpleasant.

The contrast ignores the seamy side of nineteenth-century civilisation, the slum, the insanitary cottage, sweated labour, inhuman prisons and workhouses. And it ignores the fact that this civilisation has ended in an outburst of international anarchy more extensive and more comprehensive than any outbreak of war or anarchy witnessed by Medieval Europe. If the latter suffered from constant warfare, it knew nothing of total war. The wars and factions whose grim record is contained in the pages of Salimbene's chronicle did not interfere with the philosophy of St. Thomas or St. Bonaventure, or with the art of Giotto. Despite his exile and personal danger Dante achieved the *Divine Comedy*. The Hundred Years' War, it is true, brought French architecture to a halt. But it had already achieved its best and would resume its course.

Above all, the contrast, with its disparagement of the Middle Ages, ignores the superiority of the medieval ideal over the modern. Dr. Susan Stebbing is no apologist for a Catholic culture. Yet she writes : " In the thirteenth century it was the religious and spiritual aspect of human activity that was emphasised . . . in the nineteenth century the economic aspect." [1] In other words, the *summum bonum*, that is the deity of medieval man was God, of modern man it is wealth.

The hovel, metaphorical and actual, below the medieval cathedral does not convict the latter of hypocrisy or make void its beauty. For it was inevitable. The ideal order conceived by the medieval mind and expressed in its philosophic, literary and artistic achievement could not be realised for want of the requisite wealth, technical resources and political unity. In a world of scarcity living under the threat of famine the resources necessary to support a cultured leisure, free for intellectual or artistic pursuits, were of necessity

[1] *Ideals and Illusions*, p. 202.

4

confined to a minority. Even so by dint of privation
heroically born, poor scholars could receive a university education. And art and architecture, since they were devoted
to the service of the Church, not of private luxury, were accessible to all. The dweller in the hovel worshipped in the
cathedral.

A state so strongly organised that it can suppress internal
anarchy and ensure the security of its citizens presupposes
technical instruments which were not available. They are
direct or indirect products of applied science. And medieval science was rudimentary. The medieval religion culture
lacked the services of science. No culture, however well
planned the dwelling it erects, can run its house efficiently
without a capable scientific servant. That is why the modern
worshippers of efficiency, such as H. G. Wells, are so con-
temptuous of the cultures of the past. They prefer the
uncultured civilisation in which we live, where the scientific
servant does his work admirably, but there is no master to
direct his services to the purposes of an organic religion-culture.
To their delight the servant is attempting to run the house
himself. Religion is to retire superannuated and philosophy to
abdicate her throne in the order of knowledge and accept
service under her former servant, as the ratification of
scientific truth and the arrangement of scientific data. Science,
however, though an excellent servant is a bad master. If indeed
it attempts, as at present, to play the master, it becomes the
servant of irrational human will, be it of an individual or a
group. And at present its principal function is to equip
criminal lunatics with lethal weapons. No one in the Middle
Ages, not even Roger Bacon, dreamed of making science
master of human knowledge. Above the sciences philosophy
and above philosophy theology bore sway. Nor, on the
other hand, was science disparaged. In the medieval curriculum the sciences were studied as a preparation for
philosophy and it was recognised that their method is experi-
mental. But in practice interest was elsewhere and progress,
though real, was very slight. What passed for science was in
the main the uncriticised and incomplete legacy of Greek
science. Science was too undernourished and too immature
to do her work in the speculative or practical sphere, to be an
efficient servant in the house of culture. Natural philosophy,

confused, as Maritain has pointed out, with natural science, presided over a void of learned ignorance. Metaphysics, to be sure, suffered no serious detriment. At worst it employed false illustrations. But the vision of a universal order could not be realised in the field of speculation without scientific truths to co-ordinate, in the sphere of practice without the tools provided by applied science.

The Church, moreover, had continued the policy adopted since the conversion of the Roman Emperors, the policy of receiving into her fold masses of people who became Christian because their rulers did so. These mass conversions from above had serious consequences. These spiritually immature men and women could grasp the Catholic faith only in a crude and highly imaginative presentation. They could not penetrate below its surface. And they inevitably contaminated its understanding and practice with their credulity and superstition. An interior, a spiritual and a better instructed Christianity inevitably became more and more the monopoly of a minority of specifically religious interest or thought, that is roughly the clergy and the technically " religious," itself a revealing term. The vast mass of the laity were more than ever the brute beasts St. Gregory had termed them. And the Church was rendered too dependent on the support of the secular rulers. Only by a desperate struggle could the Popes emancipate her from the imperial yoke and prevent a Latin reproduction of Byzantine Caesaropapism. And this they could achieve only by asserting a supreme dominion over the entire fabric of an ecclesiastical and a secular organisation too closely interwoven to be cut asunder. Pope Paschal's attempt to take the way, in itself more excellent, of surrendering the feudal privileges and domains of the clergy in exchange for liberty was a step towards the ideal of a free Church in a free state which attracted Dante, but which is even now realised only in a few countries. But it proved impracticable and was abandoned immediately.

For no other course was possible. These masses of converts were too immature to find Christianity for themselves or perceive its spiritual meaning, its " interior." Yet this mass conversion alone had made possible the united Christian society without which Europe must have foundered in barbarism and anarchy.

The medieval intertexture of secular and religious, Church and state as different aspects of the same society produced indeed grave abuses. The bishops became largely secularised on the model of their fellow-lords. To overcome heresy the Church relied upon the more immediately effective method of state repression rather than the slower but genuinely Christian method of preaching and example. Bishops and Popes wasted their spiritual power on political struggles waged by political and even military weapons. But this intertexture alone maintained a higher unity between the warring cities and provinces of Catholic Christendom. The religious organisation so closely wrought into the framework of secular society held the latter together. And when all is said the power wielded by the Pope and the clergy was in the very nature of things spiritual. For they owed it to the Catholic faith of the rulers and peoples. Be it granted that excommunication and interdict were on occasion used as political weapons. Yet the very fact that they were efficacious political weapons was itself a witness to the supremacy of religion. When they became ineffective, damp squibs, it was evident that Europe had taken the road towards secular humanism. If to-day the police cannot be put on the track of fugitive friars and the Inquisition has become impossible, the spectacle is equally impossible of Europe's proudest and most powerful ruler baring his back to the lash of monks to do penance for the murder of a Bishop, and moreover, a penance forced upon him by the moral pressure of an indignant Christendom.

It was this acceptance of a state-fostered conversion, of state establishment and of the consequent interweaving of the religious and political orders that enabled the Church in these ages of semi-savagery to erect and maintain cities of refuge in which holiness and a culture inspired by Christianity could survive and grow, treasuries of a religious and philosophic wisdom available there for all and sundry who wished to share it. In the shelter of cathedral, cloister and university there accumulated from generation to generation a deposit of spiritual and a deposit of intellectual truth. The former did not consist only in a developed and organised dogmatic theology. It was also an ascetic theology and a mystical theology crowning the ascetic and guiding those who followed its instruction to the heights of God. This deposit could be accumulated only in the asylums secured by the favour of rulers and people who feared and reverenced what was too lofty and too spiritual for their understanding. In these asylums there accumulated also the intellectual deposit of classical studies crowned by a developing philosophy. And the two deposits were bound together as closely as were the secular and the religious societies.

Only the new vernacular literatures belonged in part to the world outside and even these were linked in many ways with the clerks.

It is neither possible nor necessary to defend in detail the conduct pursued by the Church's rulers. While appreciating the powerful motives that induced the step, we must deplore the final abandonment in the thirteenth century of the ban, till then officially maintained, on the death penalty for heresy and the sanction of judicial torture. Even a policy sound in principle is liable to err in its practical application. Nevertheless the policy which produced the medieval religion culture was radically sound. The price paid for baptising the immature masses, violent, ignorant and undisciplined, that composed medieval society was indeed heavy. But it purchased nothing less than Christendom. And Christendom meant a Catholic religion-culture with a social and a political order to frame and protect it. And it meant the achievement of Catholic art. Above all, it meant opportunity and security for the free development of Catholic thought and Catholic spirituality. The alternative was sheer barbarism and a hostile paganism. In any case the squalid hovel would have existed. Nothing else was possible in an age of scarcity, strife and scientific ignorance. But the Cathedral would have been absent. Who shall say the price paid was too high ?

> " Mortal Prudence, handmaid of divine Providence,
>   hath inscrutable reckoning with Fate and Fortune.
>
> We sail a changeful sea through halcyon days and storm,
>   Our stability is but balance, and CONDUCT LIES
>   *in masterful administration* of the unforeseen."

No one who has not taken to heart this shrewd wisdom can judge fairly an institution or an historical epoch. Nor can he judge fairly the course pursued by Peter's bark as it has made its way through " the changeful sea," " the halcyon days " and " the storm " of history.

Let us then raise our eyes above the hovels which absorb the attention of so many critics of the Middle Ages, and view the cathedral which they erected.   There is the literal cathedral of stone, the social cathedral of a Christendom united at least in theory and ideal under the twofold sway of Pope and Emperor, the intellectual cathedral of Scholasticism and its highest achievement, the Summa, crowning a course of inferior disciplines, and the literary cathedral of Dante's *Comedia* which, on the brink of its disintegration, embodied the medieval synthesis, its entire religion culture in a poem of imperishable beauty.   Of these Dante's cathedral and the architect's present to the imagination what the social and the intellectual cathedrals present to thought.   To know thoroughly a great Gothic cathedral or the *Divina Comedia* is to know the medieval achievement.

The medieval synthesis was produced by an enlargement of the horizontal movement of the human mind still, however, subject to the predominant vertical motion.   The security and order, such as they were, achieved here and there by a powerful and able monarch such as Henry II or St. Louis and maintained in those religious asylums of which I have spoken, permitted man's natural acquisitiveness for knowledge to expand in every direction open to it.   Never has there been greater zeal for knowledge than that displayed by the poor clerks who thronged the universities from every part of Europe, cheerfully enduring cold and hunger and the dangers of the road, begging and brawling their way, sleeping in miserable garrets, seeking as best they might their daily pittance, thronging draughty lecture rooms to hear the lectures of a celebrated master, and eagerly devouring whatever books they could lay hands on. Learning, it would seem, like precious stones, is prized in proportion to its rarity.

Philosophy, with the theology it served, was the most engrossing intellectual interest.   But philosophy is not confined to its summit, natural theology.   On the contrary, it studies being at every level, human and subhuman, as well as angelic and divine.   As metaphysics gradually emerged as a discipline distinct from theology, a process not complete until St. Thomas, the width as well as the height of its vision became increasingly evident. And below metaphysics, ethics, logic, rhetoric, music, law and medicine were eagerly studied, as also what passed for astronomy and natural science. The very name " university " testifies to the universality of the medieval order of studies. It was fed by contributions progressively pouring in. The number of classical authors studied was not indeed substantially increased till the Renaissance. But they were studied widely and zealously, particularly, as we have noticed, in the twelfth century. Aristotle's philosophy, more earthly and more scientific in temper than Plato's, became known and superseded the earlier Neo-platonism, more exclusively religious in its inspiration. The soul was regarded, as Aristotle taught, as the form of the body, no longer Platonically as its reluctant captive. The change set a greater value on the body, and on that life of the senses which the soul lives precisely as the principle of the body. Aristotle came as a gift of the Moslem culture and accompanied by Moslem interpreters, in particular Averroes. Their pantheism provoked an outburst of rationalism which in turn rendered Aristotle suspect. But it was not long before St. Albert and St. Thomas used him as the foundation and framework of their Catholic philosophy. Emphasis was now laid on the relative independence of the secondary causes through whose agency God maintains and administers the world.

Catholicism, the universal religion, can be content with nothing less than a universal knowledge, knowledge of everything knowable, *de omni re scibili*, if it is to acquire the necessary material in which to embody, realise and display its principles. Nothing less was the medieval ideal. Dante opens his *De Monarchia* by declaring the purpose of humanity to be the actualisation of the potential intellect of the human race, that is to say, the realisation of man's entire capacity for knowledge. His ideal, the ideal of medieval thought and aspiration, is the utmost possible extension of the horizontal movement, of man's knowledge of nature and himself as well as the utmost extension of the vertical movement towards God. For only by knowing God and creatures to the fullest possibility of mortal life can the potential intellect of mankind be actualised, man's capacity for knowledge realised and satisfied. This medieval ideal of knowledge to the utmost breadth and height has left behind it the exclusive verticalism of the thinker who

ruled the previous epoch, St. Augustine.   For it did not overlook, as he had overlooked, the fact that although knowledge of
God as He is, as we shall know Him in the beatific vision,
involves a knowledge of creatures in Him truer than our
knowledge of creatures in themselves ; on earth, where we
cannot know God thus, direct knowledge of creatures is
necessary if we are to know as much of God as is open to our
knowledge.

Dante also knows, what the bitter lessons of contemporary
experience have failed to teach us, that this universal ideal
of a universal knowledge requires, if it is to be realised, a universal peace secured by a universal government, a supernational state.   Under medieval conditions the universal
sovereign was conceivable only as a monarch, a universal
Emperor.   A voluntary federation of subordinate nations lay
beyond the medieval purview.   But this does not detract from
the merit of perceiving so clearly a truth still hidden, with
far less excuse, from the majority of our contemporaries, the
truth that the sovereign state is no more defensible than the
sovereign family, and that if the world is to be saved from
international anarchy, the national state, while remaining
internally autonomous, must accept the superior jurisdiction
of a supernational government equipped with the means to
enforce its authority.

The Popes had always perceived this truth, as is proved by
the papal revival of the Roman Empire and the liturgical
prayer for the Emperor, " That God may subdue to him all
the barbarous nations " (those outside the pale of Christendom)
" to our perpetual peace."   A universal political community
and a universal intellectual synthesis correspond and mutually
support each other, and both draw man's gaze to the farthest
visible horizon, though he also looks up to the zenith.

The combination of wide travel on lower ground with
ascent to the heights, of humanism and theocentrism was embodied in the medieval curriculum, a curriculum wider and
deeper than any that has since taken its place.   It opened with
the Trivium : Grammar, Dialectic and Rhetoric.   Grammar
which embraced the study of Latin literature provided the
literary instruments of culture.   Dialectics, logic taught ac-
curate thinking, how to handle the tools of thought.   Rhetoric
taught men how to express thought and emotion, and, more-

over, by imitating the masterpieces of Latin eloquence. Medieval rhetoric, like the classical it continued, was excessively formal, and rigidly conventional. It repeated hackneyed themes *ad nauseam*, and in a hackneyed phraseology. But it disciplined utterance, and, when itself disciplined by logic, promoted accuracy of thought and its statement. Medieval education was not like our own, confined to the written word. It taught men to speak as well as to write. There followed the Quadrivium : Arithmetic, Music, Geometry, and Astrology, i.e. Astronomy, in short, the sciences of number and measurement. When we reflect that mathematics vanished later from an exclusively classical education, and were not restored to the curriculum of our public schools till the nineteenth century, and that music is even now regarded rather as an accomplishment than a serious department of education, we shall appreciate the medieval comprehensiveness. The value set on the numerical sciences displayed an understanding of the quantitative character of science, to which Meyerson has called our attention. And it encouraged, as it reflected, the medieval insistence on the supreme need, order. Above the Quadrivium was natural science. There was to be no choice between science and the humanities. And the educational edifice was completed by metaphysics and theology. Dante compares these disciplines to the successive spheres of the Ptolemaic heaven. We may compare them to the successive architectural components of the contemporary cathedral as it rose from the foundation through arcade, triforium, clerestory, roof and tower to the crowning spire.

The intellectual expansion of interest was accompanied by an affective, the humanism of the mind by a humanism of the heart. Its sources, however, lay not among the clerks, but outside in the world of the laity. The Teutonic races, German and Norse, brought into medieval Christendom the delight in heroic prowess that found expression in the Sagas, and the Nibelungen Lied. And in the Arthurian romances the Teutonic world met the world of Celtic legend. From Moslem Spain, as Christopher Dawson has shown, romantic love between the sexes entered Christendom through the Provence of the troubadours and the courts of love. And before this Northern France had given the Chansons de

Geste. These romantic humanisms of love and valour combined to compose the Arthurian cycle, to which were loosely
attached the stories of *Tristan and Yseult*, and the *Grail*, to which
in turn *Lohengrin* and *Tannhauser* were akin.

Exalting war and love between the sexes, this humanism
was refractory to the teaching of the Church and the religious
order she sought to impose. Nor was it ever fully integrated
into the medieval synthesis. The romantic lover, Aucassin,
declared defiantly that he had rather have Nicolette, " his
sweet friend," and go to hell with the fine knights, the gallant
gentlemen and the " fair gracious ladies " than give her up
and go to heaven with " the old priests and old cripples,
the halt and the maimed, who are down on their knees day
and night before altars, who go in rags and tatters, showing
their sores."

His defiance, never silenced completely, foretold the
rebellious humanism that would eventually destroy Christendom and produce the most secular society known in human
history. But for the time it was weak. We hear of atheists
among the Florentine intelligentsia, among them the father
of Dante's friend, Cavalcante. And Salimbene tells us of a
bishop who on his death-bed threw off the mask and vaunted
his unbelief. These men, however, were rare exceptions and
were obliged to conceal their sentiments.

The Church did much to harness the new humanism of the
affections to her Divine service. The Grail seems originally
to have been a magic cup of plenty. One manuscript
identifies the mountain of the Grail with the hollow hill of
Tannhauser's Venus, " der Graal oder Venus Berg." But,
as we know it, it is the chalice of the Last Supper, and the
story of its quest illustrates the beatitude : " Beati mundo
corde quia ipsi Deum videbunt." " Blessed are the pure in
heart, for they shall see God."

Moreover, this humanism of the heart found entrance
into the sanctuary. The Incarnation, God and Man in one
Person, is the point where the two opposite directions of the
vertical movement between God and Mankind meet, the
descent from God to humanity, God is made Man, and the
ascent from humanity to God, a Man is God. Hitherto
the ascending movement had predominated in Catholic piety,
the ascent through the risen Lord to God. From the twelfth

century onwards the emphasis of popular devotion shifts and centres upon God who is our fellow man.

St. Bernard is generally regarded as the founder of the new devotion to the sacred Humanity. In fact he regards it as subordinate and preparatory to an ascending devotion to the Divine Word. In this he is faithful to the older direction of prayer through the human to the Divine Christ, *per Christum hominem ad Christum Deum*. It is in condescension to the weakness of simple and immature souls that the human figure of Christ Crucified is set before their imagination (in Cant. 62). That is to say, St. Bernard was carried only a short way on the turning tide. Devotion to the Sacred Humanity cannot effect the mystical union of the soul with God, which of its nature is a union with incomprehensible Deity. But very soon it occupied the centre of Catholic devotion, covering, so to speak, even in the prayer of many mystics, their spiritual and imageless contemplation. It centred on the human Infant and the human Sufferer. The Crucifix laid aside the royal robe and crown and presented the naked and abandoned Jesus on His cross of torment. St. Francis introduced or at least popularised the Christmas crib. Gradually the Rosary, occupied so largely with the mysteries of Christ's earthly life, replaced for the laity the Psalter and Office as their favourite devotion. Devotion to Our Lady which sanctified the romantic devotion to womanhood grew in extent and ardour. And her artistic presentment became homelier and more intimately human. She was depicted as the loving Mother of the newborn Babe suckled at her breast or fondled on her lap. Or she was shown as the suffering Mother beneath her Son's cross. Holy women of transparent and imaginative temper shared the Infancy and Passion of Jesus in visions woven by the artistry of the subconscious and, when St. Francis had led the way, some of them entered so deeply into His suffering by this imaginative sympathy that His wounds were stamped on their body. The note of tender devotion to the human Jesus, struck seven centuries earlier by Venantius Fortunatus—*vagit infans— surge sepulte meus*—now swells to a vast concert which fills the Church with its music.

Concomitant with this new devotion to the Human Jesus and its consequence was a new devotion to the Blessed

Sacrament.   The Eucharistic Sacrifice is of its nature a movement from man to God.   Jesus is offered as a sacrifice of
praise to His Father.   So long as the Godward movement
determined Catholic devotion, the altar of sacrifice was the
centre of worship.   The Blessed Sacrament was indeed
reserved, but, as still in the Eastern Churches, only to communicate the sick.   But if the sacrifice of the altar, the sacrifice
of Jesus to God, represents the upward movement from man
to God, His abiding presence in the tabernacle may be taken
to represent the descent of God to Man, Emmanuel, God
with us, God as our fellow-man.   Therefore it was but natural
that the new devotion to the sacred Humanity should bring
with it a devotion to Jesus in the reserved Sacrament.   In
his study of prayer Heiler has pointed out that hitherto the
Blessed Sacrament had been regarded as a Holy Thing, *the
Body* of Jesus.   Henceforth it is regarded as a Holy Person,
as Jesus continuing His incarnate Life among us.   The tabernacle therefore began to replace the altar in the minds of
Catholics as the holiest place in the Church.   The Feast of
Corpus Christi was instituted, the custom of making visits to
the Blessed Sacrament became common, and processions of the
Blessed Sacrament made their appearance.   It was, it is true,
in protest against the opinion that the bread was not consecrated until the chalice had been consecrated also, that the
Elevation of the Host at the consecration was introduced about
1200.   The Elevation of the Chalice followed later by analogy.
But the new devotion at once seized upon the Elevation as
a focus of devotion to the Eucharistic Jesus, though the cere-
mony breaks in upon a prayer addressed to the Father.
Very soon it came to be regarded as the centre of the Mass.
Men went to Mass, not so much to offer sacrifice to the Father,
as to see Jesus " their Maker."   And the development would
culminate after the Middle Ages in Exposition, the devotion
of the Forty Hours, Benediction and Perpetual Adoration.

The Incarnation justifies, indeed implies, both directions of
worship, upward to the Godhead, downward to the Humanity.
The altar and the tabernacle together constitute the Catholic
sanctuary.   But the latter is for the former.   The altar is
more even than the tabernacle, as the Mass is more than
Benediction.   Nor should we envisage the Eucharistic Christ
of the tabernacle, as popular devotion has too often viewed

Him, as the weak and suffering Jesus of His mortal life.   For
although among us He is no longer of us.   He is the Risen
Lord, and though His presence is corporeal, the mode of His
presence is spiritual.   In the Eucharist His body is beyond
time and space.

Whatever may have been the case with individual mystics or
with popular devotion, the liturgy which was the entire public
worship of the medieval Church and the buildings in which it
was celebrated expressed not only the predominance of theocentric religion over humanism, but within the religious sphere
of the upward as contrasted with the downward movement
and subordinated devotion to the human Christ to the adoration
of the Godhead.   The institution of Corpus Christi was
balanced by the celebration of Trinity Sunday.   Catholic
worship consisted not of the Mass and devotions to the human
Jesus, even the Eucharistic Jesus, but of Mass offered to the
Father and the Divine Office of psalmody offered to the
Blessed Trinity.   Nor was the royal Judge obliterated behind
the Infant and the Man of Sorrows.   On the contrary, the Rood
was surmounted by a scene of Judgment in which the Crucified
was depicted as the Judge.   True the joy of the Risen Lord
was in the background and the serene and gentle figure of
the Shepherd as the Christians of the catacombs had seen
Him was absent.   For this vision of assured victory the conflict between light and darkness, order and anarchy, sanctity
and gross sin, was perhaps too great.   But the human, even
the Divinely human was, as it should be, subordinated to the
purely Divine.

Let us contemplate the medieval cathedral as the epitome
and embodiment of the Catholic religion culture in its medieval
summer.   It has been aptly styled a Summa in stone.   And
our attention has been called to the architectural quality of
medieval culture, whose finest artistic expression was, correspondingly, architecture.   St. Thomas impressed the order
of Catholic wisdom as its life-giving form on the matter
provided by the classical inheritance of thought, that is on the
truest that men had hitherto conceived.   And Dante translated
his work for the imagination into poetry, into a poem fed by
the literary treasure of antiquity.   The Cathedral embodied
the same life-giving order of Catholic wisdom in a representa-
tional material of encyclopædic extent.   The sciences and the

arts, legend and history, every department of human activity and the forms of vegetable and animal life were drawn upon to provide symbols and expressions of Catholic truth, notes of praise made permanent in paint and stone.

" There has been handed down to us," Paul Clemen writes,[1] " from the first half of the thirteenth century, the *Speculum Quadruplex* of the learned Vincent of Beauvais, an encyclopædia of the things which the medieval spirit of that time has to offer. . . . In its four books it comprises the whole wealth of the subject-matter and the symbolism of Gothic plastic art. . . . Every subject and every figure is contained in one of the four specula, the mirrors of nature, science, ethics and history." " In French cathedral sculpture we find treated the heritage of antiquity and early Christianity, the whole world of the Old and the New Testaments " . . . " the Apocalypse and the Last Judgment, the lives of the Saints, the newly revived Hellenism transmitted by way of Byzantium and Southern France, and allegorical subjects in which classical stories in changed forms are mixed with folklore." The Bible was more strictly selected than Clemen suggests, and we should add the gifts of Moslem culture. But his description is substantially correct.

Observe the word speculum, mirror. The medieval Catholic regarded all these bodily creatures, whether men and human acts, if good, aspects of nature or natural objects as mirrors of their Creator and the world of spirit. Each therefore is a symbol of a spiritual, ultimately a Divine Reality. However fanciful, even arbitrary, the application of this symbolism may be, its principle is a solid fact, the fact that every object on a lower plane of being is the reflection and participation of a reality of a higher order, matter therefore of spirit. The world of man, nature and art is thus in truth a mirror of God and this spiritual order. Therefore the value of this corporeal world and of everything in it is greater as a symbol than in itself. And so in fact the medieval Catholic saw and portrayed it. But he did not therefore overlook its value and character as they are in, though not for, themselves. Indeed their use and value as symbols depend on what they are in themselves. The naturalistic foliage that wreathed the capital and filled the canopy, such foliage as that which

[1] Introduction to *Gothic Cathedrals, Paris, Chartres, Amiens, Reims.*

adorns the Lady Chapel of Ely and the Chapter House at Southwell was obviously loved and studied for its own sake. Sometimes even the symbolism is forgotten. Grotesque faces, genre scenes, animals and leaves are portrayed solely from interest in them without thought of anything beyond. But this humanism and love of nature for its own sake are subordinate. They make their appearance only in the detail of ornament or half concealed on the misericords of choir stalls, themselves an indulgence to the worshipper's human weakness. A subordinate admission of the purely natural and human testified to the comprehensive Sovereignty of God who has room in His house for all that He has made and does not disdain man's everyday occupations, even his eccentricities and follies.

A favourite theme of artistic representation from sculpture to the illuminated manuscript is the occupations of the months. A life of toil and recreation in harmony with nature's seasonal rhythm is viewed as a divine service. The order of the months and their occupations framed man's religious worship, as in Missals and Books of Hours their pictures often framed the liturgical calendar of the Church. Men's daily work also was after its fashion a liturgy.

It is often believed that medieval as opposed to classical art despised the human body and could not therefore represent it realistically. Certainly the nude was very little portrayed. Adam and Eve and men and women rising for judgment were the only nude figures represented. And in the latter case the damned were often depicted nude, the saved honoured with clothing.[1]

And the human figures in sculpture and stained glass were more or less conventionalised. For the artist was concerned to portray not the beauty and strength of the body as such, but the body as the servant and temple of the spirit, tormented even and dying in that service. More attention was therefore paid to the countenance in which the soul is most fully expressed than to the limbs. The statues are often, as at Chartres, unnaturally elongated in harmony with the vertical aspiration of Gothic architecture. Nevertheless, as Gothic replaced Romanesque and the subordinate humanism

[1] Not always, however. In the doom discovered at Wenhaston St. Peter is admitting into heaven a bishop clad only in his mitre.

and naturalism of the medieval summer advanced, the human body began to be studied and portrayed with a delighted observation of its beauty, though still in subordination to the soul. This has been pointed out by Clemen.[1] " Gradually the way leads from the heavy and constrained early works . . . to the new classic work of Rheims. . . . The figures with their over-rich drapery are filled with an individual life. One step further and we come to the master of the Visitation on the west front, perhaps the ' Peter and Paul ' master in his final maturity. . . . The influence of antiquity is visible here. It is obvious in the rich folds of drapery, perhaps derived directly from ancient statues of matrons ; but there is also a feeling of the noble, simple rhythm of the great Greek sculptors. The bearded prophet with the pointed cap . . . is of truly Greek dignity in his whole appearance, and is akin to the ancient statue of Mausolus or the Ulysses type. In the next phase of this art an entirely new feeling for the body is awakened. The new school formed the slender bodies under the close-lying drapery with obvious pleasure, and the naked body too is sculptured with a fine, delicate sensuality. A varied succession of amazingly well-observed and well-conceived nude figures is given in the two strips of the Judgment tympanum representing the dead rising from their tombs. . . . Wilhelm Worringer declared the Gothic age to be a flowering of civilisation of equal value with that of Ancient Greece. And may we not seriously compare the greatest achievements of this Gothic sculpture with the great early works of Greece ? When we follow its development, the successive phases of Greek sculpture are at once suggested. . . . Only we must not set an absolute closeness to nature as the aim [2] of Gothic culture as it was of Greek ; this new art sought to give a likeness, a symbol, not a copy. And the Gothic sculptors were not imitators of the Greek but artists of a new and equal birth. The hidden Hellenism in their work is worth seeking out and grasping. If it was the task of the Gothic age to overcome Hellenism, it was at the same time its task to fulfil it." To overcome Hellenism by includ-ing it and going beyond it, in short by fulfilling it : this defines

[1] *Op. cit.*, xxiv and xxxcii.

[2] Though not the actual and immediate aim it was his misconception of the artistic ideal. See pp. 65-6.

THE ADORATION OF THE CROSS, DOMINICAN FRESCO BY FRA ANGELICO :
THE CHAPTER HOUSE, SAN MARCO, FLORENCE

The Fathers and Saints of the Church are gathered about the Tree of Life upon which hangs the Crucified One, and
nearest the foot of the Cross kneels St. Dominic, Founder of the Order for which the picture was painted.

THE ART OF THE CATHOLIC NORTH:
THE SACRAMENTS OF THE CHURCH, MARRIAGE AND
EXTREME UNCTION, BY ROGER VAN DER WEYDEN

not only the achievement of medieval art, the physical cathedral and its ornament, but the medieval religion-culture as a whole. It describes scholastic philosophy and the Divina Comedia as truly as Rheims Cathedral. And in this eminent fulfilment of Hellenist humanism, as God, the Divine Word, is the eminent fulfilment of all created forms, the flowering summer of Catholic culture realised the promise of its spring, the vision of Clement who saw Hellenism as the Gentiles' pedagogue [1] to the school of Christ, the classical Good Shepherd of the catacombs, and the joyous, yet dignified figures moving in a vernal landscape who foretold to Hermas the future glory of the Church.

We must not suppose that the simple and childlike spirit of the medieval man was conscious of the exact nature of his achievement. He was, of course, well aware that he was the heir of classical antiquity, and, as we have seen, he cherished a universal ideal, social and cultural. But he was not equally aware of the true nature of his artistic ideal. For all his devotion to symbolism he wanted art to be the mirror of nature, though, as Clemen has pointed out, he did not carry this ideal into practice. He selected from nature significant forms embodying spiritual ideas, the symbols in which he delighted. But he did not perceive that this selection of significant form, this symbolic view of art, is inconsistent with the theory that the aim of art is to copy nature exactly. For this was in fact the artistic ideal he cherished. And he entertained it, no doubt, because he was a child. For it is the child's view of art.

For Dante the divine workmanship of the sculptures in the purgatory of the proud was shown by their perfect likeness to nature, a likeness so exact that they might be confused with it.

" Dead seemed the dead and the living living. He saw not better than I who saw the reality of all that I trod upon." [2]

" That circling bank I discerned to be adorned with sculptures, such that not only Polyclitus but nature would be put to shame. The angel . . . appeared so vividly graven . . . that it seemed not an image which is dumb. One would have sworn that he was saying Ave, for there she was fashioned

---

[1] The classical pedagogue was not a schoolmaster. He was a slave who accompanied boys to school.

[2] Purg. xii, 67-9.

5

who turned the key to open the supreme love. And in her attitude were imprinted these words, 'Ecce Ancilla Dei,' as expressly as a figure is stamped on wax. There were graven on the marble the cart and the oxen drawing the sacred ark. . . . In front appeared people and the whole divided into seven choirs to two of my senses made the one say 'no,' the other 'yes,' they do sing. 'In like wise, at the smoke of the incense which there was imaged, eyes and nose were made discordant with yea and no'". (Purg. x, 34-45 and 55-64). The ideal here expressed is not even artistic photography which is a genuine art employing the action of light for its pencil, but the mechanical photography whose sole concern is to reproduce everything. Or rather it is the newsreel of the films, with an aspiration after the smellies and feelies prophesied by Aldous Huxley.

That is to say, though the aim of the medieval artist was, as Clemen says, not to give a copy of nature but to present a natural form as a symbol, his naïve consciousness believed that the best symbol was in fact the exact copy, which, however, he was too genuine an artist to achieve.

"You Greeks are always children," said the Egyptian priest in Plato's *Timæus*. More truly can it be said of medieval men. They were always children. They were naughty, very naughty children, good children, rough children, gentle children, children ignorant of their alphabet or children eagerly learning and poring over any book they could lay hands on, foolish children or wise children, but all alike children. That no doubt is the reason why from the Renaissance to the present day the conceit of raw adolescence has despised them.

The childlikeness of the medieval mind is shown by a contemporary comment on Salisbury Cathedral. Did the writer admire, as we do, the superb grace of the Gothic columns? Not at all. He admired the polish of the Purbeck marble so smooth that you could see your face reflected in it. That is to say he admired an effect produced as well or better by the marble fittings of a cinema lounge or the walls of a Lyon's corner house. Even Dante, seeking to represent the glories of heaven, imagines effects of moving lights. Jewelled spirits spell out over the sky of Jupiter DILIGITE JUSTITIAM VOS QUI JUDICATIS TERRAM, and later form themselves into an eagle of lights from whose mouth music and speech issue. That is to say, he envisaged the beauty of heaven as a sky-sign advertisement assisted by a loud speaker. True it is a text, not the qualities of soap or pills, that is flashed out. But at Los Angeles texts are, or recently were, employed in this way. From dusk to midnight a sky-sign proclaims " Christ saves." Dante's heaven has a touch of Hollywood. Childlike, too, was the love of elaborate pageants such as in real life adorned church festivals or royal triumphs and such as Dante built up for the imagination in his earthly paradise.

Medieval man had also the child's credulity. No legend was too marvellous, no miracle or relic too incredible for his belief. The story of the Jackdaw of Rheims was not the invention of Barham's comic muse but was related by Caesar of Heisterbach in his collection of miracles as edifying fact. Even St. Thomas made no question that demons held carnal intercourse with men and women.[1] The mythical St. Wilgefortis, who, to escape wedlock, grew a beard and was therefore crucified by her irate father, was an object of widespread devotion. A bunch of pennyroyal gathered at dawn on the Baptist's Nativity, Midsummer Day, and kept till Christmas, will revive, if laid on the altar during the Midnight Mass. The pilgrim to the Holy Land saw at Hebron a field of the red earth from which God had moulded Adam " still malleable as clay " and sold abroad for use as such. He also saw the cave where Adam and Eve slept after their ejection from Paradise, and at Mambre the oak beneath which Abraham entertained the three Angels. On Mount Tabor he was shown the ruins of the three tabernacles Peter desired to build, and on a Galilean hillside the stone on which Our Lord sat to teach. And on his way to Sinai the dragoman showed Brydenbach and his companions the unicorn, duly depicted among the fauna of the Holy Land.[2]

For the medieval child must have every truth, every incident of sacred history or legend made visible for the imagination by some concrete embodiment or relic. At the least

[1] Burchard, however, in the previous century had rejected belief in incubi and succubae as the product of a diseased imagination and indeed a positive sin. Thurston, *Superstition*, 98-9.

[2] For all this see Brydenbach, *Pilgrimage to the Holy Land*. Though Brydenbach was contemporary with the early Renaissance (he made his pilgrimage in 1483) he is a typical medieval pilgrim.

he must know the exact locality where an event happened, for example, the spot at Jaffa where St. George slew the dragon.

And the medieval child had the child's ignorance of historical perspective. For his imagination the ancient Jews, Greeks and Romans lived the same life as his contemporaries and in the same environment. Chaucer's Theseus is a feudal prince.

Nevertheless with a wisdom deeper than ours this medieval child saw human history as the progressive accomplishment of God's saving design and the Incarnation as its centre and the key to its meaning.[1]

This childlikeness was one reason why the Middle Ages achieved so much in philosophy, so little in the sciences. For the penetrating vision of the intelligent child may explore the secrets of being, revealed as clearly in his limited experience as in the wider experience of the adult. Science, on the other hand, demands an extensive accumulation of facts and a critical attitude in verifying and interpreting them—acquired by long experience and the maturity of the critical reason. The child's vision, naturally straight and sound, kept medieval philosophy from such obvious denials of common sense and daily experience as materialism, subjective idealism, positivism, pragmatism, behaviourism and all the other false directions taken by modern philosophy. The enlightened reason of medieval cosmology showed the alchemist that all corporal substances, however diverse, are varieties of a matter identical in them all to which therefore they can in principle be reduced and are thus mutually interchangeable. Seeking prematurely and by an impossible technique the transmutation of metals alchemy anticipated fruitlessly the fruitful discoveries of contemporary physics.[2] The child's simplicity which enabled the medieval man to enter the Kingdom of Christ more easily than we in our more adult sophistication, also enabled him to enter the realm of philosophic wisdom and unite it with the higher wisdom of faith, in a world view combining mysticism with

[1] As I write this I am reading St. Thomas More's *History of the Passion* and two works by Soren Kierkegaard. The latter was no rationalist but a convinced and zealous Christian. But the contrast between the complexity and indirectness of his mind and More's simplicity and directness is the contrast between adolescence and childhood.

[2] The medical doctrine of the four humours bears an analogous relation to the modern discovery of the psychological effects of internal glandular secretions.

THE ART OF THE CATHOLIC NORTH:
MASTERPIECE OF THE TWO JOHNS, BY MEMLINC, THE
HOSPITAL OF ST. JOHN, BRUGES

*St Catherine of Alexandria kneels before the Virgin and Child, and Saint
Barbara with her symbol, the tower, is nearby.   But Memlinc spent his
imagination most freely upon the persons and stories of John the Evangelist
and John the Baptist, the picture being for the High Altar of a community
dedicated to these Saints.   Moreover the donor, brother Jan Floreins, a wine
gauger of Bruges, was also named " John."*

BRUNELLESCHI'S DOME :
THE DUOMO, FLORENCE (1420–1445)

Brunelleschi was an architect very different in type from the master-masons of the Gothic Cathedrals.   He was a scholar well versed in Catholic lore, a student of Dante, and a master of perspective and geometry.   In his Florentine Dome can be seen the architecture of Italian Humanism in its early prime, by one who borrowed, indeed, from Greece and Rome, but added features of worth which expressed the religious thought and feeling of Italy in the fifteenth century.

common sense. The child is often destructive, as were those medieval men who loved fighting for its own sake. But he is often a lover of order and construction, a builder. Such were those medieval children who elaborated ideals of political order, or an order of studies or built cathedrals. If order is the educator's primary need the child, as Madame Montessori has shown, is ready, even anxious, to achieve it by self-discipline and constructive work. From the conversion of the barbarians onward the Church conducted a Montessori school from which medieval Christendom and its achievement emerged.[1]

This childlikeness accounts also in part for the gap between ideal and reality. The inexperienced vision of the child leaps to the goal and cannot see how long and how difficult a road must be travelled before it can be reached. That is why it should, as Chesterton has said, be our task to realise medieval ideals which the medievalists could not realise. The adult's experience and his progressively acquired knowledge and skill must accomplish the vision seen by the fresh keen eyes of the unspoiled but inexperienced child.

Meanwhile, however, the medieval child built his cathedral and embodied his vision, his ideal in a splendour of colour and form. To the cathedral, therefore, as the artistic embodiment of the medieval ideal and achievement we must now return.

It is now agreed that the introduction of the pointed arch and vault which transformed Romanesque into Gothic was not, as romantic writers had supposed, imitation of the natural arch of the forest trees, or a piece of deliberate symbolism, adopted to express the soul's ascent to God. It was a device of practical engineering. The pointed arch making it possible to dispense with the thick walls of Romanesque and progressively to enlarge the window space affected a great economy in the use of material at a time when difficulties of transport made the economy most desirable. Moreover, the wooden roof which spanned the Romanesque and Norman nave and choir was liable to take fire. The pointed vault enabled the wooden roof to be replaced by stone vaulting

---

[1] I do not mean that the actual methods of educating children were in the least of the Montessori kind. Unhappily they were not. I am speaking of the education of the adult child who could not be flogged into good behaviour.

and thus reduced the risk and the destructiveness of conflagrations. It is remarkable how many Gothic cathedrals replace an earlier Romanesque building destroyed by fire.

But its engineering motive did not alter the fact that the pointed architecture of Gothic expressed, though unintentionally, a soaring aspiration, an effect enhanced by the diminution of solid mass and by the wider windows, letting in the light of heaven, transformed by the stained glass into jewelled flame. And that this effect was felt at the time is proved by the fact that, as Bond has shown, the feature which crowned this architectural aspiration, the spire served no utilitarian purpose but was pure symbolism. It was a symbol of the Godward ascent, of that " Spiretop of spirit " of which Sterry wrote.

Within the cathedral there was an upward sweep of vision past the arcade, the triforum and the clerestory to the high vault. And outside there was a corresponding ascent to the central tower or spire. And the vertical was enhanced by the longitudinal prospect. Down the avenue of nave arches the eye travels to a choir sufficiently enclosed by the roodscreen to be mysterious, but open above, with the farther suggestion of a retrochoir or Lady Chapel. Looking westward indeed the prospect is less satisfactory. Seen from the outside the west front is usually magnificent. Although in French Gothic it is too often marred by disproportionate and unbalanced towers, it was employed as the background of a host of statues, arranged in schemes of comprehensive instruction, Ruskin's Bible of Amiens. But seen from within it comes up against the eye as the meaningless and blank interruption of a graceful vista of arches which might, and should have, continued indefinitely, until the stone avenue diminished into the invisibility of distance. Eastward the cathedral comes to a natural, or shall we not say, a supernatural conclusion, the High Altar of the God Man surrounded by the adoring Saints to whom the sidechapels are dedicated, and accompanied by His Mother, patroness of the Lady Chapel. And the beginning which is also the end of the world process is fixed, God, man's Creator and last End. Westward the cathedral comes to an abrupt and an arbitrary close which is not a conclusion. The historical process of realising God's Kingdom on earth proceeds indefinitely and its end escapes our vision. It is necessarily incomplete. Therefore the Gothic Church has not the completeness, the finite perfection of the Greek temple. Nor has it its perfect balance. Tall and long, it lacks proportionate breadth. So it must be. When Infinity has been introduced a finite sum can no longer be calculated. With the Incarnation the Infinite entered human history and rendered a finite perfection impossible. Therefore the Gothic church cannot be a compact whole, intrinsically complete. For this reason also it admitted an indefinite series of enlargements and reconstructions. The transepts to be sure reach out in breadth in token of that universality of interest of which I have spoken. Actually the proportionate breadth of the transepts exceeds that of the Greek temple. The medieval world included much which was lacking in the Hellenic. Romance, for example, entered antiquity only here and there, the alien prophet of a world unborn. But the breadth of the church as a whole could not correspond with the height or the length. For the vertical movement Godward overshadowed the horizontal that terminates in creatures. And the Incarnation of Infinity set going a movement towards its embodiment that can never be completed and which is aptly symbolised by the length and the inconclusive westward extension of the Gothic cathedral. Perfect symmetry implies and demands the finite vista which the Infinite destroys.

Thus height and length combine to raise our vision when we enter the cathedral to a point from which we can look down on the world, " terrena despicere," and on the unfinished course of its history. But not in contempt. On the contrary, the wealth of natural ornament and human representation combine with the detachment of this view from above and beyond the world an appreciation of all that it contains of truth, of beauty and of good. But everything is subordinate to the choir and altar of God's liturgical and sacrificial praise. In this subordination all these natural and human forms, all these representations of work and study are drawn into this praise of God. The mirrors of nature, science, ethics and history, praise the Divine glory by reflecting it. Medieval thought, exemplified by the twelfth-century prophetess, St. Hildegarde, saw man as a microcosm of the universe. For the many levels of its being are represented in him. And the Man who is God, Head of the Church, His mystical extension and body, is the microcosm of humanity. As such, in the sanctuary of the Gothic cathedral, He offers to God the entire creation, and, above all, the thought and the practical skill of man presented and portrayed throughout the building. It is to be regretted that freemasonry has rendered suspect the description of God as Architect of the Universe. For it was thus that He was seen by the Catholic masons who built and carved the Gothic cathedral. And in Christ He had begun to build another edifice, of architecture at once human and divine, the Church and the world re-ordered within her.

As in the view of the world which it embodies, everything in the cathedral is directed to God. Everything in its mode and measure is an incarnation of the Divine Wisdom that " extends from end to end mightily ordering all things graciously," and thus the fulfilment of Its personal Incarnation.

This is not to say that medieval architecture was faultless. The proportions are sometimes unsatisfactory. For example, Ely Lady Chapel, that defaced miracle of medieval stone carving, is too broad for its length and height, certainly a most unGothic defect. The triforium of Exeter Cathedral is too low for the arcade beneath it. Had the Bishop's throne in the same cathedral been carved in the nineteenth, not the fourteenth century, instead of being acclaimed as a superb example of the carver's art it would have been condemned as a typical instance of clumsy Victorian Gothic. For it crushes into insignificance the occupant whose dignity it should enhance. And Gothic painting is often extremely crude, little better than the work of children. Particular examples of modern Gothic are more satisfying than particular instances of genuine medieval work. Sir Giles Gilbert Scott's nave at Downside is better proportioned and therefore better architecture than the neighbouring nave of Wells. But we lose sight of these flaws of detail and these individual failures when we contemplate the Gothic achievement as a whole. Gothic art is a mighty prayer of consecration, consecrating to God the entire world of nature and man in unison with the Eucharistic consecration for which its Cathedral was built.

The consecration of man and the entire world to God in Christ, the sacrificial Victim, so that the consecrated Gift is received by the offerer as a medium of communion with God,[1] the meaning of the Eucharist, is also the meaning of the medieval Cathedral, the literal and the spiritual alike.

From the summit of the vertical movement, from the spire-top of spirit, the medieval mind looked down on the human and earthly scene. But it was not to despise it. On the contrary, from this altitude the eye sweeps horizontally from horizon to horizon across the world below and refers its wide prospect to the central height of God whence it is surveyed. True, much detail is lost by a vision reluctant to bend down close to earth. But the time for detail is not yet. What detail is seen is but a point seized here or there, in passing moments of descent. A spray of oak-leaves it may be, the tendrils of a vine, a lovely or a grotesque countenance. Nor does the eye linger too long on such things. It soon reascends and takes with it what it has seen for a symbol of the loftier vision.

St. Francis' attitude to the world did not, in fact, as Gilson suggests, differ substantially from this cathedral synthesis of medievalism. He did but carry it forward, breathe into it the power of his unique personality, and invest it with the poetic beauty of a life which was an acted poem. We may therefore quote Gilson's account as descriptive, not only of St. Francis' attitude and temper, and of the Franciscan spirit, but of the medieval ideal, such as I have sought to depict it. " The more he despised the world the more he loved it." That is to say, he did not despise but looked down upon the world. " He saw in it the clear mirror of the goodness of God," as Vincent of Beauvais also did in his fourfold Mirror. " In each one of the works of the Lord he recognised the hand of the workman and his soul was filled with joy ; everything that seemed to him good shouted in his ears the goodness of God ; that is why seeking everywhere his Well-Beloved in the traces of Him . . . he used all things as steps to mount to Him. . . . St. Francis lived continuously in the midst of a forest of symbols." [2] So did the architects and masons of the cathedrals, the writers of hymns such as Adam of St. Victor, the exegetes and the devotional writers.

[1] Dom Wesseling has brought out this significance of the Mass in writings to which Catholic thought and spirituality are much indebted.

[2] *Philosophy of St. Bonaventure*, pp. 71-2. English translation.

Gilson should have written " *the medieval man* " lived in a forest of symbols.

St. Francis' successor and biographer, St. Bonaventure, true to his master and true to the medieval world that produced him, composed on the sacred Mount of Alvernia his *Itinerarium Mentis in Deum* (The Mind's Journey to God). Secluded on this Tabor from a world of strife and raised above it, the Saint sought to receive and to give to others the peace of Divine contemplation, the peace that is ecstasy. The journey to this peace of the spire-top vision at the summit of the Godward ladder is an ascent through creatures seen and valued as God's works and tokens to mystical and ecstatic union with their Creator. " The soul," writes Pr. Gilson, " has reached the goal. In one single mental perception compenetrate—yet each still discernible—the first and the last, the highest and the lowest, the circumference and the centre. The mind has worked at the deciphering of the two books, of nature and the soul, with such mighty effort ; and now at last both books are before its eyes, held in their totality in one single act of vision, living with all their content transparent to the mind's gaze in the word that explains them. The soul has become again the image of God that it once was in the earthly paradise, as it were a perfect thing which has just been brought to the completeness of its per-fection, like creation on the evening of the sixth day." [1] These words describe not only St. Bonaventure's ideal, nor simply the medieval mystic's, but the ideal of the medieval religion-culture, of the medieval " cathedral."

Thus the medieval ideal united detachment with appreci-ation under the religious and Christian primacy of detach-ment. For in his vertical knowledge medieval man was aware that the creature in its distinction from God is nothing, a mere capacity to receive God. All its positive being and worth are God's communication to it. Thus whatever his horizontal vision saw and appreciated was appreciated by the vertical vision for God in it. Sometimes this was rightly understood. The creature was not appreciated for itself apart from God, but for itself as a communication and a manifestation of God. Viewed thus, there is indeed no difference between loving creatures for themselves and loving them for God.

[1] *Philosophy of St. Bonaventure*, E.T., pp. 457-8.

Unfortunately, medieval religion was often blind to this truth, a blindness shared by too many devout Christians before and after the Middle Ages. It failed to appreciate creatures, or at least large classes of them, for this Divine communication of their positive value. Theoretically, however, and ideally, in the conceptual realisation of the Summa, in the artistic realisation of the *Divina Comedia* and in the cathedral the medieval religion-culture achieved a harmony of the vertical and the horizontal movements of the human spirit, reconciled detachment with appreciation, built and ordered the earthly city with a vision directed to the heavenly. Even the secular ruler, Dante declared, must behold " at least a tower " of the heavenly Jerusalem.

Such was the medieval ideal in the summer of the Catholic religion-culture. And such was the finest expression of that ideal, in thought, in poetry, in painting, in sculpture and in architecture. But it was not the actuality of the medieval world, lay or clerical.

The matter was too recalcitrant to the idea which the medieval artist, whether the artist of speculation, of politics, and economics, or the artist of word, brush, chisel, glass or building, strove so valiantly to impose upon it. Social order and therefore security were insufficient, instruments were lacking, scientific knowledge was too scanty, and education, confined, as it was to a small minority, too restricted. The tensions, political or theoretical, above all the tension between the religious and vertical and the secular and horizontal movement, could not be overcome in practice by a synthesis achieved only as an ideal and in the finest speculative and artistic accomplishment. The least additional momentum in one direction or another and the medieval order, a cathedral whose structure was poised too insecurely, would collapse.[1] Its collapse and an attempt to rebuild it, an attempt successful only in part and for a time, will be the history of the Catholic religion-culture in the ensuing period of its late summer and autumn.

[1] Firm foundations, however, upheld the Christian religion-culture for several centuries after the collapse of medieval Christendom. Indeed, a considerable portion of the fabric survived and was strengthened by the work of the Counter-reformation.

LATE SUMMER

THE DISINTEGRATION OF THE MEDIEVAL ORDER :
THE RENAISSANCE

THE fourteenth and fifteenth centuries were centuries of disintegration. Centrifugal forces were striving in many directions to destroy the medieval synthesis completed, as we have seen, only in the realm of idea and imagination.

In the political order the victory over the Hohenstaufen Empire which had vindicated Papal supremacy over the Christian commonwealth was short-lived. It broke the power of the Empire and permanently saved the Church from the danger of that Caesaropapism which had enslaved the Eastern Church. But in place of the Empire arose powerful national states. And one of these, the France of Philip the Fair, within half a century after the defeat of the Hohenstaufens, successfully defied Boniface VIII and carried a French successor to the " Babylonish captivity " of Avignon. Thus as the result of their strife the two factors of supernational unity were weakened, one of them to a virtual death. The Holy Roman Empire entered on the decline which left the Emperor a merely nominal sovereign over the host of petty rulers who divided Germany. And the Papacy was weakened in face of the national state by Philip's victory, by the seventy years at Avignon under the shadow of France, though the French control of a French Pope was in fact largely nullified by the war with England, and by the great schism which followed. The latter indeed produced the conciliar movement which sought in a general council a centre of unity above the warring Popes and strengthened the power of the national monarch who decided which claimant to the Papacy his subjects should acknowledge.

No doubt the rise of the national state, which from 1300 to the present day has progressively increased its power and its

THE ANNUN-
CIATION BY FRA
ANGELICO, THE
PRADO, MADRID

*Those whose heart
was given to the
Mother of God would
not prefer Venus.*

THE LAST SUPPER, BY FRA ANGELICO:
THE LIBRARY OF THE MONASTERY OF SAN MARCO, FLORENCE

hold on men's loyalties, was an immediate gain of peace and order. A strong national government could and did provide a security which the nebulous and remote sovereignty of the Holy Roman Emperor had never provided. But it bore within it the seed of that international anarchy which has rent Europe in pieces and has replaced the insecurity of fighting barons and cities by the insecurity of total war which takes a larger toll of wealth, works of art and human life, and is more detrimental to religion and culture than the former.

Thus loyalty to the national monarch grew. And it was supported, as Bergson has shown, by the evolutionary inheritance of a herd instinct uniting a social group against potential foes. It made men lose sight of the Christian commonwealth and resentful of interference by a foreigner even in the religious sphere. It therefore threatened to abolish or at best restrict Papal authority. And it was an earthly loyalty concerned with interests wholly of this world. To strengthen it, therefore, was to strengthen the horizontal at the expense of the vertical movement. A human loyalty was encroaching on the Divine.

The synthesis effected by thirteenth-century Scholasticism and most perfectly by its greatest representative, St. Thomas, was a synthesis of human wisdom and divine revelation, and in philosophy between Augustinian Neoplatonism with its one-sided emphasis on the vertical and spiritual movement and the more humanist and scientifically rationalist philosophy of Aristotle. St. Thomas vindicated the autonomy of philosophy, the power of the human mind to attain truth by its natural light and the relative independence of created causes. In some points even, I venture to think, he inclined too far in the rationalist and Aristotelian direction. For example, he regarded the senses as the sole ultimate source of human knowledge. *Nihil in intellectu quod non prius in sensu.* Rather, I hold, from the outset the intellect apprehends directly even the outer forms of corporeal objects in and through the atomic data of sense. And by denying spiritual matter and therefore making the body the principle of man's individuation, he rendered it very difficult to understand how the individual can survive death. We may prefer in some respects the teaching of the more Platonic Bonaventure. But in the main, St. Thomas held the balance between Platonism and Aristotelianism, the vertical and the horizontal, spirit and reason, and successfully harmonised them.

The Thomism synthesis, however, did not long dominate Catholic philosophy. The philosophy of the fourteenth and fifteenth centuries pressed one aspect of truth to the detriment of others and divorced what Thomism had happily wedded.

Pr. Moody has indeed shown that the greatest fourteenth-century thinker, William of Ockham,[1] did not teach the nominalism with which he is usually credited, which confines knowledge to the particular object and denies universals. But he pressed the Aristotelian element in St. Thomas's thought, to which St. Thomas had himself conceded too much, to the detriment of the Augustinian and Neoplatonic factors. Though Ockham did not confine knowledge to the concrete and individual phenomenon, by denying the metaphysical status of the universals, whose reality he admitted, he undermined its foundation. He thus, however unwittingly, prepared the way for empiricism and positivism. The secularist temper of his philosophy is noticed by Pr. Moody. " He was a secular philosopher in comparison with his scholastic predecessors. St. Thomas was a theologian primarily "—also a philosopher—" and a man of science only secondarily. Ockham was a man of science." [2] The shift of interest between St. Thomas and Ockham is significant. It forecasts the same change of interest to be made by western civilisation, the progressive expropriation of theology and metaphysics, that the natural sciences might usurp their vacant throne. And it was surely no mere coincidence that Ockham also anticipated the political secularism of modern Europe by maintaining the ecclesiastical supremacy of the civil power as represented by the Emperor Louis and defying Papal excommunication. From the outset political and philosophic secularism advance hand in hand in their campaign against the Catholic religion-culture of Europe.

Because Ockham's view of knowledge was empirical and rationalist in temper his successors could go forward to the nominalism which did in truth deny universals which, it was taught, are simply convenient labels to denote a number of

[1] Though Duns Scotus survived until 1308 he may be regarded as a thirteenth-century thinker.

[2] E. A. Moody, *The Logic of William of Ockham*, p. 307.

similar objects. Gradually philosophy would come to be regarded as the product of man's autonomous reason, and would lose its consecration as knowledge of the Divine Wisdom reflected in created being, by an intelligence which is itself illuminated by the Light which enlightens every man. Between philosophy and theology there was now a wide gulf. Reason, it was held, could not elucidate revealed truths and relate them to the conclusions of reason. They were solely matters of faith, sundered from reason. An opposition was thus set up between faith and reason which would culminate in Luther's denunciation of philosophy and " the whore reason." Moreover, within the sphere of reason itself, Nominalism, though this was not at first realised, confined knowledge to the individual phenomenon. Anything beyond this could be no more than a useful and probable generalisation. Philosophers had entered upon the path that would lead ultimately to Comte's rejection of philosophy in the name of empirical science, and to Mills' empiricist logic which could not be certain that the natural laws valid on earth hold good in the stars. This empiricism was the goal of one tendency of late medieval thought, as Luther's fideism earlier reached had been of another.

As we have seen, the *Summa Theologica*, the *Divina Comedia* and the cathedral represented a harmony of the vertical and the horizontal movements of the human spirit, of transcendence and immanence, detachment and appreciation, supernature and nature, the divine and the human. But it is doubtful whether anyone, even their makers, fully grasped the implications of this harmony. In the scale of practical valuation the exaggerated verticalism of Augustine desiring to know only God and the soul was still dominant. It may be questioned whether St. Thomas would have welcomed the humanism deduced from his philosophy with impeccable logic by certain modern Thomists. He probably emphasised man's fallen nature rather than the goodness of his nature as such. Even if he did not, certainly his contemporaries and his successors did. The monastic movement as St. Bernard and his contemporaries had viewed it was a flight from a world where the Christian life was impossible. The friars indeed went out into the world. But it was primarily to rescue from it recruits for their monastic life or, where this was impossible, to gather men and women who, though remaining in the world, would live in it according to the rule of a Third Order which *in its original form* was more austere than the rule followed to-day by many professed religious. It was in St. Bernard's spirit that St. Dominic's successor, Blessed Jordan of Saxony, congratulated his postulants on having escaped from bondage to the devil. That is to say, the friars sought to render escape from the world to religion more widely accessible. They did not envisage a type of Christian life more suited to men and women living in the world than the traditional monastic spirituality and ascesis. When the medieval Catholic was not lax he was a Puritan frowning on dances, on the drama, even religious drama, on romances, vernacular poetry—the classics were educational—and amusements generally. Puritanism was not made in Geneva, or in Edinburgh for that matter. The Protestant Puritans did but discover its nakedness and display its inhumanity by isolating it from the poetry and humanity of Catholic devotion and worship and by seeking to impose it by force on the entire community. A typical instance of this tension between two extremes is the note of recantation which Chaucer appended to the *Canterbury Tales*. Certainly the worldly Chaucer had allowed himself in places an indefensible licence. But the repentant Chaucer has become a Puritan. " I revoke . . . my translations and enditings of worldly vanities as is the book of Troilus, the book also of Fame, the book of the Nineteen Ladies ; the book of the Duchess, the Book of Saint Valentine's Day, of the Parlement of Birds, the tales of Canterbury, those that ' sounene into,' tend to sin, the book of the Lion. . . . But of the translation of Boece de Consolatione and other books of legends of saints and homilies and morality and devotion that thank I Our Lord Jesu Christ." It seems clear that the only writings which approved themselves to Chaucer's conscience were the specifically religious or moral. Of all the immortal tales we should probably have had from the converted Chaucer, besides the Prologue, only such as the good Parson's insipid dissertation on the deadly sins. Those who present Chaucer as representative of medieval Catholic culture should remember that had he been a more devout Catholic, he would not have been the Chaucer we know, the poet of humanity. That is

THE DISPUTA,
BY RAPHAEL,
THE VATICAN
STANZE, ROME.

"The frescoes with
which Raphael adorned
the Vatican are in the
authentic tradition of
the mediæval cathedral.
Raphael enforces this
truth by painting both
a 'School of Athens'
and a 'Disputa.'
The School of Athens
does not array Greek
philosophy in opposition
to Christian theology.
On the contrary, in the
spirit of Origen and
St. Thomas, it is de-
picted as the forerunner
of the higher wisdom
and its preparation."

THE CREATION
OF ADAM.
FRESCO
BY MICHAEL
ANGELO IN THE
CEILING OF THE
SISTINE CHAPEL,
ROME

"Adam stretches out
his arm towards God,
who, in turn, bends His
arm down to Adam.
But their fingers do not
touch. Man's nature
and history are a search
for God. . . . 'Here
Hellenism in the naked
Adam confronts He-
braism in his Divine
Creator.'"

to say, the Catholic conscience, though prepared to accept creatures, required their explicit reference to religion. It was not enough that within a framework of Catholic belief, therefore within a universal reference to God, they should, simply by being what they are, display His beauty and worship Him by it. Actually the cathedral expressed this wider view, but hardly in the intention of its pious architects.

The same tension appears in the attitude adopted towards human, and in particular, sex love. When the Albigenses explicitly denounced sex as evil the orthodoxy of Catholic doctrine, divinely protected from passing fashions of thought, condemned the heresy. But an Encratism of feeling, an Encratite attitude of mind that fell short of explicit teaching, had long prevailed within the Church. Its fount was the apocryphal writings which had circulated since the second century. It had been fostered by the excesses of Augustine's teaching on sex. Roswitha had voiced it in the tenth century when she dramatised legends presenting sex in the foulest light, its excesses and even perversions, and in contrast with them, praising celibacy, even of the married. The Sarum calendar reflected the same spirit when in defiance of the facts it honoured Sts. Perpetua and Felicitas as Virgins or the Queen Mother Bathildis. A fifteenth-century life of St. Radegunde transforms her justifiable separation from a husband, no better than a monster, into a refusal from the outset to be his wife in more than name. When Margery Kempe was converted from worldliness she looked back on her wedded life as unclean. If Jesus went to the marriage at Cana it was, so medieval writers said, to separate the bridegroom, St. John, from his bride, Mary Magdalen. St. Thomas refused to endorse St. Augustine's condemnation of sexual pleasure as such. But even he taught that the use of marriage —purely for sexual pleasure—is a venial sin. And the Dominican St. Catherine did her utmost to persuade her married friends to live as brother and sister. Love is the ultimate of morality and religion. Accordingly by its attitude to love we may judge the ethos of a culture or a society. Therefore this opposition and tension between the lower love of the flesh and the higher love of the spirit, carried far beyond the subordination of the former to the latter, and its paradoxical consequence that marriage was considered by

6

the pious in the words of Patmore's daughter " rather a wicked sacrament," witness to a divorce between flesh and spirit, nature and grace, which survived and was active, beneath the ideal synthesis to which medieval culture aspired and in its greatest achievement did in such large measure attain.   Though the cathedral was no work of Puritans, the religion of the most devout worshippers in it was in many respects Puritan.

It was therefore only to be expected, however deplorable, that those who rebelled against this Puritanism, those who prized the visible world, humanists who loved man's body and mind, his literature and art for their own sake, failed to reach a wider understanding of Catholicism, an understanding veiled by the puritanism of the ascetic tradition, and revolted more or less consciously against the Catholic religion.

The older schoolboy, like the youth who has left school behind him, is apt to be conceited, disobedient and disrespectful, critical of his teachers. And his interests are most commonly on the surface.[1] The knowledge he values is the knowledge of facts, what he would regard as particularly hard facts, and especially knowledge which yields practical fruits.   How keen boys are on machines, how interested in motors and aeroplanes.   He plays, as Plato observed, with philosophic arguments, tearing them to pieces to display his own cleverness and sceptical of any truth below the empirical surface.   He has lost with the child's simplicity and inexperience the child's rectitude of vision.   He has exchanged wisdom for cleverness.   He has left the kingdom of heaven into which only little children have entrance for the kingdom of earth.

Precisely the same phenomena can be observed in the adolescence of the European culture which began in the last two centuries of the Middle Ages.   The delight in argumentative dexterity, in logic chopping shown by the later and degenerate Scholasticism has been often charged against the scholastic philosophy.   It was in fact the decadence of that philosophy, as it fell a prey to the adolescent cleverness of an age that would soon cast it scornfully aside.   For as yet it is but the schoolboy stage of European adolescence.   On the other hand, the practical and the scientific interest has awoken.   Its first beginnings go back to the thirteenth

[1] There are, of course, many deep and religious boys. But they are a minority. It was the same with the boyhood of Western Europe.

century to Grosseteste, Albertus Magnus and Roger Bacon. Bacon indeed displayed much of the adolescent temper which would prevail later. Though he professed the subordination of science to philosophy and theology, his heart was with science and, moreover, for its practical utility. His ideal, his dream of the future was just such a world as that in which we live, a world of horseless carriages, ships that need no sail and a conquered air. " An apparatus," he wrote, " may be devised ' for sailing without the aid of rowers . . . with greater velocity than if a full crew were on board. . . . Cars may be constructed to travel with incalculable speed without any animals to draw them. . . . Flying machines may be built in which a man, sitting in the middle of the machine, may drive some engine, by means of which artificial pinions can be made to beat the air.' " [1] Nor did he shrink from the destructive aspect of applied science. On the contrary, he experimented with gunpowder and has left the earliest known recipe for its manufacture.[2] As the Middle Ages advance it becomes evident that the march of science has begun. Gunpowder, clocks, and spectacles will be followed by the compass and printing. Before the fifteenth century closed Leonardo da Vinci studied the principles and possibilities of aviation and sketched wings attached to the body. And he devoted the best of his endeavour to planning scientific devices.

It must not be thought that I would belittle science. Its advance was indispensable, if man were to master his environment and translate into reality his ideal of order and universal knowledge. Only the adult can realise his childhood's dream. And only through adolescence can the child become the adult. Man had to follow to its utmost the horizontal movement, if the vertical were to yield all its fruit, if the world in and through man were to be subdued to God's human service and worship. But the process of growing up involved grave loss. For many a century the horizontal attraction would draw man's vision downward to earth. The mind is limited, and pride is strong. And the triumphs of scientific knowledge and its practical application must needs

[1] *Opus Tertium.* Quoted and translated by H. Thurston, S.J. *Superstition*, pp. 21-22.

[2] For use, however, as an explosive not as a propellent. See *Enc. Brit.*, Ed. 13, Art. *Gunpowder*.

foster pride. Man, lord of a world in which he has, and can have no peer, is likely to be proud. To be humble a man who lives with inferiors must possess exceptional virtue or receive special grace. And humility is the fruit of wisdom, not of adolescent cleverness.

The recovery at the Renaissance of the complete cultural inheritance of Greece and Rome brought the schoolboy it would educate into contact with a humanism that encouraged and flattered its beginnings in himself. Now at last the man of the Renaissance decked out in an intellectual suit cut by the most skilful tailors of antiquity felt really grown up. Scholarship had opened to him the world of the past, exploration was opening up the entire world of the present, science offered the alluring prospect of a brave new world in the future. Nevertheless for the moment it was the antique classical inheritance that weighed most. For it was a world of actual achievement, whereas the worlds of exploration and science were mainly worlds of promise as yet unrealised. The new art of printing was valuable primarily because it made the classics more accessible and insured them against the risk of further losses.

But the European was still but a schoolboy. He felt very grown up, despised his childhood and enjoyed defying or at least cheeking his masters. Nevertheless in the main his mind was still a child's. His adolescence was only beginning. Though he might discard in patches beliefs and ways of his childhood, he was not only on the whole faithful to the Christian tradition, he retained the child's credulity. He could still believe in impossible monsters dwelling in lands still unexplored, indeed in barnacles which turned into geese off his own coasts. Protestant prejudice might reject unexamined on *a priori* grounds all post-Biblical miracles and the cult of Saints, itself a naïve and extremely credulous incredulity. But otherwise the schoolboy of the Renaissance and even his senior of the baroque period was as ready as the medieval child had been to accept without examination the most incredible marvels, miracles, legends, relics, folklore, an imaginary and authoritarian " science." There was no doubt an increasing number, more advanced in intellectual age, who were critical of such untested beliefs. But they were a minority of pioneers.

It was not until the seventeenth century that the progress of science and the birth of historical criticism introduced the full adolescence of the European mind. And it was not until the rationalism of the eighteenth-century Enlightenment that the western European left his boyhood definitely behind. Henceforward, though he will entertain credulities, many of them negative, he has outgrown the unquestioning belief of the child, and still, in the main, of the schoolboy. He will be the undergraduate at the University, sceptical of everything he has been taught, yet dogmatic and confident of his own views and not a little conceited. But for the present he is still at school.

We must not therefore exaggerate the extent of this incipient revolt of humanism against Christianity, this affirmation of the horizontal to the detriment of the vertical movement.

Looking back we can discern ominous cracks in the Catholic religion-culture of Europe during the later Middle Ages. But they were hardly noticed at the time. The edifice was still so strong and so imposing. It would indeed require half a millennium to demolish it completely. Only in Italy was there any explicit paganism. And as Pastor has shown, its extent has been grossly exaggerated. The prevalent philosophy of Renaissance Italy was indeed Platonism. And Platonism might seem a return to the earlier and more narrowly vertical philosophy of the Augustinian Platonism which had prevailed before the rediscovery of Aristotle. But it had now a classical colour which tended to assimilate it in temper, though not in aim, to the Neoplatonism which had fought in the last ditch against Christianity. The philosophic schools closed in Athens by Justinian were re-opening in Italy. Ficino was a devout priest. But the lamp he lit before the statue of Plato was, or at least might easily become, a threat to the distinctive character of Christian sanctity. Pico de la Mirandola, Ficino's brilliant disciple, was himself a holy man. St. Thomas More translated his life for our edification. But his famous challenge to dispute theses on every topic, *de omni re scibili*, is marked unmistakably by the arrogant self-confidence of the brilliant young man, for whom truth holds no secrets and who is prepared to uphold his own view on any and every subject against the world. Certainly it was of no good augury that Pope Calixtus III protected Valla who frankly defended Epicureanism and demolished the Donation of Constantine with a glee which proved that his critical acumen wanted that deeper insight which would have shown him its practical value in the long struggle of the Papacy against enslavement by a barbarous nobility or an Emperor disposed to claim earthly omnipotence.[1]

If the open irreligion of such men as Valla and the more serious Pomponazzi was exceptional, there were many who cared far more for the humanist classics than for the religion they quite sincerely professed.

As we have seen, classical literature and philosophy had always provided the material of the Christian religion-culture, the stuff which the Catholic religion must dominate, transform and employ. We have observed in the last centuries of the ancient world the sheer mass of the classical material threatening to stifle the new Christian form. The amount of that culture and its weight on the mind had been considerably reduced by the barbarian invasions and the overthrow of the old political order, assisted probably by the new blood and foreign traditions of the invaders. It had therefore been easy for the Christian form to subdue and transform it. The conflict was no longer between the new religion and the old culture, but between a religion-culture and barbarism. The classical material had been reinforced, at first in the sphere of philosophic speculation when Aristotle was rediscovered, now in the sphere of letters when more Latin classics came to light and the revival of Greek opened the literature of Hellas to the western scholar. No wonder this larger mass of classical material once more threatened to prove too much for the Christian form to master and mould.

Though St. Thomas had incorporated Aristotle the later philosophers emphasised, even exaggerated, the rationalist and scientific character which characterised Aristotelianism in contrast to the Augustinian Platonism of which St. Thomas had retained so much. With Pomponazzi Aristotelianism was frankly irreligious. And the new Platonism tended to be more Platonic than Christian. The humanism of classical literature was more insidious, an intellectual atmosphere and a spiritual ethos.

---

[1] We cannot apply to past ages a standard of literary honesty which was not generally acknowledged.

The new material whether philosophic or literary was, however, now confronted by a Christian culture already achieved, and achieved by incorporating classical literature and philosophy.

The Christian form, therefore, could more easily, than in the autumn of antiquity, subdue and transform it by building the new classical culture into an edifice which already contained so much from the same quarry. A Christian humanism would be achieved and would defeat the pagan. We have only to recall St. Thomas More to see Christian humanism embodied in flesh and blood. And he was far from solitary. The Italian Latin poet, Baptista Spagnuolo of Mantua, was a Carmelite and a Beatus to boot. Whatever the shortcomings and excesses of Erasmus he was a faithful Catholic to the end and More's " darling."

Moreover, of its very nature this literary and philosophic culture was confined to the few. It could not affect the mass of the people. These everywhere remained, what they had been before, ignorant, often superstitious, but until the Reformation devout Catholics and, save for the countries infected by the heresy of Wycliffe and his Hussite successors, with no thought of any other belief. And the Lollards and Hussites were not humanists. It was only when the humanism of letters was reinforced by the humanism of science, whose outlook and still more its practical results have exercised an attraction far wider than a literary culture could exercise, that the revolt against Christianity could spread beyond a comparatively small circle of intelligentsia and undermine the religious allegiance of the European peoples. And the time for this was not yet. The Renaissance, the period during which the new classical culture was introduced, was but a transition between the Gothic and the Baroque cultures. And these cultures were phases of the same religion-culture. In both alike the material of the culture was classical thought and literature, the form Catholic Christianity. Only the amount of this classical material differed. It was less in the Gothic, more in the baroque phase of the Catholic religion-culture. The Renaissance tensions were thus largely due to the imperfect assimilation of the new matter, not yet digested.

Moreover, as though by some unconscious presentiment of the humanism she must face and the humanist culture she

must dominate, a presentiment in which we may see the action
of the Holy Spirit, the Church during the last two centuries of
medievalism had reinforced her spiritual resources, the resources of mystical religion. For mysticism is an intimate
union with the Word who is the source of her life and truth,
the Divine exemplar whose image she seeks to impress upon the
world and therefore on culture and the Light in which she
will see and appraise all forms of human wisdom and knowledge,
the Light of her philosophy, her literature and her art.

The imaginative and emotional devotion to the human
Jesus, his Mother and the Saints and in particular to the
Blessed Sacrament spread ever more widely to safeguard the
imagination against the seduction of a purely human ideal,
such as classical humanism would offer. Eyes fixed upon
One fairer than the children of men were not likely to be
dazzled by the beauty of Apollo. Those whose heart was
given to the Mother of God would not prefer Venus.

It was during the fifteenth century that the Rosary assumed
its present form as a method of prayer, fixing the imagination
on the mysteries of the Word Incarnate to meet a challenge
to His rule more insidious than the Albigensian heresy against
which St. Dominic was believed to have employed it. That
the devotion spread with the assistance of unhistorical revelations is regrettable. But never was an evil overruled to
greater good.

Fifteenth-century Italy, the Italy of the humanists, witnessed the spread of devotion to the Name of Jesus. Thus
the self-deification of man was met at its first and still mainly
unconscious beginning by devotion to the Divine Humanity.

And beyond this imaginative devotion mystical religion
whose object is the Incomprehensible Godhead above image
or concept, flourished. Dionysius' Mystical Theology, his
" hid Divinitie," spread, we are told, like wildfire among the
devout in fourteenth-century England.[1]

It inspired that classic of pure mysticism, the anonymous
Cloud of Unknowing, which recommended to those capable
of it a simple prayer of pure love to the inconceivable God,
a prayer in which the active exercise of the will yields to a

[1] An old writer reports that " Dionysius' works . . . walked up and
down " (England) " at deer rates." Dom Justin McCann. Introduction
to the Cloud of Unknowing, p. xvi.

more passive and a conscious reception of the Divine action
in the centre of the soul, that is to say, passes from acquired
to infused contemplation. England also produced Hilton's
Scale of Perfection, the writings of Rolle and Dame Julian's
Revelations of Divine Love. In Germany, Eckhart's ill-expressed
but powerful mystical preaching was tempered by Tauler and
Suso, and the Netherlands produced one of the two princes of
mystical theology, Ruysbroek, who described the soul's ascent
to the summit of prayer and that earthly deification in which it
shares the life of the Trinity, going forth with the Persons and
returning with them into the Godhead. A high contemplation inspired those great women who, in the dark days of
schism and war, rebuked and encouraged princes, changed
the history of a nation, shaped the policy of popes, founded
or reformed orders, St. Bridget, St. Catherine of Siena, St.
Colette, St. Joan. This mystical religion was spread in
Germany by the Friends of God and in the Netherlands a
century later by the Brothers of the Common Life. In face
of humanism reborn and its reinforcement of the horizontal
movement the vertical movement thus rose aloft with renewed
vigour to God to find in Him a life fuller than any humanism
could promise, a light no shadow of earth could darken.

The devotional and mystical movement of the later Middle
Ages was the power-house from which the Church drew strength
to combat humanism with such success that it would be largely
transformed into a Christian humanism and the final triumph
of secular humanism delayed for three centuries.

Meanwhile, throughout Western Europe until the fifteenth
and, save in Italy, during that century, Gothic art continued
to develop. True, the Hundred Years' War produced a long
hiatus in the architectural history of France. But its close
was followed by a new florescence, the Flamboyant style.
In contrast with the Flamboyant the Decorated style in England
had been followed by the plainer and geometrical Perpendicular. Perpendicular, however, cannot be judged, as we
now see it, simply as architecture. The architecture, as Bond
has pointed out, was intended to be the frame of stained-
glass windows. The Perpendicular Church was a glasshouse.
When its glass is destroyed it loses its soul. The splendour of
Perpendicular glass is the counterpart of the architectural
luxuriance of Flamboyant. Both in their different ways display

the spaciousness, the lightness of the final stage of Gothic. Indeed Perpendicular showed a tendency to replace the architectural divisions of the Church, nave, aisles and chancel by wooden screens, though it was a tendency which had not been carried to its conclusion, when the Reformation fell upon Church building in England and blighted its development. Flamboyant and Perpendicular alike show a pride of human life and work and embody a temper for which the horizontal movement of the spirit counted for more than it had in the earlier Gothic. Nevertheless, in architectural expression as, in fact, the horizontal was still subordinate to the vertical movement, humanism was to theocentrism.

In the Italy of the fifteenth century Gothic was replaced by the classical style of the Renaissance. The horizontal architecture of antiquity was revived in conformity with the horizontal outlook of humanism. For the first time since the defeat of paganism, secular subjects, chiefly taken from classical mythology, are themes of painting and sculpture. And they are treated for their own sake, not, like the mythological representations in Dante's Purgatory, to illustrate Christian teaching. Nevertheless art reflected the abiding supremacy of Christianity. Christian subjects far outnumbered the secular. The highest achievement of art was still devoted to the adornment of churches. And even more than Florence, Papal Rome became the artistic capital of Europe.

Were these sacred subjects mere cloaks of secular? Were the Madonnas of Renaissance art no more than representations of human motherhood? No general answer can be given. At one extreme Fra Angelico dwelt in the heavenly places and had eyes and brush only for holiness, for Christ and His Saints. At the other Perugino was evidently more interested in landscape than in the sacred figures he placed in it. Had he lived a little later he would undoubtedly have been a landscape painter. And he left a repute of atheism. Many Madonnas were no more than the glorification of an earthly model or beloved. Nor can I believe that Catholic faith meant anything to Leonardo da Vinci. The famous Christ of his Last Supper is simply the handsome and, to our thinking, somewhat effeminate young hero who was the artistic ideal of Renaissance humanism. He bears no relation to the Incarnate God of history and Catholic belief. Imagine

Leonardo's Christ speaking as Jesus spoke to the Pharisees.
It is unthinkable. Nevertheless the simple fact that the
majority of Renaissance artists were sincere Catholics made
it impossible for them to paint or chisel as pagans. They
could not, even if they would, forget that Christ had come
and that man has an immortal soul to lose or save. With
the Christian faith a new soul capable of God had taken
possession of the human body.[1] It could not be cast out.
Never again could the human form presented by art be the
athletic animal which the Greek sculptors had portrayed.

We may think Raphael's art too naturalistic, too frequently
a colour photograph of beautiful peasant women and children.
But the frescoes with which he adorned the Vatican are of
another order. They are in the authentic tradition of the
medieval cathedral. The school of Athens does not array
Greek philosophy in opposition to Christian theology. On
the contrary, in the spirit of Origen and St. Thomas, it
is depicted as the forerunner of the higher wisdom, and its
preparation. And in the Disputa theology and philosophy's
ancillary wisdom represented by the great Doctors and Sacred
Art in the persons of the painter Angelico, the poet Dante and
the architect Bramante meet to adore and celebrate the Eucharistic Presence of the Word made Flesh.[2]

The Renaissance indeed was to conclude with an artist
who more perfectly than any other, more perfectly even than
the Gothic cathedral, embodied the synthesis of Christianity
and humanism, of nature and the supernatural, the vertical
and the horizontal movements. He is Michelangelo.

The heart of the Catholic church, the private chapel of
her head, is the centre of Catholic art.

As Matthew Arnold pointed out our culture is a com-
pound of Hebraism and Hellenism. The Hebraism, transmitted and fulfilled by Christianity, is its Christian form, the
Hellenism with its Latin derivative, its matter. On the Sixtine
roof Hebraism and Hellenism meet in perfect harmony. The
naked youths revive the Hellenic love of the nude male body.

[1] Of course I am speaking the language of appearances and about
man's knowledge. In fact man has had an immortal soul from the beginning.

[2] In his introduction to the Phaidon Raphael Mr. Suida notes the
contrast between the vaulted roof covering the School of Athens, human
philosophy, and the open sky of the Disputa, truth divinely revealed.

Female nudity had been admitted only by the later classical art and even then but half-heartedly. There is no naked Hera or Athene. And Michelangelo is not so successful with his female as with his male nudes. His Eve is inferior to his Adam. But these naked men are not the athletes, the healthy animals of Praxiteles, Polyclitus or Myron. Their faces bear the character of spirit. And they attend on Prophets and Sibyls proclaiming the mysteries of God. Above these is depicted the Majesty of the Divine Creator, as the Jews, first of all men, knew Him. No Greek thinker, not even Plato, attained the knowledge of creation *ex nihilo*. It has been learned, not from the *Timæus*, nor from Aristotle's first Mover, but from Judaism. And creation is the central theme of these decorations. Michelangelo loved man's physical as well as his mental and spiritual nature, and without prudish shame delighted in the body as God has made it. But he did not forget that man is the creature of God to whom, therefore, he owes all he is and has whether in body or soul. God, not man, is supreme and the centre of all. Nor is He a merely immanent force, a spirit bound to nature. He is transcendent, wholly other, above the light and the earth He creates. In the background of Genesis we discern Dionysius.

Blake will revive Michelangelo's manner and share his temper. But he will confuse God with his human creation. For him the human form will be divine. For Michelangelo it was but the noblest visible creature. Yet Blake the neo-Gnostic will regard the present condition of the human form as evil, thus fluctuating between excesses, where Catholic truth keeps the centre. Catholic truth be it observed. For Catholics have not yet attained Michelangelo's Catholic " wholeness." [1] They are still half-ashamed of his nudities, not perceiving that they are pure in their reference to God, temples of the Holy Ghost built divinely in flesh. Therefore we should return to this artistic centre and learn its lesson.

The centre of the centre is the greatest religious picture in the world, the creation of Adam. Adam lies naked on the earth, wakening to existence, to life and consciousness, to man's long history. He lies on bare ground. Nowhere does Michelangelo do more than indicate natural forms.

[1] I owe this phrase to a friend's suggestion.

Of all artists he is the most remote from the landscape painter. For lower nature might distract the beholder from the crown of her beauty, man. The landscape, therefore, must be simplified to the uttermost that man may be confronted with his Creator, alone in face of the Alone. Wrapped in the dark cloak of His transcendence God bends down over His creature. In the folds of the cloak angel forms appear, to remind us of the pure spirits that occupy the interval between God and the lowest spirit, man's embodied soul. But overshadowed thus they do not withdraw our attention from the two protagonists. The face of one wears, it would seem, a look of horror. It is as though he were contemplating the suffering and the sin awaiting God's human creature, the price of his freewill. Adam stretches out his arm towards God who in turn bends His arm down to Adam. But their fingers do not touch. Man's nature and history are a search for God, for the union with Him in which alone he can find satisfaction and fulfilment, be the search conscious or unconscious, straighforward or perverse. For sin itself seeks good and therefore unwittingly the Good. But man cannot in this life know God as He is. Even to the greatest Saint He is hidden in the Cloud of Unknowing. Therefore the fingers do not meet. Yet God is close to man, blessing and aiding the search He has inspired, and not only by grace but by man's nature as a spirit. Therefore He hovers above him close at hand and bends down to him. This is the truth of human nature, of human history, of human religion, natural and revealed. That is why the picture is the greatest of all religious pictures. And its meaning is inexhaustible, being no less than the meaning of humanity as the creature and as the son of God. Here Hellenism in the naked Adam confronts Hebraism in his Divine Creator. Humanism is reconciled with theism. Man fulfils himself by seeking God. And this meeting hints at the personal meeting of Humanity and Godhead in the Word Incarnate foretold by the Prophets and the Sibyls. For creation, and preeminently the creation of man, is an incarnation of the Divine word. And man is an intelligence and can therefore decipher the objective intelligence inscribed in the forms of nature.

But not even Michelangelo has depicted satisfactorily the Word made Flesh, not even in the Risen Christ of the

Minerva, still less by the Apollo armed with Jove's thunder-bolts who presides over the Last Judgment, a work disappoint-ingly inferior to the superb frescoes of the Sixtine roof. After all, we know much of God as Creator. For we see His creation. Of God as Judge we know very little. For we have not yet been judged. Neither Michelangelo nor any other artist has given us a truly satisfying Christ, not even the anonymous sculptor who carved the Beau Dieu of Amiens. For devotion I prefer the unpretending and frankly allegorical Shepherd of the catacombs.

Was Michelangelo a spirit too tormented to attain the centre which is the repose of the human soul ? He does not *always* attain it, certainly not in the Last Judgment. But on occasion he attains it. In the Creation of Adam he attained it. The centre, however, does not and cannot exclude tension. For it is not the perfect centre of beatific vision but an earthly centre where darkness still hides the face of God and man's hand is not yet clasped in His. On earth man's life is always a warfare and the supreme human artist must be a man of strife, a Michelangelo, a Beethoven, a Dante, and, as we darkly divine, a Shakespeare. But at this centre the tension is the fruitful tension which is not opposition, but the aware-ness of a harmony which, however, can be achieved and held fast only by unremitting struggle, waged, not as in the less fruitful tension of more exclusive attitudes and tempers, against any constituent of the human and Divine whole, but against the forces whether external or in the soul of the artist that make for disintegration, for the assertion of one factor at the cost of another. And this struggle to express and preserve harmony, to keep and display the centre, is also repose in the centre above the conflict. Such was the struggle of Michelangelo and such his repose. That he could not always express the centre proves only that even the supreme artist cannot always keep and express it. He would be super-human else. In the Sixtine roof the centre is kept and displayed. Also I am told,[1] in St. Peter's Dome. But I cannot see the dome in isolation from a building not of Michel-angelo's design. And, as I shall argue later, St. Peter's is not central.

[1] By Robert Sencourt in his *Consecration of Genius.*

The Sixtine frescoes and above the rest the Creation of Adam are at once the achievement and the promise of a comprehensive reconciliation of all things in a centre in every sense Catholic, in Christ and His mystical body, in the complete Incarnation of the Word, begun by creation and perfected in the new Creation which fulfils it. Was the promise kept ? Was the ideal maintained ? The spiritual disintegration and the political anarchy of modern Europe proclaim its defeat. Hardly had Michelangelo finished the Sixtine roof when the religious unity of Western Christendom was rent asunder by the Reformation, and when he died in 1564 it had been permanently divided into two hostile camps, Catholic and Protestant. And the polemical temper aroused by the doctrinal strife led inevitably to an impoverished and narrower perception of Catholic truth where it was still maintained. The truth Protestants denied was insisted upon to the detriment of the truth they professed in common with Catholics. For example, whereas devotion to the Blessed Sacrament became more intense, Bible reading, which for the Protestant was almost a sacrament, was neglected by Catholics. Because the Reformers rejected the Catholic priesthood, the priesthood of the laity, rightly understood, ceased to be a living belief among Catholics. On the other hand, the incipient revolt against Christianity by a pagan humanism was checked. The Church gathered her strength not only against the Reformation but against " humanism " within her own fold. The counter-Reformation was far more than the assertion of Catholic doctrine against Protestant denials. It was an effort to re-establish in every sphere the Catholic culture of the Middle Ages in forms and by methods suited to the novel conditions. The attempt was never more than partially successful and finally failed. But it was so far successful that it established and maintained for more than two centuries in the countries which had remained Catholic or were recovered by the Church, a living Catholic religion-culture continuous with the old. We may call it from the name of its art baroque.

AUTUMN : THE AGE OF BAROQUE

Until recently it has been customary to oppose baroque art to Gothic and often to condemn it on that score. There are signs of a welcome change of view. It is being recognised in many quarters that baroque art, far from being opposed to Gothic, was its legitimate heir and continued it as the culture it expressed continued the culture of medieval Europe. Walter Schubart [1] has truly described baroque as " a continuation of Gothic . . . self-conscious Gothic . . . a renaissance of Gothic." We have travelled far from Ruskin's view of baroque as the antithesis of Gothic.

As we have seen the material of the older Catholic culture was classical. This is true even of its art, though not to the same degree as it is true of its literature. For the themes of Gothic art in so far as they were not directly religious were taken from the deposit of classical learning. The Norman column—the parent of the Gothic—was derived from the classical. " Norman columns and shafts are based on classic tradition ; the base, usually simply moulded and standing like the classic base on a square plinth, was a modification of the classic Attic base." [2] The decoration of the Gothic capital could trace its descent from the Corinthian acanthus. And an illustration, to take another example, in the twelfth century Winchester Bible, which depicts David leaping upon the lion to kill it, derives from a classical representation of Hercules.[3]

The Italian Renaissance introduced an art so classical that in its major works at least the Gothic spirit was for a time repressed by the classical. But it was not defeated, even in Italy. It soon took possession of these classical forms and remoulded them in accordance with its temper, as it had done already with a scantier classical material.

[1] *Europa und die Seele des Ostens*, p. 63.
[2] E. E. Howard, *The Mediaeval Styles of the English Parish Church*, p. 44.
[3] Walter Oakshott, *Introduction to the Artists of the Winchester Bible* [8].

BORROMINI'S BAROQUE CHURCH OF S. CARLINO, ROME

The Gothic spirit of Baroque art imparted a new movement to the classical forms. It rounded contours and bent them in contrasts of convex and concave.

ENTRY OF ST. IGNATIUS INTO PARADISE, BY POZZI, CHIESA DI S. IGNAZIO, ROME

"Though Baroque architecture lacked the aspiration of the Gothic spire its place was taken by the painted vault or dome. Upward and upward into a far heaven of serene and boundless light floated the figures of the Blessed, the flat surface by skilful perspective producing the effect of an actual and unbounded space . in which they move."

In a most valuable study of Roman baroque, T. H. Fokker describes baroque art as the art which employs mass and space as means of expression. " The Baroque artist expressed himself in mass and space."

Though he is at times too subtle in distinguishing the three phases into which he divides Roman baroque, Fokker has proved that a particular school of baroque employed mass and space as their means of artistic expression. And much that he says of its work seems to me applicable to baroque as a whole. Nevertheless his criterion of baroque art is unacceptable. For it excludes work every whit as baroque as that which it includes. The Fountain of Trevi and the painting of Pozzi are as baroque as the work of Bernini and Borromini. Fokker, however, will not recognise them as such. Of the architecture, painting and sculpture, reproduced in Werner Weisbach's volume on baroque art only a portion is accepted as baroque by Fokker. Though he says nothing of German baroque the fact that he places those Roman buildings which approach it most closely on the verge and at the conclusion of baroque, suggests that he would not regard it as genuine baroque. In any case he sharply distinguishes from baroque the final stage into which German baroque developed so gradually that demarcation must be arbitrary, the style known as rococo.

That Fokker's exclusions are untenable can be proved from the analogy of Gothic. The work he describes as Academic rather than baroque is far more closely akin to the work he recognises as baroque than Perpendicular architecture is to Early English. Yet all agree in regarding Early English and Perpendicular as varieties of Gothic. To be consistent we must say the same of Fokker's Academic and baroque. These styles, as also the rococo which occupies much the same place in baroque art as Flamboyant in Gothic architecture, must be regarded as varieties of baroque, and we must conclude that Fokker has given us not a study of baroque, even Roman, but of that variety of Roman baroque which employed mass and space as its means of expression.

Fokker's definition is thus too narrow. But it is at the same time too wide. Mass and space were the means by which the art of ancient Egypt achieved its effect, mass above all. And the art that is emerging in our own time from the artistic

7

anarchy of the nineteenth century aims at nothing save effects of mass and space. Decoration, so luxuriant in baroque, is reduced to a minimum, if not dispensed with entirely, that mass and space may produce their effects undistracted. But the spirit of Egyptian art was not in the least baroque and contemporary art is its antithesis. Fokker's definition is therefore at once too wide and too narrow.

It is impossible to define baroque satisfactorily by any external character. For it was not confined to the visible arts. We can recognise a baroque music and a baroque literature. How, then, are we to define something so elusive ? Baroque should, I suggest, be defined as the employment of classical forms by Gothic feeling. In art at least Gothic had made little direct use of classical forms.[1] Baroque employs all the classical forms recovered by the Renaissance. But they are employed and remoulded by the spirit which had built the Gothic cathedral. Though the matter of baroque is classical, its " form," its spirit is Gothic. From classical materials the Gothic soul wove its baroque body. Not to see this is to be blind to its nature.

It was the same with baroque literature. The classics at the disposal of the medieval European had been comparatively few. And he did not write a classical Latin. In the baroque period the Gothic spirit of the medieval European disposed of an enormously increased classical library, which, moreover, now included the Greek as well as the Latin classics. The baroque writer is at pains to render his Latinity unimpeachably classical and to copy classical models. And his vernacular writing is steeped in classical reminiscence and imitates the classics.

But he employs this classical material and manner in the same Gothic spirit which had inspired the laxer Latinity of his medieval forbears.

Moreover, baroque art and literature were expressions of a culture inspired by this Gothic spirit working upon a matter of classical inheritance.

There was a baroque style of living, a baroque temper of mind, and social and political institutions in harmony with them. All these were Gothic and classical, a classical embodiment and expression of the Gothic soul.

[1] See, however, above, p. 96.

My definition of baroque is therefore interior, because its criterion is not technique nor any language of external form, but the spirit which inspired and moulded the outer forms. And that spirit was Gothic, the outer forms classical. Being interior our definition is, as we have just seen, equally applicable to baroque literature and in general to baroque culture. We are in no danger of forgetting that every genuine art is the organic expression of a culture. And the culture in turn is informed and inspired by a view of reality which must be religious or, since a pure negation can inform nothing, pseudo-religious. That is to say, it must be, as every culture has always been, a religion-culture, or what Fascism and Communism seek to impose, a pseudo-religion-culture.[1] We also see baroque in its organic continuity with Gothic, baroque culture as a later phase of the Catholic religion-culture of which Gothic was an earlier phase, baroque art as the continuation, though also the metamorphosis, of Gothic art. Between them for a brief space, and mainly in one country alone, lay the Renaissance art and culture in which the new classical forms have not yet been assimilated by Christianity and therefore not yet remoulded by the Gothic spirit.

Never indeed did Renaissance classicism completely hold the field. North of the Alps baroque succeeded Gothic. And even in Italy we can detect baroque below the classical surface. That is to say, even when the accession of classical material was the greatest in volume and its weight heaviest, the Gothic spirit was already beginning the work it would soon achieve, the work of employing and refashioning the new classical forms. It was not until 1584 that what is usually considered the first baroque church, the Gesù in Rome, was consecrated. But its consecration was far from being the birthday of baroque.

Weisbach in his standard account of baroque art [2] regards the shell ornament as typically baroque. It was not until the seventeenth century that it became with Borromini a characteristic architectural form. But at least from 1500 we find it in book illustrations and in the background of paintings. The architecture shown both in pictures and in book illustration is baroque many years before actual architecture became

[1] A civilisation, however, not strictly speaking a culture.
[2] *Die Kunst des Barock.*

baroque. In the full Renaissance these imaginary baroque buildings seem as though awaiting the day when the power of the new classicism will have weakened sufficiently to permit them to be realised in fact. Many, however, of these fantastic designs, such, for instance, as appear in the illustrations to Nadal's meditations on the liturgical Gospels, were never translated into stone.

That the latest phase of the classical culture was itself, as we have seen, decidedly baroque in temper and manner, afforded the Gothic spirit an entrance into the order of classical forms, what the Germans would term the classical form language (Formsprache), to create the new baroque. The late classical ornament, putti and fantastic animals, and the luxuriant foliage in which they disport themselves, which was taken over by Renaissance ornament, was baroque.

In literature also baroque made an early appearance. Italian poetry, it is true, as Mario Praz has pointed out, never became fully baroque. The tradition of classical formalism was too strong. But the romance published by Aldus in 1499, the *Hypnerotomachia Polyphili*, is baroque in the rich and free fantasy with which it treats classical material. And the illustrations are inspired by the same baroque spirit. When in fact Bernini mounted an obelisk on an elephant's back, he borrowed the design from a woodcut in the Hypnerotomachia.[1] The contemporary pastoral Sanazaro's *Arcadia* created an Arcadia unknown to antiquity, the Arcadia of nymphs and shepherds playing in a golden age. His artificial and theatrical, but romantic Arcadia would haunt the literary imagination of Europe until the close of the baroque age, concluding on the eve of the debacle with the Trianon pastoralities of Marie Antoinette. This Arcadian pastoralism was thus a distinctive feature of baroque culture in its imaginative aspect. We can hardly deny that its source was already baroque. An instructive volume might be written on the prehistory of baroque during the Renaissance. It would teach us to observe everywhere behind the classical foreground, in books and their illustration, in ornament, and literally in the background of pictures, baroque forms and motifs, and thus detect the Gothic spirit, aided, as we have seen, by the baroque quality of the latest classical phase, already laying hold on

[1] Max von Boehn, *Lorenzo Bernini*, pp. 79, 94.

S. BERNARDINO, BY EL GRECO, THE PRADO, MADRID

" *Since in the fifteenth century Saint Bernadine had preached devotion to the Holy Name, the device, ' I.H.S.' has been commonly depicted aureoled with rays. There could be no better symbol of the Baroque religion and its culture.*"

" *Mystical contemplation is ecstasy, a tense concentration of the spirit, of the energy which is its very being. Therefore the mystical predominance in Baroque was the presence in it to inspire and move it, of ecstasy, an ecstasy of the human spirit aspiring to God. The flame-like figures of El Greco are embodied ecstasies.*"

the classical material and beginning its work of transformation.

The Gothic spirit of baroque art imparted a new movement to classical forms hitherto fixed and sharply defined. It rounded contours and bent them in contrasts of convex and concave. In this Borromini was a master. It blent part with part, outline with outline. As it advanced, baroque architecture,—as in the Gothic culture, architecture is the predominant art—abolished boundaries which paradoxically are nevertheless visible. " Limits seemed to be metamorphosed, to shrink away or dissolve in light instead of being forcibly asserted. This result was the consequence of a combination of opposing effects. Space would not be recognised as such, if its bounds were not perceptible ; on the other hand, its expression would remain simple and direct if it were not enriched by an illusory negation of its limits." [1]

" The interiors of the churches and piazzas which these masters built exercise an irresistible, though at first inexplicable, fascination within their vanishing circumferences. . . . Their spaces seem immense and infinite though their main outlines are strictly regular and rigorously defined." [2] " The fascination which the principal buildings of Bernini, Borromini and Cortona exercise is based on an inherent contradiction between their strictly regular and limited area and the apparent immensity of their interiors." [3]

Fokker shows that analogous effects were produced in painting and sculpture.

Though baroque architecture lacked the aspiration of the Gothic spire its place was taken by the painted vault or dome.[4] Upward and upward into a far heaven of serene and boundless light rose in tiers or floated the figures of the blessed, the flat surface by skilful perspective producing the effect of an actual and unbounded space in which they move. If in Gothic all the arts united in the Cathedral, in baroque their limits seemed to have been obliterated and one imitated the other, as it sought to produce an effect proper to the other. Painting must produce an illusion of sculpture or of architecture. Architectural features were continued and enhanced

---

[1] Fokker, *Roman Baroque Art*, p. 143.   [2] *Ibid.*, p. 8.   [3] *Ibid.*, p. 13.
[4] The painted dome does not seem to have been common until the later rococo phase of baroque.

by a painted architecture. The unity of the arts is more complete than it had ever been in Gothic.

In the Gothic cathedral the eye, and with it the body, were drawn by an involuntary motion towards the choir of the Eucharistic sacrifice. Baroque exposes the high altar to view that the attraction to it may be the greater. But the loss of mystery in its unveiling is compensated by the mystery of light and shade, of space and of contrast. Of the earliest baroque church, Vignola's Gesù, Fokker writes, "The chief purpose of the design is to attract the visitor's eye to the high altar. The interior of the church is so divided and arranged that attention is immediately focussed on the altar-recess. The side walls of the nave and of the Greek cross . . . lead up to it rapidly. The continuity of this approach is arrested by an open space ; yet beyond this sudden obstruction, we soon attain the altar, a haven of rest and a promise of mercy within its apse." [1]

The exterior of the baroque church was not at first so satisfactory. Many churches of the earlier baroque lack external unity. The elaborate façade seems to be attached arbitrarily and without genuine bond to a structure hetrogeneous in its bald and stark outline, and inferior material. This in my view is the outstanding fault of this architecture, in other respects so lovely. And for this reason no doubt Fokker's description of church exteriors is confined to the façade. Only in a few instances, such as Bernini's San Andrea al Quirinale, Borromini's San Ivo alla Sapienza and San Giacomo nel Corso by Francesso da Volterra is the disjunction overcome and an organic external unity achieved.

With the rococo baroque of Central Europe in the following century it was otherwise. Here the linear rhythm which moulded the interior was extended with due modification to the exterior and made it an organic whole. Zimmerman's churches at Wies and Steinhausen are eminently successful examples of an organic exterior.

Within, the rhythm of flowing lines and intricate curves is an architectural music. If Pater was right and music is the limit to whose perfection the other arts aspire baroque must be the most consumate of architectures. For it is the most musical— and most musical in its concluding phase " Every quality of

[1] *Roman Baroque Art*, p. 24.

Rococo " Spengler has written " censured by those who have
not understood its muscial character was born from the spirit
of counterpoint. . . . The absence of measure and definition,"
more truly their simultaneous affirmation and negation,[1] " the
daring sweep, the insecure poise, the undulation, the scintilla-
tion, the abolition of visible surfaces and articulate divisions—
all this is the victory of tunes and melodies over lines and bodies.
. . . They are edifices no longer, these abbeys, palaces and
churches. They are petrified sonatas, minuettes, madrigals,
preludes : chamber music in stucco, marble, ivory, and precious
woods, cantilenas of volute and scroll, cadenzas of cornices and
stairs. . . . Architecture dissolved and was drowned in music.[2]
And Barthel experiences the interior of Wies as the music of an
orchestra."[3]

We have already noticed in Gothic architecture a motion
towards an unattainable goal. And we have observed the
same Infinity at work in the religion-culture whose summer
built the Gothic cathedral, setting it in an analogous motion
towards an end never to be achieved. On the other hand, we
have also observed the strict order which was the medieval ideal,
alike in art, in thought, and in social organisation. That we
observe precisely the same motion, the same infinity, the
same tension, and the same order and definition in baroque
art as in Gothic proves that they embody the same spirit
—I have termed it the Gothic spirit—and are successive
phases of the same artistic expression. And we expect and
shall find the same movement, infinite aspiration, tension, and
formality in baroque culture as in its art. How should it be
otherwise ? A living art is an organic expression of its culture
and they cannot embody a different soul. Gothic culture and
baroque are successive phases of the same culture.

In baroque both factors of the Gothic culture are reinforced. The horizontal movement is more vigorous and
more extensive and the vertical receives a fresh impetus.

Both movements have become self-conscious, fully aware of
their nature and their contrast. The very strength of the
former evokes, as it demands, a more potent effort of the
latter to master it. The baroque culture therefore is in a

[1] Fokker, *Roman Baroque Art*, 24, 143, 153, 157, 253-4.
[2] Spengler, *Der Untergang des Abendlandes*, vol. i, ch. 4, pp. 383-4.
[3] *Barockkirchen in Altbayern und Schwaben*, p. 40.

higher state of tension than the Gothic. And the higher tension is expressed in its art.

In the Christian view of things the finite is definitely finite. It is never confused with the Infinite, as pantheism in all its forms confuses it. But it is seen as grounded in the Infinite, utterly dependent upon the Infinite, existing only by and through the Infinite. Moreover, the finite is a communication and a reflection of the Infinite. Therefore the finite is intelligible only through the Infinite.[1] And it leads the mind and the heart, in short the human spirit, to the Infinite. The spirit is aware of the Infinite in the finite, yet beyond and wholly other than the finite and of the finite as an incarnation of the Infinite.

As we have just seen, baroque art, while defining boundaries, the finiteness of things, their definite outline with the utmost strictness suggests and constantly makes us aware of the Infinite beyond these strictly defined boundaries and implied by them. In this, therefore, it is essentially a Christian and a Catholic art, an expression of the Catholic world view. And this is equally true of the baroque culture which its art presupposes. Moreover, in this baroque art and culture continue Gothic art and culture. But the classical forms taken into baroque emphasise the finite, even more than Gothic had done. The boundaries, human and intelligible to the human reason, " the human measure " in thought and in art which the classical culture of antiquity had expressed consummately and with supreme achievement found expression in baroque by the classical forms and material, artistic and literary, which it had taken over from the ancient world. But the Christian awareness of the Infinite was maintained and indeed heightened by the religion of the Counter-reformation. Thus in the very definiteness of the human boundary there was implied and expressed the Divine Infinite beyond it.

After the emblem book, of which I must shortly speak, the most typical expression of the baroque spirit was the garden, at once formal and fantastic. The apparent size of a small garden can be doubled, if it is divided by hedges

[1] Fully and ultimately intelligible, intelligible in the ground of its being. Partially and relatively, finite objects are intelligible without reference to the Infinite.

of such size and shape as to suggest the further garden on the other side of them. The eye is aware of a beyond which is nevertheless within the garden. The baroque garden, as we see it in engravings, survivals, or in the delightful gardens imagined by Dekker, was divided and subdivided by clipped hedges and cut shrubs. They are as sharply defined as the lines, partitions and ornament of the baroque church. But they are so arranged and cut that, like the latter, they suggest a beyond which is boundless. The boundary in its very emphasis implies the boundless. The contrast is the peculiar charm of the baroque garden, as of baroque art, and the culture they express. We may indeed picture Baroque culture as a formal garden adorned with statues, the artistic legacy of antiquity, brought to a subtle perfection by generations of successive labour, at every point presenting strict boundaries and well-defined shapes, yet pervaded by a sense of the Infinite beyond, yet within it. And the garden is bathed in the mellow light of autumn, the autumn of a mature and fruitful religion-culture.

The contrasted implication of boundary and infinity in the baroque garden is enhanced by another contrast. It is the contrast between the formality of the close-clipped hedges, and the patterns in which plantations, hedges and flower-beds are laid out, a formality and restraint imposed even on water compelled to flow in the design of an elaborate fountain, and the fantasy of these patterns, beds which are arabesques of intricate curvature, an architecture of bushes, walls, columns or alcoves, cut also on occasion, certainly in Holland and Britain, into quaint shapes of bird or vessel, an endless curiosity of form in the parterres, water flowing in every conceivable figure, fanciful or grotesque. The word " grotesque " is indeed derived from the grotto of the baroque garden, with its fantastic ornament and devices of water. The formality of design enhances the free play of fantasy in the shapes of which the close-trimmed plant or captive water is the material, shapes in which plants paint a picture, there is an embroidery of flowers,[1] an architecture, even an orchestra of water.[2] In short the strict definition of these rigid forms becomes by the fantasy of

[1] The *parterres de broiderie*.
[2] The water organ and the water theatre were common adjuncts of the baroque garden.

their employment the suggestion of an infinite freedom and possibility, freedom in their bondage, possibility through their fixation.

The formal garden, it is true, was not created by the baroque culture. It had been the garden of the Roman Empire, the " baroque " garden of pagan " baroque." The art of topiary, it would seem, was invented in the reign of Augustus. The formal-fantastic garden of the ancients, however, was rudimentary. Its full development, the realisation of its possibilities, was reserved for Christian baroque.

When the baroque culture collapsed and was succeeded by the amorphous " civilisation " of the nineteenth century, the new freedom had no understanding of the formal garden. Its place was taken by the landscape garden. It was, it is true, in the eighteenth century that the landscape garden was introduced in England and attained its perfection as baroque art yielded to Neoclassical. But it was not until the nineteenth that, after the final collapse of the baroque culture, it superseded on the Continent the formal fantastic baroque garden. Now, however, both in England and on the Continent it must compete or blend with a formal garden by no means fantastic, a garden which expressed the empty formalism of prosperous self-complacency and social respectability. Thus the nadir was reached of geranium and lobelia bedding with shrubberies of Portugal laurel. Whatever the romantic beauties of the landscape garden, with the formality the infinity also departed. In its place there is but an indefinity, the indefinity of a nature conceived neither as finite nor as infinite, but as a formless confusion of both. What then, it may be asked, of actual nature ? If we did not already know God by reason or faith, we should find in it a purely immanent indefinity. Modern nature mysticism has been in fact for the most part a romantic, vague and merely natural pantheism. Thus the modern landscape garden expresses the indefinity of the pantheist immanence of Romanticism which declares the finite creature, nature and man, divine and therefore somehow infinite. The baroque garden, like the culture which created it, expressed the true view, the view of Christianity, the Infinite beyond the finite, never to be in the least confused with it, yet its ground, implication and end, in short the creative incarnation of the Infinite in the finite which has been crowned by the personal Incarnation of God.[1]

We have observed towards the close of the Middle Ages a widespread movement of spiritual religion, both as an affective and imaginative devotion to the humanity of Christ and the Saints and in its purely mystical form as a contemplative union with the formless Godhead. To meet the advance of humanism this devotion and mysticism advanced also. In baroque culture mystical religion is that infinite perspective whose artistic expression we have already noted.

The Jesuits who, more than any other body, determined the devotion of the Counter-reformation, fostered the prayer of imagination and human affection. They have often been blamed for this. But it would have been impossible and dangerous to preach the prayer of pure contemplation to the masses ignorant hitherto of any prayer beyond vocal petition for needs mainly physical. Those who object to the Jesuits that they put forward the human Jesus as the way to God should logically take offence at Jesus for putting Himself forward as the Way. True, a most intelligible attachment to the form of devotion they had found so profitable and which they had come to regard as the special devotion of their Order led many Jesuits to oppose the soul's advance to a simpler contemplation beyond image and concept. They would have confined all souls to the imaginative and reasoning prayer of St. Ignatius' Exercises. But the Order produced many, such as Alvarez, Guillorè, Surin and de Caussade, who practised and taught contemplative prayer. The understanding and practice of contemplative prayer could not have been lost precisely at the epoch when mystical theology attained its perfection, the age which produced the Doctor of mystical theology and prince of Christian mystics, St. John of the Cross. From Spain at the close of the sixteenth century the mystical movement spread to France and dominated the spiritual life of the French Church. It was that mystical " invasion " and " conquest " of which the Abbè Bremond is the historian. When towards the end of the seventeenth century the reaction against Quietism brought mystical religion into

[1] For a detailed account of the baroque garden copiously illustrated, see *A History of Garden Art*, Marie Luise Gothein, trs. Laura Archer Hind (2 vols.). The author devotes the greater part of her book to the formal garden of the baroque culture.

suspicion and produced what Bremond called the " retreat " of
the mystics, the virtue went out with it from Catholic spirituality. The source of its power, the river that maketh glad
the city of God, diminished to a rivulet, and the ruin of the
Catholic religion-culture was at hand. Meanwhile it flowed
full and strong and provided the spiritual strength that enabled
baroque culture to resist the advancing forces of rationalist
humanism and rebellious states. Never in fact, not even
during the later Middle Ages, had mysticism played such
a powerful part in Catholic life, been so widely known among
Catholics or exercised such supremacy over Catholic devotion
as during this early autumn of the Catholic religion-culture.
And devotion passed easily from the Divinely human to the
pure Divinity. St. Theresa, who first demarcated clearly the
stages of the mystical ascent, was distinguished by her devotion
to the human Jesus, as also was Angelus Silesius, the German
mystic and convert, whose flights to the incomprehensible
Godhead impelled him to use language so daring and so
paradoxical that it sounds pantheistic, even blasphemous.

Mystical contemplation is ecstatic. It is not, of course,
always or most commonly literal ecstasy. But it is ecstasy
in the wider sense of the term, a tense concentration of the
spirit, of the energy which is its being. Therefore the mystical
predominance in baroque was the presence in it, to inspire
and move it, of ecstasy, an ecstasy of the human spirit aspiring
to God. As the fixed outlines of baroque, artistic and
cultural, imply and suggest the Infinite, so, too, its forms
in their very formality are invested with the ecstatic quality
derived from the contemplation of the Infinite Godhead.
For the first time art attempts to express ecstasy. Zurbaran's
" St. Francis " portrays the Saint in the ecstatic pain and
bliss in which he passed his last years. The flame-like figures
of El Greco are embodied ecstasies. About 1740 an anonymous
German artist carved the figure of a saintly beggar in ecstatic
adoration. It brings to the mind his living contemporary,
Saint Benedict Joseph Labre, as if not the body but the soul
of the Saint at prayer had been the artist's model.[1]

This Godward ecstasy of the Spirit was confronted with
human ecstasies released by the humanism of the Renaissance.
In these man's energy is tense and concentrated in his natural

[1] *Das Meisterwerk Deutches Rokoko*, No. 12.

SANTA THERESA, SCULPTURE BY BERNINI, IN SANTA
MARIA VITTORIA, ROME

" Live here, great heart, and love and die and kill,
And bleed and wound and yield and conquer still ;
Let this immortal Life, whene'er it comes,
Walk in the crowd of loves and martyrdoms."
Richard Crashaw : " Upon the Book and Picture of the Seraphical Saint Teresa."

BERNINI'S ALTAR OF THE CHAIR, ST. PETER'S, ROME

" *Here the glory centred in the golden window, where the dove hovers, balances the Chair, flanked by the Doctors of the Church and investing it with its radiance.*"

and human fulfilment. There was an ecstasy of knowledge, knowledge already beginning to widen out towards the ocean of knowledge over which man's mind voyages to-day. We need but think of the vast astronomical prospect opened up by the telescope. There was an ecstasy of power, the power of the victorious hero, free, like Machiavelli's prince, from all law, human or divine. He is depicted in Marlowe's *Tamburlaine* aspiring to rule the Earth. " Is it not brave to be a King Techelles, is it not passing brave to be a King and ride in triumph through Persepolis ? " Seated on a chariot drawn by captive monarchs he will cry in the intoxication of victory, " Holla ye pampered jades of Asia." Spain and Portugal achieved vast colonial empires and dreams of an empire overseas were stirring in the soul of Elizabeth's England.

There was the ecstasy of a proud and dazzling luxury, in which the wealth of a kingdom displayed its possessor's glory, pageants and banquets, fields of cloth of gold. And there was the ecstasy of a romantic human passion, of a Romeo and Juliet, an ecstasy which rebelled against the divine love with which it seemed to compete, as it had rebelled from its Provençal birth centuries earlier.

Against all these human ecstasies the divine ecstasy reacted. The human hero of Renaissance art became the ecstatic saint, the hero of divine love and pre-eminently that favourite subject of baroque art, the ecstatic martyr whose ecstasy of love triumphs over the torments realistically portrayed. Baroque delighted to depict the tortures of martyrdom. San Stephano Rotondo in Rome, whose walls are covered with horrifying martyrdoms, is a veritable chamber of horrors. And it portrayed with the same realism the torments of the Passion. It must be admitted that the motive of this realism was not solely the desire to depict the triumph of charity over the fiercest assaults of human cruelty. An age of such contrast and conflict as the baroque could not escape the neurosis such tension produces. It found expression in a sadist pleasure in the contemplation of suffering. This sadism was obvious when the flogging of a prostitute was made a subject of poetry. And it found free play in the hideous epidemics of witch-mania which disfigured the sixteenth and seventeenth centuries, and which significantly raged most fiercely in countries that were the scene of barbarous and devastating

wars ; in Germany during the Thirty Years' War, and in
France during and after the civil wars of religion.   In Spain,
on the other hand, which enjoyed a strong government and
freedom from internal strife, the Inquisition early adopted
a policy of dealing with alleged witchcraft so sensible
and so just that the Spanish Empire was spared these
horrors.[1]   It can hardly be denied that this nervous sadism
was unconsciously at work in the preference of baroque art for
scenes of torment.   But above and beyond it there was the
conscious desire to display the victories of ecstatic love.

Against the ecstasy of passion the ecstasy of charity reacted
by employing the imagery and language of the earthly lover
to express its intenser passion.   Against the ecstasy of display
it reacted by the lavish adornment of churches, that luxuriance,
indeed riot, of colour and form and, where possible, opulence
of precious materials which offend the taste of many whose
temper is less ecstatic.

Dr. Mario Praz has studied two of those English baroque
poets termed by Dr. Johnson, not very happily, " metaphysical," Donne and Crashaw.   In this essay he applies
to baroque a phrase often employed by Swinburne, " the
spirit of sense."   The spirit of sense does, indeed, express
very well this meeting of spiritual and sensuous ecstasy.   It
is on the frontier between sense and spirit.   And it may
penetrate into either territory.

It may signify the spiritualisation of sense, the sublimation
of man's passionate energy in an ecstatic love of God.   And
it does signify this when baroque achieved its aim.   This
was its meaning in Crashaw's hymn to St. Theresa and its
artistic counterpart, Bernini's sculpture in Santa Maria
Vittoria of her ecstasy, the transverbration of her heart.   Dr.
Praz introduces his study of Crashaw by reproducing and
describing Bernini's masterpiece.   " In Rome there is a work
of art which may be regarded as the epitome of the religious
spirit of the Seicento.   The Angel, whose visage glows with
the radiance of a triumphant smile, launches his gilded dart
at the heart of the Saint, stretched in languorous abandonment on a pillow of cloud.   The alluring violence of the
Seraph's gracious and cruel gesture, and the voluptuous bliss
in which the Saint's entire body is dissolved from a counten-

[1] See Charles Williams, *Witchcraft*.

ance inebriated with heavenly delight, to the heel of the naked foot, soft and flaccid like a flower, whose strength has been sapped by the sun, suggest a blend of the human and the divine, possibly best defined in a Shakespearian phrase dear to Swinburne, ' Spirit of sense.' . . . There is a refined and Alexandrine quality in this Christian Love whose nature is not the savage violence of a conflagration, but the lambent caress of flame, so tender and so feminine is it.   The Angel's gesture is graceful, gallant, his violence adorable as the wrath of a youthful cherub.   He seems to be engaged in an exquisite and cruel game with the Saint and twists his dart as though he were playing a madrigal.   And his victim surrenders herself with a consuming pleasure to the inebriating martyrdom ; transformed by her ecstasy into a weary Maenad, not visited by a fury, but caressed by the grace of God." [1]

Dr. Praz has described not only Bernini's and Crashaw's St. Theresa, but the ecstatic religion of the baroque culture, as it descended from the summit of mystical contemplation to lay hold upon the human world of insurgent and ecstatic sense and subdue it.

Equally ecstatic is the Saint Scholastica modelled in stucco a hundred years later by Feichtmayr for the Benedictine church at Zwiefalten. [2] Indeed the ecstasy is, if possible, even more profound.   The Saint clasping a crucifix reclines, her head thrown backward, her eyes closed.   She is lost in a swoon of love, the slumber of sense and reason in which the spirit alone is awake to the Divine Presence.   " Ego dormio sed cor meum vigilat.   Ne suscitetis neque evigilare faciatis dilectam donec ipsa velit."   " I sleep but my heart waketh.   Wake not nor arouse the Beloved until she will."   She is the bride of St. John's poem of mystic union.

> Quedème y olvidème
> Cesò todo y dejème
> Dejando mi cuidado
> Entre las azucenas olvidado.

" There I abode and forgetting everything I left my care behind, in oblivion lost among the lilies."

---

[1] Mario Praz. *Secentismoe Marinismo in Inghilterra*, pp. 145-6.
[2] Sacheverell Sitwell, *German Baroque Sculpture*, Plate 21.

The flame of the spirit's ecstasy has rapt into itself the earthlier fire of sense. Sense is transmuted wholly into spirit. But before this point is reached there is an entire scale of partial transmutations and various blendings throughout the religion of baroque, its art and its literature. For the spirit of sense can also signify the sensualisation of spirit, the investment of earthly passion with the aureole of religious devotion, the portrayal of sensual desire under sacred forms. And between these extremes there was wide scope for an admixture of both passions, indistinguishable even by its subject, or the artist who represented it. This ambiguity of the spirit of sense inevitably found expression in the art and culture it inspired.

If mystical religion was the Infinite in baroque religion and its creations, the boundary found expression in three ways. Of these the first was a powerful reinforcement of the hierarchical and legal organisation of the Church. The second was that growth of devotion to the human and the Eucharistic aspects of the Catholic religion to which I have already called attention. Here, however, the effort to attain and express the Infinite in and beyond the finite took shape as a process of mystical interiorisation by which these creature-linesses and humanities were divinised by reference to the transcendent and purely spiritual Godhead. The third was the free employment of classical art forms, natural objects and secular knowledge and activities in the service of religion.

In the baroque age the Church was faced by the open revolt of the Protestants, and the masked revolt of a secular humanism. She was faced by the growth of the strong and centralised national state tending more and more to claim the undivided, or at least the ultimate allegiance of its subjects, and therefore, even when the rulers remained Catholic, disposed to interfere in the province of religion and exercise control over the government of the Church. She was faced by the confident self-assertion of intellectual adolescents, men sure of themselves and their capacities. Moreover, individual experience was valued and exalted in isolation from the religious community and to its detriment, and not only by the Protestant doctrine that an experienced faith is the sole and sufficient guarantee of salvation. For centuries ignorance

SAN CARLO ALLE QUATTRO FONTANE : BORROMINI

The fascination which the principal buildings of Bernini, Borromini and Cortona exercise is based on an inherent contradiction between their strictly regular and limited area and the apparent immensity of their interiors. Borromini built his walls in concave and convex curves which suggest that substantial parts of them are giving way to centrifugal pressure or that they are being compressed to bursting point.

B. Cæsar. De
Bus.

Ite. om
docēte. nes
gentes

In
Doct
rinis

glori fi
cabo
domi
num

Congregationis. P.P. Doctrinæ
Christianæ Instituor in Gallia.
noctu orans, lucæ visibilis solis Circumfusus
ad lucem rapitur inaccessibilem.
Michel. van lochom excu

CAESAR DE BUS

of Latin had debarred most laymen from active or mental
participation in the liturgical offices and had fostered private
devotions. The sense of corporate worship, above all of the
Mass as the common sacrifice offered by the entire Catholic
community, had been lost. And the Protestant insistence
on the priesthood of the laity did not, though it should have
done so, encourage an attempt to restore it. The interior
solidarity of membership in Christ's mystical body was lost
sight of. If, therefore, pure individualism were to be avoided,
the exterior unity of the Church, its means and instruments,
must be placed in the foreground.[1] For her defence against the
forces making for disintegration the Church was obliged to
depend upon her external organisation and her legal code. She
must improve and enforce canon law and centralise her government on the model of the centralisation affected by the secular
governments and in competition with it. And she must draw
closer her bond with these governments whose support alone
could save from heresy the countries they governed. And she
must do this even at the cost of ominous concessions, turning,
for example, a blind eye to Gallican tendencies in France, and
allowing the Spanish king to appoint to all the bishoprics
and abbeys in his wide dominions.

The Catholic anti-clericalism, widespread in the Middle
Ages, such as it is found, for example, in Dante, in Petrarch,
in Matthew Paris, and in Langland, disappeared. A stricter
discipline forbade this outspoken public criticism of the clergy,
above all of the bishops and the Pope. It was a striking
and significant difference between medieval and baroque
Catholicism, though in this respect Saint Francis had anticipated the latter.

The index and the censorship of books were instituted by
the Counter-reformation. The liturgical services were regu-
lated by elaborate rubrics authoritatively imposed and were
placed under the supervision of a Congregation of Rites.
Local liturgies were replaced by the Roman Use. Popular and
local canonisations were forbidden and the right to sanction
the cultus of a saint was in future reserved to the official judgment of the Holy See. The Roman bureaucracy was extended
and reorganised.

[1] Calvin and his Church met the same danger by analogous methods,
a strict ecclesiastical organisation and discipline.

8

That is to say the individualist revolt was necessarily met by emphasis on the government and the law of the Church, on her external authority. In the religious sphere this was that strict demarcation of boundaries which we have noted as one of the two factors of the baroque religion-culture. Its most massive artistic expression was Saint Peter's. In Saint Peter's, it is true, there is much that is purely baroque and completely satisfying. Such is Bernini's altar of the Chair. Here the glory centred in the golden window where the dove hovers balances the Chair flanked by the Doctors of the Church and invests it with its radiance. The symbol of external authority is thus balanced by the symbol of the Spirit and the interior life He communicates to the Church, or rather it is subordinated and related to the latter and clothed with its light. In and beyond the finite and human we are aware of the Infinite and the Divine. But this subordination and deification are not expressed by the Basilica as a whole. It is not pure baroque, but a baroque enlargement and overworking of a classical plan. In Saint Peter's, therefore, the boundary to a considerable extent excludes the infinite. The Basilica is primarily an embodiment and artistic expression of the external authority of the Church and her rulers' power and pomp. The expression of interior religion is repressed by their predominance. We are not, as in the medieval Gothic or the pure baroque church, impressed first and foremost with the glory of God as the aim and inspiration of the building, but with the earthlier glory of the Pope. Under the circumstances this was inevitable. For it was only by insistence on the power of the Papacy that God's glory could have been asserted against the rebellion and usurpation of incipient humanism and its secular state. But the church which expresses it produces in me at least a sense of oppression and confinement. I am conscious of the ecclesiastical materialism which subordinates the soul of religion to its body, whereas the body exists only by and for the soul. And I do not believe that I am alone in this impression. But Bernini's Chair corrects it and asserts the truly Catholic relation between the body and the soul, the boundary and the Infinite, as it was embodied in baroque art and culture.

In the religion which inspired and fashioned baroque culture, contemplative and mystical prayer represented, in a sense was the Infinite. The boundary, in and beyond which the Infinite was presented, was the human and sacramental devotion whose extension during the baroque age we have already noticed. This devotion, therefore, met the baroque emphasis on the definite boundary and the human measure. Humanism was met by the divine humanity of God Incarnate and the deified humanity of His members, and was sanctified as a Christian humanism. The cultus of the Saint sanctified the cult of the hero. Passionate love for the human Jesus, the Infant and the Sufferer, and for His Mother, sanctified erotic passion. The splendour of ritual and religious pageantry in churches where every art made its appeal to the senses, sanctified the love of rich material and brilliant display.

Baroque religion, however, was not content merely to continue and foster the Eucharistic and devout humanities bequeathed to it by the later Middle Ages. They were subjected by the dominant mysticism to a process of interiorisation, of spiritualisation. Devotion to the human Jesus and to His Eucharistic presence was referred to His Godhead in and beyond them. What Bremond has termed the French school of spirituality, Cardinal Berulle and his disciples in the Oratory and outside it, imparted a theocentric character to this devotion. The soul must no longer rest in the outward and visible mysteries of God Incarnate, His acts and His words. She must go inwards and contemplate the state, the disposition they expressed. And beyond this she must contemplate the total disposition of Jesus of which these particular dispositions were but the effects, His " interior." Berulle instituted in the French Oratory a feast of the Interior of Jesus. When before St. Margaret Mary, St. John Eudes propagated devotion to the Sacred Heart of Jesus and instituted its feast together with that of His Mother's heart, his intention was to honour and celebrate their disposition, their interior under a more concrete form. And this disposition was primarily not love for men, but adoration of God. The disposition or the interior, the state, in short, of the human Jesus both in His life on earth and still in the Blessed Sacrament, is the state of a Victim and Priest, offered and offering Himself to God's glory. This aspect of the sacred Humanity was the particular devotion of Berulle's fellow Oratorian, Père Condren.

Such a view of the Eucharistic presence assimilated the tabernacle to the altar, sacramental devotion outside the Mass, to the Mass itself. For in this aspect the Eucharistic presence in the tabernacle continues permanently the sacrificial offering of the Mass. In both alike, Jesus is the Priest and Victim of His Father's glory. The abiding presence in the tabernacle is the sacrificial state of which the sacrifice of the Mass is the act. And the Apocalyptic Lamb slain before the foundation of the world represents a state rather than an act of sacrifice. For this theocentric devotion Jesus is not present in the tabernacle primarily to help and console us, nor even to be adored by us there, but to offer among and with us and on our behalf the sacrificial worship of God which is the essence of religion and prayer. Thus the Eucharist with all its concreteness and its sensible visibility, and all the pomp surrounding it, and images, actual or mental, of Our Lord in His earthly life, are seen as so many expressions of the one disposition or state of Jesus, the state of sacrificial worship He offers to God as the human Head of redeemed humanity, God's Divine-human Victim and Priest. There is no room here for sentimentality, for a barren luxury of self-pleasing emotion. Everything is referred to the glory of God to which everything is a means. The most sensible beauties of worship, the most humanly attractive mysteries of the Sacred Humanity adore the Infinite and Incomprehensible Godhead. The formless prayer of the mystic's contemplation is approached in and through, yet beyond the images and emotions of every religious creatureliness and humanity. It is indeed doubtful whether those responsible for this interiorising fully grasped the close union that should exist between the corporate adoration of the Divine Office and the worship of God by the Eucharistic Priest. They probably regarded the Office rather as an assistance to personal devotion. But the connection lies close at hand. The adoration of the Office, its praise of God's glory, should be united with the state of sacrificial praise offered by our High Priest.

After the defeat of mysticism this theocentric understanding of the Sacred Humanity and the Eucharistic presence gave way to the anthropocentric view closer to human emotion and self-interest. The Sacred Heart no longer represented the adoring " interior " of the Priest and Victim, but Our Lord's human love for His fellow-men. And the presence of His humanity in the tabernacle was no longer seen as a state of sacrificial worship offered by the Head and Representative of redeemed mankind. Its purpose is rather to aid and comfort man or, at most, to receive our worship. It is this relapse from a theocentric and interior to an anthropocentric and more exterior understanding of it, that has invested modern devotion to the Sacred Heart and the Blessed Sacrament with the sentimentalism and the all too human emotion which have disfigured it. And these in turn have produced the weak and sugary images and hymns which have made the popular imagination of the Sacred Heart a veritable caricature of the historical Jesus, the Incarnation of the Divine Wisdom.

Reaction against this sentimentalism and anthropocentrism has alienated many Catholics, zealous to revive a deeper and a wider religion, from extraliturgical devotion to the Blessed Sacrament and from devotion to the Sacred Heart. In this, however, they run counter to the mind of the Church. What is needed is not rejection but interiorisation. We must return to the theocentric understanding of the Sacred Humanity taught by the French school. We must once more direct every form of devotion to the human Jesus towards the adoration of the Triune Godhead, and see in the Eucharistic presence an abiding state of sacrificial adoration, in the Sacred Heart that state of adoration symbolised and Incarnate. That is to say we must return to the highest ideal and practice of baroque religion. But we must complete it and socialise what at best was excessively individual, by linking with this devotion, in particular with our Eucharistic devotion, the corporate adoration of the members in union with their glorified Head, and moreover as it is expressed by the liturgical worship of the Divine Office. Thus every form of devotion will be reduced to adoration, the adoration offered by Christ in His Eucharistic and His mystical body, and identified with it.

This interiorisation whereby the finite is referred to the Infinite, thus displayed in it and beyond it, found artistic expression in that suggestion of a boundless space in and beyond fixed boundaries which, as we have already seen, was characteristic of baroque art. Fokker shows how in the period which he terms full baroque, this suggestion of the infinite, this interiorisation of the boundary was effected architecturally in the interior of churches. " The limits " of space " seem to be metamorphosed, to shrink away or to dissolve in light . . . this result was . . . the consequence of a combination of opposing effects. Space would not be recognised as such, if its bounds were not perceptible. On the other hand, its expression would remain simple and direct, if it were not enriched by an illusory negation of its limits." The negation is illusory because a closed building must actually be bounded in every direction.

" These contrasts were of three different kinds, invented by three different masters. . . . Cortona concealed the walls of his church behind columns, piers and pilasters, with recesses and altars of varying form differently combined and by breaking up the remaining wall space with doors and balconies. Borromini built his walls in shapes," concave and convex curves, " which suggest that substantial parts of them are giving way to centrifugal pressure or that they are being compressed to bursting-point ; he covered his vaults with ornaments which exaggerate effects of perspective so as to suggest infinity. Bernini made use of the perplexity caused by the introduction of a screen of bright light between a comparatively dark space and a luminous background." [1]

In the garden of Buen Retiro the designer, Cosimo Lotti, " hit upon the ingenious idea of constructing the stage of the open-air theatre so that by removing a wall at the back the view was thrown open into the park." . . . This " had the merit of allowing people to sit in an enclosed place and at the same time to see the picture before them in a sort of frame." [2] Thus, beyond the restricted stage a wide vista was opened up, the background of the narrowly confined action. The prince of garden architects, Le Notre, restricting the view at the sides by alleys and copses, fixed the gaze upon a far-stretching prospect in front. As in the Gesù, Vignola had drawn the eye to the altar,[3] Le Nôtre, in the garden of Vaux Le Vicomte, drew it to the horizon.[4] The architecture of church and garden alike presents the infinite in and beyond the finite.

[1] *Roman Baroque*, p. 143.   [2] Gothein, *History of Garden Art*, I, 379-80.
[3] See above, p. 102.
[4] Gothein, *History of Garden Art*, II, 52-56 (with illustrations).

If in baroque churches the finite is represented by the definite outlines and by the statues and paintings, the portrayal of the human, it is interiorised, as it were deified, by this suggestion of boundless space. "Effects of perspective." Throughout baroque art, in its churches, town-planning, gardens, painting, they refer the finite to an infinite beyond, as in its religion mystical contemplation interiorising the human aspects of Christianity produces in every devotion an effect of perspective beyond and beyond to God. Besides perspective light. Fokker has shown how Bernini employs light to suggest infinity. A concealed window, as in the Raymondi chapel in San Pietro in Montorio or above St. Theresa's ecstasy in Santa Maria della Vittoria or a lantern, as in the sanctuary of Sant Andrea nel Quirinale, projects a flood of light beyond the shadow [1]. "Limits dissolve in light" in those vaults where the ranks of saints and angels vanish in it. And in the landscape of such painters as Claude and the Poussins, Caravaggio and Domenichino, the lighting plays perhaps the most important part.

Christian art, like Buddhist, had very early adopted the nimbus from classical art as a sign at first of distinction, later of sanctity. The splendour of light is the obvious symbol of supernatural radiance and its Luminary. Baroque art had a predilection for this symbolism of light. A dissolved aureole invests the painted figures of saints. A heaven of light opens to the dying eyes of the martyr. Nothing is commoner in the books of religious engraving so popular at this epoch than to depict a saint looking upward to a sun or to rays of light. The halo is often a sun, for token that holiness is a communication to the soul of the Divine Light. Saint Charles Borromeo, for example, is depicted with a solar halo crossed by a ray of light descending upon him. Caesar de Bus looks upward in prayer to a sun. Gilt rays frame pictures and altar-pieces. Rays descend from above on the figures represented, as, in Bernini's masterpiece, upon the angel piercing Saint Theresa's heart. Beside Saint Ignatius the device of his order, I H S, appears within a frame of rays, the Godhead beyond the Humanity of Jesus.[1] In fact, since in the fifteenth century Saint Bernadine

[1] Fokker, *Roman Baroque Art*, 153, 157, 253.

[2] For these saints, see *Summaire des principaux Fondateurs et Reformateurs des Ordres Religieux*, a book of engravings, Paris, 1635.

had preached devotion to the Holy Name, it had been commonly depicted aureoled with rays. There could be no better symbol of the baroque religion and its culture, indeed of the Catholic religion which produced the latter as its most perfect cultural expression.

Here also contemplative interiorisation and theocentrism lead the imagination from the human figure, be it even the figure of Jesus, to the light which symbolises the Infinite and Incomprehensible Godhead whose darkness to the mind of mortal man is a boundless excess of light. Without the light symbolism baroque religious art would not have sufficiently expressed the Infinite Deity. Without its abundant and most human humanities it would not have sufficiently expressed Its Incarnation. With the Catholic faith baroque religion moves to and fro between its two poles, pure Godhead and Godhead Incarnate in Its creation, between God and God made Man.

Another means of giving artistic expression to this mystical interiorisation was to portray in attitude and countenance contemplative, even ecstatic, prayer. This, as we have seen, was peculiar to baroque art. And it was often combined with the light symbolism, for example, in the illustrations I have just mentioned.

Gothic art had already suggested the Infinite by the height and length of its cathedrals and had employed the infinite suggestion of light by depicting the figures and scenes of its windows on the background of the light pouring through them. Baroque art, inspired by the same spirit, sought the same effect by other means, and more consciously. More consciously, because baroque religion was aware of the growing threat of humanism, the revolt of the finite against the infinite and its intention, as yet not fully aware of itself, but destined to triumph hereafter, to shut out from man's vision the perspective and light of the Infinite and confine it within the boundaries of creatures, as such finite, even if decked with an illusion of infinity. Baroque religious art in its purpose and finest achievement is thus an interiorisation of the outward, a spiritualisation of the sensible, indeed of the sensuous, the spirit of sense, taken in its upward direction, a reference of the finite to infinity, a deification of the human.

To combat a secular humanism and convert it into a

Christian, baroque religion accepted humanism more widely than Catholic religion had previously done. It carried further the incorporation into a Christian order of man's earthly studies and interests and the nature and humanity with which they are concerned that we have observed in the Gothic cathedral, in the philosophy of Saint Thomas, and the *Divina Comedia*.

The decoration of the baroque church made lavish use of the pomp and splendour so dear to the Renaissance, of rich material and the forms of mundane pageantry. The Court of Heaven as represented in painting and stucco is the celestial counterpart of an earthly court. The rococo churches of Austria and Southern Germany are gay as the theatres and ballrooms they resemble. Worship celebrated in such buildings seems veritably a dance.

In consequence the religious art of baroque has been condemned as disguised worldliness. The critics forget the unearthly light investing that heavenly court, the suggestions of infinite space, the prayerful and ecstatic countenance of the saint so richly robed amid a luxury of marble and gold.[1] These material pomps are not accepted that the spirit may rest in them, but that by spiritualising sense it may rise to the realm of spirit.

The religious architecture of baroque is often regarded as a distinctively Jesuit style. This is a misconception. Had any other style been popular the Jesuits would have employed it. But in truth the baroque style in its free and lavish employment of splendid display and earthly beauty was congenial to the spirit of the Society. For the Jesuits, the shock troops of the Counter-reformation, were determined to conquer humanism for Christ. Saint Ignatius' life may be divided into three portions. In the first he was a man of the world, in the second a man of God, in the third a man of God and a man of the world and a man of the world to win the world for God. The Society he founded has perpetuated the final phase of its founder's life. The Jesuit has been a man of God and a man of the world for God. The Jesuit ideal is to employ humanism in the service of religion. The Jesuits would take men where they found them that they might not leave them

---

[1] More often than not imitation marble and gilding. Nothing more could be afforded than the semblance of costly material.

there. To wean them from sin they would comply with whatever is not actually sinful. The end, the greater glory of
God justifies not, as their enemies allege, all means, but all
means not immoral. Those who blame the Society for this
should at least have the justice to arraign St. Paul who a millennium and a half before St. Ignatius declared that he would
be all things to all men to save some. And the Jesuits were
attempting to save nothing less than Christendom, to save it
from the disintegration of heresy and a rebellious humanism.

Since the European child was now an adolescent schoolboy
he must receive a suitable education. The Jesuits therefore
became the educators of Catholic Europe, imparting an
education better than any hitherto available. His tastes
must be gratified and given a Godward direction. He loved
display. Architecture and painting, pageantry and music,
must delight eye and ear—in the worship of God. He was
erotic and passionate. He must have a passionate and erotic
religion to sublimate and redirect his passion. He loved the
theatre and the dance. The Jesuits staged religious or morally
edifying dramas with the utmost elaboration of stagecraft.
They even fostered the development of the ballet. He was
proud of his knowledge. The Jesuits were men of letters
and learning, able to play their part in every field of literature
and study. In the seventeenth century he became interested
in science and its practical applications. Jesuits were scientists.
The Jesuit Lana designed a flying ship whose principle at
least was sound (1670). And it was the Jesuits' astronomical
knowledge which opened China to them. He was proud of
his independent will. The Jesuits championed free-will against
an older theology which seemed to deny its rights. But they did
so to win it for the free service of God. In moral theology they
demanded the least they could from men little disposed to
obedience. But from that minimum of observance they sought
by the sacraments, devotional exercises, preaching and ritual to
raise men to heights of sanctity. For this they have been and are
severely censured, even by Catholics. If the Church were
better confined to a devout minority, Christian in every fibre of
their being, the censure would be just. If, however, there were
to be a Catholic Christendom, that is to say, a society of Catholic
peoples, where the universal profession of Catholic faith
provided for all a Catholic environment with its religious

privileges and possibilities, they could have adopted no other policy. In fact their policy had been decided in principle long since, when the Church baptised societies *en masse*, the Roman Empire first, then the barbarian tribes that conquered it. The decision involved a Church not confined to mature Christians but composed of believers who were in the main but raw material for a long and necessarily very imperfect process of education and sanctification. The Jesuits and the Counter-reformation on which they set their seal did but pursue this predetermined policy under novel conditions by extending its application to meet them.

In the end the humanist revolt proved too strong. The Counter-reformation was defeated. Christendom exists no longer. Has its demise proved a benefit to religion ? In some respects no doubt. But on balance ? Unless we are prepared to answer with a confident affirmative we are not entitled to censure the policy pursued by the Society of Jesus.

Gothic art employed in its symbolism the natural and the human contents of Vincent's mirrors. The Gothic spirit of baroque enlarged enormously the number and variety of these human and natural symbols. If the Gothic cathedral is a microcosm of the medieval religion-culture, the baroque religion-culture which continued it offers the student a microcosm far smaller and more accessible. It is the emblem book. Even more than the Church or the formal garden the emblem book is an epitome of baroque. There is no quicker way of entering into its spirit than by poring over the illustrations of an emblem book and reading the explanatory text.

The emblems, charming, quaint and more fantastic than anything possible in architecture or topiary, are drawn from every department of nature and human life. The emblem is the symbol, because it is the reflection on the sensible plane, of a moral or religious fact. As we should expect in the literature of the adolescent, the erotic emblem is the commonest. Images of earthly passion, never coarse or suggestive but conceived according to the mythological fancy of late antiquity, symbolise every phase and aspect of love, sacred and profane. Cupid appears constantly, to represent either the heavenly Eros or the earthly Eros he defeats.

Ingenuity is taxed to the uttermost to discover emblems and analogies and with this end in view searches the entire

world of nature and man. The literary counterpart of the
emblem is the conceit. It is in fact a verbal emblem, sought
with equal ingenuity. It was not, as Doctor Johnson maintained with his too blunt common sense, the perversity of a
misapplied erudition that made the baroque poet strain his wits
devising elaborate conceits. It was his appreciation of the
truth, believed with equal conviction by the medieval Catholic,
that everything below is the symbol of something above,
every object of sense the symbol of a spiritual reality. This
was as true of the designer of emblems. It was the same
principle that fostered in such men as Paracelsus, Boehme
and Thomas Vaughan the belief that in consequence of this
analogy between the physical and the spiritual orders knowledge of the one would throw light on the other. The transmutation, for example, of the spirit by God's grace warranted
a corresponding transmutation of the elements and experi-
mental knowledge of the latter would illuminate the former.
Mysticism justified alchemy. Alchemy in turn threw light
on mysticism. This, indeed, was a mistake. We know too
little of the spiritual order to derive from it scientific illumination. And the Church frowned on this " theosophy." It
has no place in the teaching of the great Catholic mystics.
But the emblem and the conceit, belonging as they do to the
order of imagination and of art, not of science, require only
knowledge of religious and moral truth and of the visible
aspects of the objects which are to symbolise it. That they
are out of fashion with modern Catholics is evidence that
the latter have lost this powerful conviction of the unity of
all knowledge and of all things knowable, the unity of a
creation hierarchically ordered towards the supernatural
creation of grace.

To be sure our emblems and conceits could not be those
of the Seicento. The world from which they must be taken
has changed, is incalculably more extensive and more complex.
Science has discovered a vast universe of natural knowledge.
The world we know is not the world our ancestors knew.
But we should not discard the fundamental Catholic principle
they brought to its understanding, no less in truth than the
principle of Divine Incarnation. Meanwhile we could do
worse than return for a leisured hour to the emblem book and
its companion the baroque poem and enter into the " joyful

wisdom " of their elaborate fancies which so often convey profound truth. And if we understand the emblem book, we appreciate baroque art and culture, we appreciate the Counter-reformation and we appreciate the Jesuits. For we shall see in all alike a Catholic religion-culture extending to every department of human experience, and relating it to God, the Infinite in and beyond the boundary, the Christian form of a classical matter, the vertical motion of the spirit dominating the horizontal. That is to say, we shall appreciate the entire religion-culture of which the baroque culture was the vintage, the religion-culture of Catholic Europe as under particular historical conditions it extended the Incarnation by expressing it in a given cultural material, the inheritance of classical antiquity. Truly there is much to be learned from the emblem book, and, I think, from a teacher of no slight charm.

We shall perhaps best understand the Christian humanism at which baroque culture, continuing the Gothic, aimed, and which at its best it achieved more completely than the latter, if we consider an example studied by Bremond in that volume of his *Histoire du Sentiment Religieux en France* devoted to Christian humanism—" humanisme devot " he termed it, the Platonist Capuchin, Yves de Paris. That his writings are still unobtainable encourages me the more to dwell upon a writer of singular charm and, what is more important, so comprehensive and centrally Catholic in his interests. He seems in fact the human incarnation of those Vincentian mirrors, presented by the decoration of the Gothic cathedral, and later by the emblem book. Nor has Yves merely the interest of the scholar or the dilettante of knowledge. He displays a passionate love of beauty in every form. And the entire range of his interests is unified and rendered an organic whole by his Christian Platonism, which beholds in the objects of sense and in men's secular occupations shadows, and there-fore revelations, of the Divine Beauty and Government above them.

This Capuchin might have said with truth, "Nihil humanum a me alienum "—nothing human is foreign to me. Nor any natural beauty. As he describes it, we share his enjoyment of a walk, " Right against the eastern gate where the great sun begins his state," as the English poet was writing at this very time. " As soon as you leave the house you are embraced by the west wind that delights you with its freshness and closing the pores of the skin renders the spirits more intent upon the splendours of a spectacle of which the leaves already advertise you by a rustle of admiration. The light which fills the air with its delicious and ever-increasing flood, whose source is as yet invisible, shows us by this dawn of a new day what the dawn of the world was like before the stars were created. Assuredly it seems as though all things were being given their being as they emerge from the indistinction of darkness with their diverse shapes and colours. . . . The pleasure the eye receives as it beholds the vast spaces of the atmosphere whiten with the light and bodies adorned with divers colours incites the wise man to look for the source of these glories and without long reflection he turns, as by a natural sympathy, to the East. What treasures and wonders he sees there ! Those little clouds whose rivalry is too weak to obscure the daystar put on his liveries and become the harbingers of his advent. They curl and twine in wavelets of fire, they compose thrones of crystal, long porticoes of rubies and diamonds, streets paved with agate, tapestries embroidered with gold and pearl, and fancy pictures them a throng of luminous dwarfs marching in front of the sun's triumphant chariot.

"At last the sun becomes visible as a zone of burning light which in less than no time has grown into a semicircle and is soon a perfect orb. Do not lose these moments when for a brief space you may fix your gaze on this fair sun, since the vapours rising from the ground and extending from the horizon to the place where you stand have woven for him a transparent veil tempering his brilliance to your weak vision. Marvel at this wheel of flame whose borders redder and more supportable by the eye leave in the midst spaces that whiten as they spread out and are lost in remote depths, impenetrable abysses of light." [1] A bed of flowers delights Yves and he is charmed by the sight of violets, " robed in royal purple and richly scented, growing in a wood " or " anemones spread out over the ground whose bright colouring better than the tallest trees represents the orb of day." [2] And he takes pleasure in

---

[1] *Histoire du Sentiment Religieux*, vol. i, pp. 434-5. Since the English translation (S.P.C.K.) is inaccessible I have translated directly from the French original. [2] *Ibid.* p. 446.

watching a bee, a line of ants, two snails meeting. He would like specimens or at least pictures of natural objects from every order. He enjoys the sight of a gallant vessel leaving port. Those were the days before the sailing ship had yielded place to the ungainly monsters of steam and oil. He enjoys travel, in particular his visit to Italy, when he saw the ruins of ancient Rome, side by side with the fresh beauties of the new emerging from the hands of Bernini, Borromini, and Cortona.

Yves' view of humanity is perhaps too optimistic. He dwells by preference on the goodness in men and is indulgent to their follies. He seems unaware of the hideous cruelty which then, as now, made men behave as fiends. In his day soldiers murdered civilians by hand, in our own by bombs dropped from the air. But it is an amiable excess. For he contemplates humanity in God and therefore sees rather what God can make of man than what man can become when he revolts against God.

For Yves humanism is Christian, not secular. Every spectacle, human or natural, raises his mind to God. When we contemplate a star-lit sky on a calm night, " All our feelings surpass nature. Our thoughts rise above the earth into a boundless expanse of light that holds all our powers in suspense and makes us marvel at something more than we behold and enjoy a bliss we do not understand." And " If we plunge into the solitude of a forest amidst the silence and in sight of those great trees, majestic in the height of their trunks and the wide expanse of their branches, our mind is straightway rapt into itself, our heart is sensible of unwonted emotions and the entire body, trembling with a reverent awe, makes us aware of an infinite greatness that demands the free homage of our will." [1] In this sensitiveness to wild beauty, however, Père Yves is not baroque. He anticipates Rousseau and the romantic love of nature he inaugurated. But, as Croce has pointed out, the individual is not perfectly and exclusively representative of any aspect of human thought or culture, least of all men of outstanding endowment. But for Yves there is no danger of pantheism, of the romantic substitution of the indefinite for the Infinite. To the Infinite his mind and heart, even his very senses, are directed. It is the goal

[1] *Ibid.* p. 488.

of all his appreciation of man and nature, even of his delight in human beauty and love, considered, however, as objects of contemplation, not of vital union. For he is well aware of the distinction between æsthetic appreciation of human beauty and the desire to possess it by a physical union.

Yves does not contemplate God only through creatures, but directly by contemplative prayer. God is apprehended in " the highest part of the soul without the aid of reasoning. . . . Climb to the furthest point of your intellect and your own unity will make contact with this sovereign Unity and you will grasp something of the Infinite Being that holds you in its grasp." " It is for Him that our hearts sigh by sudden aspirations whose nature we cannot conceive because they rise to the infinite and the subtle point of our souls approaches this indivisible Being by a concept that exceeds reason "— concept seems hardly the right word for what is in fact an obscure intuition—" and by a love which forestalls the search of knowledge." [1] Here is the transcendent Infinity attained by the contemplation of baroque religion which crowns and unites its wide humanist culture, as in art its representation dominates and pervades the wealth of visible forms and colours. Yves, the humanist and the lover of nature, is a mystic and his knowledge and enjoyment of creatures are directed to the knowledge and praise of the Creator. He combines the detachment which made him choose the life of a bare-foot friar with an appreciation of creatures as intense as it was comprehensive. In this he exemplified the ideal and the fullest achievement of Catholic religion and the culture it has inspired, above all, of the baroque culture which combined most fully the two factors, detachment and appreci-ation, the vertical and the horizontal movements of the human spirit, mysticism and humanism. His singularly attractive figure may well remain with us to justify Christian humanism against the Puritanism, Catholic or Protestant, which looks askance at man and nature, and because God, could we know Him as He is, would suffice all our needs, concludes that on earth, when as yet He is invisible, we can dispense with His mirrored reflections. Specialists of the vertical movement, such, for example, as the Curé d'Ars, whose call and attrait are an exclusive devotion to the direct service

[1] *Histoire du Sentiment Religieux*, vol. i, p. 488.

THE ROCOCO CHURCHES OF AUSTRIA AND SOUTHERN
GERMANY—

*" Gay as the theatres and ballrooms they resemble."   The example is the
Nepomok Kirche of Munich, designed by the brothers Adam.*

THE IMMACULATE CONCEPTION BY PIERRE PUGET:
THE ORATORY OF ST. PHILIP OF NERI, GENOA

The Gothic and the classical factors in Baroque were not mixed everywhere in equal proportions. The sculptor, Pierre Puget, subdued his neo-classical tendencies when he carved this statue in 1665, as did his contemporary, Nicholas Poussin, in his Baroque religious paintings, though the classical tendency was dominant in the secular work of both artists.

of God, though they rise to the summit of holiness, are narrower
and less imitable by the majority of Catholics than humanist
contemplatives such as Père Yves.   Nor were all the saints men
of such exclusively vertical attrait.   St. Venantius Fortunatus
has his place among them beside St. John Vianney.   " Wisdom
is justified in all her children."

In his monograph on Bernini Max von Boehn speaks of
the passion for the drama which possessed the Romans of
the seventeenth century.   " Clement IX wrote the merriest
comedies which Michael Angelo de Rossi and Abbatini set
to music " : [1] Sullivans to the Papal Gilbert.   Imagine, if
you can, a Victorian Archbishop of Canterbury composing
librettos for Sullivan.   Gilbert no doubt would have been
highly diverted by the spectacle of Archbishop Tait writing the
libretto of " Iolanthe."   And Boehn tells us of a bloody brawl
in a convent occasioned by a confessor who pronounced it
sinful for nuns to act. [2]

This love of the theatre was not confined to Rome.   It was
universal throughout the baroque culture.   Drama expressed
and relieved the emotional tension of an age when the ecstasies
of sense and spirit met in conflict.   And it gratified the self-
assertive exhibitionism of the adolescent European.   Moreover,
the stage gave plentiful scope to the baroque love of pageantry
and the tendency to unite several arts in the production of a
common effect.

Drama, however, was not confined to the literal stage.
The entire baroque culture and way of living was a drama,
religious and secular.   And its stage was the church, the
street, the public place, the palace of wide rooms richly
appointed and reached by princely staircases, and the formal
fantastic garden.   The elaborate dresses were the costumes
of the characters in this perpetual drama, the elaborate
etiquette its book of words.   The peruke was the actor's wig,
the rank and precedence observed so meticulously the parts
assigned to the players at their birth.   This baroque drama
was polite.   It was composed and performed in accordance
with strict rules.   It observed unities accepted as obediently
as were those of the French classical stage.   For it was not a
tragedy, enacted beneath a sky overcast with cloud, in a world
open in every direction.   It was a comedy of manners whose

[1] *Lorenzo Bernini*, p. 39.   [2] *Ibid.* p. 46.

9

action was bounded on all sides by the frontiers imposed by the Catholic view of the world. Its infinity was upward only, the infinity of that heaven of light painted on the vaults of churches. Below, it was played in the garden of hedges and topiary, the baroque culture.

The garden was, in fact, a favourite stage. Most princely gardens were furnished with an open-air theatre whose walls were clipped hedges. And it was to be the stage of dramas, masques and pageants that Le Nôtre designed the gardens of Versailles.[1]

Religious worship observes a ritual fixed in every particular. Rubrics minutely detailed are enforced by Rome. Treaties are made and wars waged by rule. For all the ingenuity displayed in devising conceits and surprising effects, literary equivalents of the devices and surprises of the baroque water-garden, poetry employs a stereotyped vocabulary, and an unvarying material, drawn chiefly from classical myth and history and seeks always the same type of effect. If painting, sculpture and architecture are freer than poetry, the rule is bent rather than broken and we are sensible of the boundary, even when it is transcended. The Gothic spirit must always reckon with the classical forms it employs. Baroque culture is closed in every direction save one, towards heaven. The knowledge, indeed, was being accumulated and the forces gathering strength which would demolish these boundaries, uproot these trim hedges and throw the garden back into wilderness. Meantime, however, fancy sported in the security of its enclosure. And the drama was played with the decorum of its prescribed movements.

The Gothic and the classical factors of baroque were not mixed everywhere in equal proportions. On the contrary, baroque art displays an entire range of their mixture from the predominantly Gothic to the predominantly classical. Consider, for example, German baroque sculpture. Guggen-bichler's statue of a Benedictine saint at Mondsee [2] is almost purely Gothic. There is nothing save a heightened expression of prayer on the face, a greater mobility in the hairs of the beard thrown back over the shoulder, and the detail of a book held half open, to differentiate it from the statues of

---

[1] Gothein, *History of Garden Art*, esp. Chapter xii.
[2] Sacheverell Sitwell, *German Baroque Sculpture*, Plate i.

saints in a late Gothic façade.   Gothic also is his wooden
statue of Our Lady.[1]   Its repose in particular is Gothic,
not baroque.   These images obviously belong to a continuous
line of development from Gothic sculpture.   On the other
hand, Ignaz Gunther's St. Kunigund at Rot am Inn,[2] though
the expressive face, gesture and clothing are of Gothic inspiration, has a worldly manner, akin to the secularism of pagan
religious art, when it had degenerated into an elegant
mythology.   In this it belongs to the classical and horizontal
aspect of baroque.   Ubhlherr's St. Elizabeth at Wilhering,[3]
seems to me intermediate between the statues of Guggenbichler
and Gunther as also is the typically and centrally baroque
group by Straub [4] at Reisach which depicts St. Simon Stock
receiving the scapular.   Notable here are the Saint's ecstatic
countenance and the rays above the Madonna and Child,
symbol of the Godhead beyond Its Incarnation.   Dietrich's
carving of the Ascension [5] presents a classical Christ of the
Jove Apollo type which Michelangelo had depicted in his
" Last Judgment."   Wenziger's sleeping Apostle, from a group
at Staufen,[6] like Guggenbichler's statue, is Gothic intensified
by baroque emotion.   Though asleep he seems to be aware
subconsciously of His Master's agony.   On the other hand,
Meisner's Hercules and Omphale [7] is purely classical without
a touch of Gothic.   And the same may be said of Beyer's
Venus and the Dolphin in the Baroque Museum, Vienna.[8]
But perhaps we ought not to call these examples at the classical
pole baroque.   For the Gothic factor is the form whose
union with a classical matter constitutes baroque.   When,
therefore, as in these instances, the Gothic form is absent, we
can hardly speak of baroque any longer.   All these sculptures,
ranging from the Gothic pole in which the classical matter is
almost absent, to the Classical in which the Gothic form of
baroque is replaced by a classical spirit belong to one region
of baroque art,   German baroque of the later seventeenth and
the eighteenth century.

[1] Berlin Kunst Museum, Weisbach.   *Die Kunst des Barock*, p. 415.
[2] Sitwell, *German Baroque Sculpture*, Plate 23.
[3] *Ibid.*, Plate 20.   [4] *Ibid.*, Plate 22.
[5] *Das Meisterwerk Deutches Rokoko*, Plate 4.
[6] *Ibid.*, Plate 17.   [7] *Ibid.*, Plate 16.
[8] Sitwell, *German Baroque Sculpture*, Plate 8.

There are, however, important distinctions in this respect between the national provinces of baroque. The art most central between Gothic and Classical, in which the Gothic form has most perfectly mastered the most extensive classical matter, is the art of Seicento Italy. But even here when the art is secular, the architecture of a palace or the picture of a scene from Pagan mythology, we observe a classical predominance. German baroque is also central. But the wide range of individual fluctuation we have just noticed between the Gothic and the Classical witnesses to an acuter tension here between the Gothic and the Classical factors of baroque. Roughly speaking the Gothic baroque is older, the Classical of later date. As the eighteenth century advanced the classical factor gained at the expense of the Gothic until a neo-classicism superseded baroque.

France and Spain represent respectively the two poles. During the early seventeenth century French art and literature were baroque. The age of Louis XIV, however, witnessed a victory of classicism. Though on technical grounds Weisbach illustrates the art of Louis Quatorze as baroque, such buildings as Versailles and the interior decoration he reproduces from contemporary chateaux and " hôtels " are entirely classical in spirit. The sole truly baroque features of this period in France were the formal fantastic garden and the dramatisation of manners. And even in the garden the formal factor was developed at the cost of the fantastic. A widely influential manual of garden design, written by Le Nôtre's pupil Le Blond, condemns " porticoes of many kinds cut in greenery, the winding trellis " . . . and " the extravagant clipping of trees into the shapes of animals . . . and many other things," in short, fantastic topiary.[1] Though he did not see it as a victory of classicism over baroque, Brèmond has related the change in French literature, as it affected the style of religious composition. He often calls attention to the re-writing in the style of Louis Quatorze of books originally written in the quainter and less " correct " French of Henri Quatre or Louis Treize. What he describes is the re-writing in classical, of books written in baroque, French. For religious literature at any rate the change was loss not gain. For the Gothic form whose presence differentiates the baroque

[1] Gothein, *History of Garden Art*, II, 113.

THE CHURCH OF THE SORBONNE, PARIS :
ARCHITECT, JACQUES LEMERCIER

Designed and built to the order of Cardinal Richelieu, and a classical composition design of rare beauty, with its façade of classical columns and its delightful dome. It is the first important domed church in the French Baroque and was associated with a hostel for poor theological students founded by Robert de Sorbon, the Confessor of St. Louis.

*THE COURT OF HEAVEN, AS REPRESENTED IN PAINTING
AND FRESCO, IS THE CELESTIAL COUNTERPART OF AN
EARTHLY COURT*

The Choir of Weltenburg Church, designed by the brothers Adam.

from the classical was, as we have seen, the Christian form of the Catholic religion-culture. To classicise religious literature was therefore to force the religious form which determined its content into an infelicitous union with a literary form of secular quality.

In Spanish baroque, on the other hand, the Gothic factor predominated. Its architecture, Weisbach observes, was deliberately intended to harmonise with the older Gothic. And in his lectures on Spanish baroque he points out that its architecture emphasises the vertical.[1] That is to say, it represented the vertical movement of the spirit by the same architectural means as Gothic had employed before it. It is not, therefore, surprising that such work as the West Front of the Cathedral at Compostella is strikingly Gothic in effect. Though in painting this Gothic intention was absent, such painters as Zurbaran and El Greco were Gothic in carrying to its utmost the artistic expression of the transcendental and vertical movement of Gothic, its Godward movement, as pre-eminently ascetic and mystical painters. And the repose of mystical contemplation is impressed upon the sculpture of Mora and Mena.[2]

In Spanish America baroque architecture lingered latest. Even after the French Revolution and its sequel had over-thrown the political and social order which had framed and supported baroque culture and had brought its art to an end in the Old World, the Spanish missionaries were erecting in California mission churches which are fine examples of baroque art in its more austere form. Their baroque is perhaps the most Gothic baroque anywhere in existence, more Gothic even than the baroque of metropolitan Spain. There is one interior in particular which strikes me as purely Gothic or rather as belonging to the primitive Gothic which is emerging from Romanesque. Thus the final examples of baroque architecture are close in time and space to the hideous mass-civilisation which has succeeded baroque. The land of Hollywood is the land where baroque art drew its last breath.[3]

[1] Weisbach *Spanish Baroque* 9.   [2] *Ibid.* 36-39.
[3] Little information is available about Spanish American baroque. The lacuna is most regrettable. For the surviving spirit of indigenous art entered into it and, reinforcing a tendency already operative, produced a luxuriance of fantastic ornament.

The complete baroque culture was necessarily confined to Catholic countries and districts. For it was a Catholic religion-culture and its form Catholic Christianity. Nevertheless the Protestant countries shared incompletely the baroque culture and its art. For they had its matter in common, the European inheritance of classical culture. Nor was this all. They also shared, though imperfectly, its religious form. Their religion was a dogmatic Christianity professing many Catholic doctrines. Moreover, in spite of the theological and ecclesiastical barrier, Catholic spirituality at this epoch profoundly affected Protestant. In his study of pietism Ritschl has proved that from the latter part of the sixteenth century onwards Protestant spirituality reacted towards the Catholic past and through the gap left by Luther's and Calvin's admiration for St. Bernard, the type of devotion the saint had inaugurated entered Protestant religion, fashioned its devotion and produced pietism. True, devotion to Our Lady and the saints and to the Blessed Sacrament was excluded by Protestant doctrine. But devotion to the human Jesus flourished. The hymn by the Evangelical Newton, "How sweet the name of Jesus sounds," echoes the Catholic hymn, "Jesu dulcis memoria." Rous, a Puritan divine of the Commonwealth, applied the Song of Songs to Christ and the soul. The Spiritual Directory by the Jesuit Parsons was adapted without acknowledgment for Protestant use. A chaplain of Cromwell's, Thomas Goodwin, published a treatise on devotion to the Sacred Heart. It appeared in 1642. It was, therefore, an instance, not of borrowing from a Catholic source, but of an analogous development. It was entitled "The Heart of Christ in Heaven towards Sinners on Earth. A Treatise Demonstrating the Gracious Disposition and Tender Affection of Christ in His Human Nature unto His Members under all Sorts of Infirmities Either of Sin or Misery." "The drift of this discourse," Goodwin wrote, "is to ascertain poor souls that His Heart in respect of pity and compassion remains the same as it was on earth ; that He is as meek, as gentle, as easy to be entreated . . . so that they may deal with Him as fairly about the great matter of their salvation . . . and upon as easy terms obtain it of Him, as they might, if they had been on earth with Him and be as familiar with Him in all their requests, as bold with Him in all their needs." It is particularly significant that although his theology forbade belief in a Eucharistic presence of the Sacred Heart, he attempts nevertheless to offer what equivalent he can. " The Holy Ghost," he writes, " follows us to the Sacrament and in that glass shows us Christ's face smiling on us and through His face His Heart ; and thus helping us to a sight of Him, we go away rejoicing that we saw our Saviour that day." Goodwin's devotion, indeed, as Bremond has pointed out,[1] is St. Margaret Mary's anthropocentric devotion to the Heart of Jesus in its love for us, not the theocentric devotion of St. John Eudes to the Heart of Jesus as embodying His state, His " interior " of priestly adoration. But the mystical movement did not leave the Protestant world untouched : Boehme was a Lutheran. Translations were published in England of Cusa and in part of Benet Canfield's *Rule of Perfection*. Even under the Commonwealth Hilton's *Scale of Perfection* could be openly published in London. This is less surprising in view of the wide and detailed acquaintance with scholastic theology displayed by such Puritan divines as Goodwin. The Quakers represented a one-sidedly interior type of religion carrying to excess and exclusion the doctrine of personal inspiration and individual guidance which Father Baker had expounded shortly before in a balanced and Catholic form. Theological hatred combined with a large measure of spiritual and even intellectual communion was the attitude of English Protestantism to the Catholic religion. And it was as a spiritual force and as a teacher of the intellect that Catholicism informed baroque culture and art.

The Christian Platonism of an Yves de Paris was paralleled by the Cambridge Platonists. One of them at least, John Smith, does not descend from his serene flight in the stratosphere of contemplation to the stormy atmosphere of anti-Catholic polemics. Such polemics grievously disfigure the writings of Henry More who in the width of his interests and in his love for natural beauty and meditation in the open air might otherwise have been Père Yves' spiritual brother. " One summer morning . . . having rose much more early than ordinary and having walked so long in a certain wood that I thought fit to rest myself on the ground . . . I reposed

---

[1] *Histoire litteraire du sentiment Religieux en France*, vol. iii, 641 n.

my weary limbs amongst the grass and flowers at the foot of a broad-spread flourishing oak where the gentle fresh morning air playing in the shade on my heated temples and with unexpressible pleasure refrigerating my blood and spirits and the industrious bees busily humming round about me upon the dewy honey-suckles to which nearer noise was most melodiously joined the distanced singings of the most cheerful birds . . . these delights of nature conspiring together . . . charm my wearied body into a profound sleep " which, however, was the occasion of a philosophic dream inculcating an optimistic view of God's providential government, such as was held by Père Yves.[1] With this morning in the wood we may compare Yves's morning walk when, so he believed, " the plants, trees, and stones shed a constant, though imperceptible, effluence of their virtues for a certain distance around wherein, if we walk, we shall receive these effusions in their purity and enjoy this delightful operation of nature's chemistry on our behalf." [2]

If English religion in the seventeenth century had had the good fortune to find such an historian as French has found in Bremond, we should be able to trace in detail analogous developments of speculation and spirituality, ranging in height from an imaginative devotion to the human Saviour upward to mystical contemplation, and in breadth comprehending with a widely Platonic Christianity the worlds of nature and humanity as a reflection of things heavenly. Even the too exclusive verticalism of the narrower Puritans had its parallel in Jansenism and in a view of religion which, though not formally heretical, was inspired by the same spirit.

It is commonly believed that England is almost wholly devoid of baroque art. This is erroneous. There is in England a distinctive and a very lovely domestic baroque architecture. Gothic and classical forms blend in every variety of delightful and fanciful combination. Indeed, this baroque Tudor and Stuart architecture seems to me more perfectly baroque than the severe and regular palaces of contemporary Rome. Kirby Hall, for example, is more truly baroque than the Palazzo

---

[1] Marred, however, by an Origenist belief in pre-existence. *Divine Dialogues*, ed. 1713, p. 247.

[2] Brèmond, *Histoire litteraire du sentiment Religieux en France*, i. 437.

Mattei or the Palazzo Montecitorio. For this English architecture combines the Gothic with the classical in fuller measure than the architecture of a Roman palace which is still predominantly classical. Later, however, British architecture, like French, became classical though Vanbrugh, Hawksmoor and Gibbs are baroque. Vanbrugh's Castle Howard is a superb example, though pre-eminently individual, of a baroque palace. Thus the development of British domestic architecture from the sixteenth to the nineteenth century was in the main the progressive advance of the classical as opposed to the Gothic factor of baroque. And Vanbrugh's architecture is, in fact, so Roman in quality that it is rather a revival of the pre-baroque of late antiquity than Christian baroque.

Protestant iconoclasm indeed made a fully developed religious baroque art impossible. Nevertheless, it is not wholly absent. Weisbach depicts two important Protestant baroque churches in Germany, at Leipzig and Berlin. In England the Laudian porch of St. Mary's at Oxford with its twisted columns is pure baroque. St. Paul's, Mr. Sitwell maintains, is a baroque Cathedral. His judgment may be accepted. But the cathedral is well on the neo-classical wing of this Gothic-classical art.

Gothic, however, lingered among us, indeed it never wholly died, and met baroque. The latest style of Gothic, as seen, for example, in Bishop West's chantry at Ely, is thoroughly baroque in spirit, in its luxuriance of late classical ornament, foliage, faces of cherubic putti and grotesque animal forms. Far more remote from baroque than this more flamboyant style, Perpendicular was still being built in the early seventeenth century, notably at Oxford, for example, Wadham chapel.

Of particular interest is a combination found here and there of Perpendicular and baroque forms in the same building. The effect is a baroque in which the Gothic factor, here nakedly visible, dominates the classical. A charming example of this baroque is the chapel of Peterhouse, Cambridge, built when Crashaw was a fellow, and shortly to be damaged by Dowsing's fanaticism. The tower of St. Mary's, Warwick, a late work by Wren, fills a Perpendicular outline with baroque detail. St. Catherine Cree, whose consecration by Laud excited Prynne's ire, has a Perpendicular east window and baroque arcading.

Influenced by the most Gothic feature of Gothic, the spire, Wren developed a distinctive variation of baroque and made his steeples masterpieces of architectural beauty and baroque art. They represent a Gothic form of baroque in which its Gothic spirit has completely subdued and refashioned the classical material. There are fine examples of Wren's baroque built by his successors, St. Mary-le-Strand in particular, and St. Martin's-in-the-Fields by James Gibbs. But Wren's interiors disappoint the promise of the exterior. The religion for which they were built required, not a temple of sacrificial praise, but an auditorium for sermons. Not even such fine appointments as Gibbons' carving compensate for the baldness of a design so misconceived.

If its baroque art is restricted England produced the most perfect baroque poetry. As we have seen, it was in Crashaw that Dr. Praz found the literary counterpart of Bernini's St. Theresa. And when Crashaw adapted Marino's poem on the slaughter of the Innocents he left it far more baroque than he had found it. As Dr. Praz has shown by a detailed comparison, he elaborated the conceits and fancies, restrained in the original by regard for the classical tradition. Other baroque poets were Donne, Herbert, Vaughan and Cowley. Milton was too classical and too Hebraic to be baroque.

If we represent to the imagination the baroque religion-culture as a continental Empire, England was an island lying off its coast, independent of its sovereignty, but entertaining close relations with it. And in one department, namely, poetry, England could boast the finest baroque achievement. We can but regret the more the probable achievement of English baroque architecture had our country remained Catholic. What magnificent churches Inigo Jones and Wren would have given us! Whether a Catholic England would have achieved much in painting and sculpture is more doubtful.

" Heaven lies about us in our infancy," Wordsworth wrote. It lay about the old age of the art of Catholic Europe, the final phase of baroque, the rococo of the German eighteenth century. It is the Dantesque paradise of light, dance and music presented by every device of convergent, even blending arts, architecture, painting and sculpture. To this heaven at Rohr Mary soars in exultant bliss, below her the empty tomb and astonished Apostles. From it at Weltenburg St. George rides forth to slay the dragon and release the doomed maiden. Sculptures both by Egid Quirin Asam.

And everywhere joy.

" Rich curves," writes Mr. Harold Speed, " that is curves farthest removed from the straight line seem to be expressive of uncontrolled energy and the more exuberant joys of life." [1] The rococo riot of curves, in which Mr. Speed can see only an earthly voluptuousness, expresses, when employed in sacred art the exuberant joy, not of natural but of supernatural life," " the joy of the Lord " into which, like the faithful soul, the art of Christendom entered at the end of its course. It exults in the masterpieces of rococo—in the work of the brothers Asam, of Johann Michael Fischer, of Zimmerman. In the bravura of the Nepomucen Kirche, Rohr and Weltenburg, in the counterpoint of Steinhausen and Wies, in the extravagance everywhere of colour and form, in vaults and domes where saints and angels rise rank above rank until they fade into the light of God which clothes them with its glory, suffering and sin seem already vanquished and transmuted, the joy of Christ's victory manifest already in souls and bodies blessed ever-lastingly. Now, as never before, Christian art copies and displays the eternal sport of Wisdom before God in the motley of the various forms embodied in time, ludens coram eo omni tempore, ludens in orbe terrarum. What in Roman baroque was as yet a comparatively sober happiness is now jubilee. We have remarked already the music of rococo. It utters its joy, a joy for which, though but in semblance and anticipation, discords have been resolved in harmony. For the day, so soon to close, the day of the Catholic religion culture is " the day which the Lord hath made." Therefore the Catholic artist " will rejoice and be glad in it." The expression of his joy is the rococo church.

I have dwelt at length on baroque and devoted more space to it than to any other phase of the Catholic religion-culture for several reasons. Its merit is largely unrecognised and, even more, its nature as the heir and the continuation of Gothic. I love it. And it is good to speak of what one loves. And it was the ripe fruit of the Catholic religion-culture, when its classical matter was most extensively employed and re-fashioned by its Christian form. It was thus pre-eminently

[1] *The Practice and Science af Drawing*, p. 220.

the culture of a Christian and a mystically Christian humanism, a culture such as the religion of God Incarnate must of necessity inspire. Its accidents were local and temporary. For they were determined by the cultural inheritance and environment which gave the humanism Christianised its distinctive character. But its Christian and classical humanism is still close to us, and, whether we recognise it or not, we owe to it whatever culture yet survives in the civilised barbarism of a mechanised and standardised epoch. So we may well love baroque and learn from its spirit, often also from its letter. It will teach us how to be free without being lawless, to be humanist without being secular, to rise high yet range far, to live a life hid with Christ in God yet regard no human interest as alien.

Why then, it may be asked, did the baroque culture perish, leaving no later phase of the Christian, or indeed, of any religion-culture to succeed it ? Why was its autumn followed by winter ? The baroque religion-culture perished and with it the Catholic religion-culture which had fashioned Western Europe, because in every sphere the forces of revolt and disintegration proved finally too strong and, converging, destroyed it. What made their victory possible ?

The ultimate religious inspiration of the baroque culture was, as we have seen, Catholic mysticism. When towards the close of the seventeenth century mysticism suffered a defeat from which it failed to recover, the virtue began to forsake the culture it had inspired. Baroque religion was mortally weakened by this wound in its heart at the very time when the forces hostile to it were gathering strength and confidence. Well-meaning ecclesiastics who opposed mysticism, because its Quietist excess menaced the necessary institutional and sacramental aspects of religion were unwittingly delivering the Catholic religion and with it the Catholic culture of baroque into the hands of their foes.

From the outset, however, the baroque religion-culture suffered from a weakness which finally proved fatal. The synthesis it achieved was imperfect. Though truly organic, it had never been a perfect organism. It had always contained a considerable inorganic element, an element of artificiality and external compulsion. If the baroque religion-culture and the synthesis of a Catholic humanism which it

STEINHAUSEN : ZIMMERMAN

In the Rococo of Central Europe the linear rhythm which moulded the interior is extended with due modification to the exterior and makes it an organic whole. Zimmerman's church at Steinhausen is an eminently successful example of an organic exterior. In the counterpoint of Steinhausen the joy of Christ's victory is manifest already.

Dum tradit, attrahit.

Venus et l'Amour doucement,
Guident les ames au tourment.

Litteras ne relegas.

Bruslez ces lettres, il vaut mieux,
Qu'enflammer ton cœur par tes yeux.

FROM THE EMBLEM BOOK: *THEATRUM AMORIS DIVINI ET HUMANI*

Cupid tows a boat towards a burning city. The love   Seated before a cabinet the Divine Eros advises her to
of the sexes is the way to Hell.   burn the old love-letters unread.

achieved and in which it consisted had not been organic, it would not have been, as it was, a living culture. For only an organism is alive. Had it, on the other hand, been completely organic, which it was not, it would have resisted successfully the dissolvent forces which attacked it. This, however, is but to say that it was human. A completely organic synthesis incorporating and harmonising every constituent of human life and thought duly subordinated and co-ordinated by its vital form would be the culture of a fully deified humanity, disposing, moreover, of knowledge and practical resources out of proportion even to the vast accession of both during the last two centuries. Such a synthesis will be the kingdom of God on earth promised before human history ends and for whose advent we are taught to pray.

The Catholic religion-culture of European history, of which the baroque culture was the conclusion, was not and could not have been this perfect organism, man's distant goal. The synthesis it achieved was imperfect and only in part organic. What it lacked organically was supplied by artificial construction. It was as when a lame man supplies his physical defect with crutches. Throughout the Catholic religion-culture the transcendental aspect of religion was insisted upon to the *comparative* neglect of the immanental. This was indeed necessary. For only when God's transcendence of creatures has been fully realised can His Immanence in them be emphasised without danger of immanentism, the pantheism which recognises no divinity external to the world. But, however necessary, a one-sided affirmation of transcendence is an imperfection. And the imperfection became sensible when the reaction and revolt of a pantheistic immanentism began. From the Renaissance onwards this immanentism has been an increasingly powerful force, spiritual and intellectual. For it flatters man's pride by presenting humanity as the highest manifestation of this purely immanent process. Whether it be called spirit, life-force, or by Marx, self-moving matter is in the last resort chiefly a question of terminology. For in any case it is in man that it flowers and becomes completely self-conscious. Such was the pantheism of Giordano Bruno, and, prudently veiled, of Campanella. In its earlier presentation, when its language and, to be just, its intent were spiritual, this pantheism was the substitution for a Creator wholly other than His creation of a creative and self-evolving world-soul. Indeed, this view is very far from obsolete to-day. It should have been met by the development of a true, because transcendental, immanentism, by emphasis upon the immanent action in creatures of the God who is nevertheless transcendent of them. Belief in a world-soul should have been answered by insistence on the truth that the Holy Spirit to whom the immanental action of God is appropriated by Catholic theology, though He is not and cannot be a world-soul, performs its functions sustaining and moving from within the operation of creatures and imprinting on matter disposed to receive the impress, the form for which it has been disposed. Indeed, the Thomist doctrine that God premoves the action of secondary causes had taught this. And in the twelfth century St. Hildegarde, and Adam of St. Victor had celebrated in hymnody the work of the Holy Ghost as the ultimate and immanent principle of life.

" Thou fire of the Paraclete," wrote St. Hildegarde, " life of the life of every creature, Thou art holy, giving life to forms. . . . Thou dost combine all things and bind them together. From Thee the clouds flow forth, the æther flies, stones have moisture, streams come forth and earth transpires verdure." " Thou fillest all," wrote Adam, " cherishest all, dost guide the stars and move the heavens abiding motionless." This, however, was a rare note. And in baroque religion, where it should have been struck most loudly, it is not heard. Among a host of special devotions there was none to the Holy Spirit.[1]

Immanentism, impressed as it is with the organic unity of the world and mankind, tends in its social ideal to some form of communism. Campanella suffered imprisonment for his share in a mad dream of establishing a communist regime in Naples with the help of the Turk. And at the close of his life he was greeting the newly-born infant that would be Louis XIV as the predestined ruler who would establish communism. He was wide of the mark in confusing the Grand Monarque with Lenin. In face of this extreme, Catholics should have insisted on the principle of solidarity in the mystical body of Christ and its social embodiment.

[1] The devotion initiated by Blessed Crescentia of Kaufbeuren was too local and short-lived to be of account.

In fact this solidarity was in the main lost sight of. To be frank, Goodwin and Polhill displayed a more vital under-standing of Christ's mystical body than many Catholic writers. Even mysticism stressed too exclusively the union of the individual soul with God. Except in France, where a better tradition lingered, there was little appreciation of the corporate liturgical worship which expresses the solidarity of Catholics in the body of Christ. And even in France the liturgy was valued rather as instructive than as corporate. The Benedictine mystic, Father Augustine Baker, otherwise of admirable wisdom, is blind to the worth and meaning of the Opus Dei, so important in the eyes of Saint Benedict. Even when the Mass was viewed theocentrically as the sacrifice of praise its corporate aspect was insufficiently taught. Though baroque religion of necessity believed in the Holy Ghost and the Holy Catholic Church, it did not clearly perceive the immanental operation of the former and the organic solidarity of the latter which that operation on its highest and supernatural level produces. As we have seen this individualism made it the more necessary to insist upon the external unity of the Church, upon her hierarchy and her code of law. Only thus could disintegration be avoided. But when a living awareness of the internal and organic solid-arity of the Church is lacking, her organisation must be conceived externally and mechanically. So long as mystical and contemplative religion flourished this externalism and mechanism were overcome by their subordination to it. When, however, it fell into the background, they became an oppressive burden on the spirit. And the balance was fatally shifted as between the interior and the exterior of Catholicism. Hence-forth hierarchy and law, even the sacraments, were widely regarded as the end for which religion exists instead of as a means, however indispensable, to safeguard and foster the spiritual life of the Church, her life of contemplation and praise. Law took precedence of prayer. This de-ordination, this ecclesiastical materialism was a fatal weakness in face of the gathering assault of an exclusive subjectivism, proclaiming the unchecked and uncontrolled supremacy of personal experience, of the spirit immanent in the soul of man.

Moreover, despite the wide acceptance by the baroque culture of natural beauty and human interests, the one-sided transcendentalism it inherited had not been fully corrected. Hence the failure to realise sufficiently the work of the Holy Spirit in nature, subhuman and human, and therefore its intrinsic and organic connection with the supernatural order above it. Baroque Catholicism, therefore, tended to regard nature as profane, a recalcitrant material, which could indeed be subordinated to the supernatural religion of Christ and employed in its service, but, as it were, by force and merely to provide a symbolic language into which supernatural truth could be translated for the imagination. It was little understood that the symbol can be employed as such only because it reflects, and therefore in its measure and order partakes the nature of that which it symbolises. That is to say, the relation between the symbol and that which it represents was conceived too externally. In this respect also the organism was defective and the defect must be supplied by artifice. This artificiality of fundamental conception explains, I believe, the artificiality which too often attaches to baroque symbolism, to the emblem and the conceit, and reduces what might have been imagination revealing a vital connection between the sensible type and the spiritual antitype to an entertaining, even a charming fancy, which plays on the surface of an analogy it cannot penetrate.

Christian humanism, it is true, as in a Père Yves, hinted at a deeper and more organic view. But it was but a hint and, moreover, confined to a comparatively small circle. In Catholic as well as in Protestant Europe Puritanism was powerful. The dance and the theatre were condemned as indiscriminately by French bishops as by Presbyterian divines, by Bossuet as by Prynne. A striking evidence of the tension between the vertical and horizontal movements, between Christianity and a secular humanism, is the unrelated juxtaposition of sacred and profane art. Dante had employed themes derived from classical myth and history, but to illustrate and reinforce Christian truth. In Renaissance and still in baroque art, the pagan themes are treated for their own sake. In garden and gallery images of gods and heroes challenged the images of Saints, and often both were the work of the same artist.

The fountain of Venus in the Villa d'Este at Tivoli is a typical baroque altarpiece whose altar is a sarcophagus tank

MICHAEL HOYER: FLAMMULAE AMORIS SANCTI PATRIS AUGUSTINI
A charming little book. Many of the illustrations are Dutch tiles reproduced in engraving.

The pride of man, embracing earthly things,
Built Babylon, the seat of Asian kings,
      Now levell'd in the dust, and quite forgot.
We scorn those transient glories, fix our eye,
Upon a city which is plac'd on high,
      The new Jerusalem, the Christian's lot.

OTTO VENNE: EMBLEMATA DIVINI AMORIS

*It portrays Augustine's two cities, the diabolic city built by human pride and
self-love, the heavenly city of God built by humble charity.*

shaped like a contemporary altar, framing in place of a Christian saint the naked goddess.[1] It is the superficial harmony of an underlying discord unresolved.

To the same country and period, eighteenth-century France belong the painters of polite society, Watteau, Boucher, Fragonard and the writers of the Gallican sequences and hymns, Santeuil, Gourdan and Coffin. But the former represent the pagan and classical aspect of the baroque culture, strictly neoclassical rather than baroque, the latter its Gothic and Christian aspect, The contrast indeed is here so great that it seems scarcely credible that the Paris Breviary and *L'Embarquement pour l'Isle de Cythére* are products of the same culture.

Nowhere, however, was this divorce between nature and supernature, due to the persistence of a too exclusive emphasis on the vertical, as opposed to the horizontal movement of the spirit, on God's transcendence as contrasted with His immanence in creatures, more sensible than in the view taken of the relation between human and Divine love. And this, as I have already observed, is a point of crucial importance, where the attitude adopted is decisive for an entire culture.

The humanist challenge, asserting against the ascetical tradition the rights of human nature, of man's earthly desires, pleasures and interests made itself, as we should expect, heard most loudly in the erotic sphere. The splendour of human love, of woman's beauty and the passion it inspires was proclaimed with a triumphant defiance of religious rule and censure. Together with the glories of classical antiquity it was the theme of the *Hypnoterotomachia Polyphili.* It was also the theme of a drama widely popular in the Seicento, Guarini's pastoral play, " *Il Pastor Fido.*" First published in 1590, it became a European classic. The edition I possess is one of the Elzevir pocket classics, the Temple classics of their day, published in 1678 in conjunction with a Paris publisher. There is nothing coarse or prurient in Guarini's courtly Arcadia. "The Pastor Fido" observes a perfect decorum and has a moral ending. But with a passionate zeal and a seductive charm it proclaims the glory of sexual love. It hurls defiance at asceticism. Cardinal Bellarmine told Guarini that his book was more dangerous to Christianity

---

[1] *Le Fontane del Giardino Estense.* Venturini. Plate 6.

than Luther's heresy. It certainly uttered a revolt more
radical than Luther's against the Catholic order.

> Mira d'intorno Silvio
> Quanto il mondo hà di vago e di gentile,
> Opra è d'Amore. Amante è il Cielo, amante
> La terra, amante il mare.
> Quella, che là sù miri innanzi a l'alba
> Cosi leggiadra stella,
> Ama d'amor anch'ella, e del suo figlio
> Sente le fiamme : ed essa, che'nnamora
> Innamorata splende,
>
> .   .   .   .
>
> Amano per le selve
> Le mostruose fere : aman per l'onde
> I veloci delfini, e l'orche gravi.
> Quell'augelin che canta
> Si dolcemente, e lascivetto vola
> Hor da l'abete al faggio
> Ed hor dal faggio al mirto
> S'havesse humano spirto
> Direbbe, ardo d'amore, ardo d'amore :
>
> .   .   .   .
>
> Al fine ama ogni cosa
> Se non tù Silvio, e sarà Silvio solo
> In cielo, in terra, in mare
> Anima senza amore ?
> Deh lascia hormai le selve,
> Folle garzon, lascia le fere ed ama.

" Look around you, Silvio. Whatever the world hath fine
and estimable is the work of love. The sky is a lover, the
earth a lover, and the sea a lover. Yon winsome star that
above us is watching for the dawn loves too, and feels her
son's fire and she who makes to love herself shines enamoured.
. . . The savage beasts in the woods love, and in the waves
the swift dolphins love, and the clumsy whales. That little
bird that is singing so sweetly and flits wantonly from the
fir to the beech and from the beech to the myrtle, had it a
human voice would say, I am burning, I am burning with
love. . . . In fine everything loves, save yourself, Silvio.
And shall Silvio be the only living soul in heaven, on earth and
the sea, that is without love ? Leave then the woods, foolish
boy, leave your wild beasts and love."

Once more the refrain of the *Pervigilium Veneris*, the
swan song of pagan literature, is sung here. It is a pæan of
love's lordship and the vital force that animates all living things,

whose flower is the passion of human sex. Whatever his intentions, in such a passage Guarini voices the immanental vitalism in revolt against transcendence that was taught as explicit doctrine by his contemporaries, Bruno and Campanella. The universe is pervaded and ruled by a vital force purely natural in character that loves and arouses love and loves in the sexual love of man.

In face of the challenge the true place and dignity of natural love should have been affirmed on its various levels from the cohesion and mechanical attraction of inanimate objects through the sexual unions of plant and animal to human sex where this biological passion can be made the material of spiritual love. Natural love and sex should have been seen and valued as reflections on a lower level of spiritual and religious love on the highest. The cosmic love sung by Guarini should have been accepted and subordinated as a preparation and foreshadowing of its supernatural fulfilment.

Baroque religion, however, continued in substance the attitude of medieval. The love of the sexes was still regarded as in a derogatory sense profane, the foe, not the harbinger of Divine Love, at best tolerable because inevitable. Erotic symbolism was indeed freely employed both in writing and within the limits of decency in pictorial art. There is no commoner subject of the emblem book than the representation of Divine love by emblems of the human Eros. But the symbol is employed to exalt religious love, not merely, as it is, as higher than earthly, but at the expense and to the detriment of the latter which is disparaged and denounced. It was forgotten that human love can be a suitable symbol of Divine only if it reflects and, after its fashion, participates in the latter, and as such is good and pure, indeed, in a wide sense sacred, sacramental. For a base and unclean love must be unfit for a service so holy.

Typical in this respect is an Emblem Book entitled *Theatrum Amoris Divini et Humani*. In a long series of charming emblems it glorifies Divine love and vilifies human indiscriminately. The former is carried to its ecstatic conclusion, the ecstasy of love and this rapture of love itself concludes with the heavenly vision of Love. The latter is empty, deceitful, and perilous. Cupid is portrayed weighing down the left arm of Psyche, while the heavenly Eros raises her right arm aloft. Psyche skates with Cupid on slippery ice, in a picturesque winter-scene. This and many other illustrations remind me of Dutch tiles. Seated before a cabinet she is taking old love-letters from a drawer. The Divine Eros stands above her and advises her to burn them unread. Cupid tows along a canal a boat in which a youth lies asleep and a lady sits facing him. It is a pleasant stretch of water bordered by a wood. But it leads through a distant bridge to a burning city. The love of the sexes is the way to hell. While Psyche sleeps in the sun at the foot of a tree, Cupid shoots at her his fatal arrow, a spider spins his web from a bough and a snake lies coiled in the grass.

The illustrations are accompanied by passages of verse and prose in Latin, French, Spanish, and Flemish. They celebrate the praise of Divine, the infamy of human love. " Repentance and sorrow *always* follow " the earthly Eros. " Tis the oblivion of reason and akin to madness, a foul vice ill-fitting a healthy soul. It darkens counsel, breaks lofty and generous spirits, drags men down from the most sublime to the basest thoughts. It ensnares the soul. It defiles childhood, ruins youth, stings and teases the dying flesh of eld. 'Tis a penalty there is no escaping, a dire bane, a calamity men desire, a domestic peril, an evil coloured with the show of good, an unceasing strife, a daily mischief, a grievous burden."

The theme and its emblematic treatment were long-lived, surviving, indeed, till the death of baroque. In the following century a Flemish Augustinian, Fr. Michael Hoyer, published a series of extracts from St. Augustine, and the devotional writings which passed under his name, treating of Divine Love. He called it *Flammulæ Amoris Sancti Patris Augustini*. It is a charming little book. As in the *Theatrum* many of the illustrations are Dutch tiles reproduced in engraving. One emblem displays in the background a windmill and a boat, treated as in the tiles. Another depicts a formal garden and a fantastic fountain. The poems employ the passionate language of classical love poetry.

The very words in which Catullus expressed his passion for Lesbia are adapted to the soul's love of Jesus :

    " Vive Lux mea, vive, teque amemus "
    " Vivamus mea Lesbia atque amemus " Catullus wrote

" aeternum et sine fine perfruamur
tuis ignibus, osculisque sanctis.
Qui te deperit impotente flamma "
" Illum deperit impotente amore," wrote Catullus—
" Qui te plus propriis amat medullis.
Illi gaudia mille, mille risus
Illi basia casta, mille lusus
Et naves veniunt amoenitatum
Et messes veniunt suavitatum
Torentes simul omnium leporum.
Vive lux mea vive meque castis
Adure amplius, ampliusque flammis."

" Live my Light. May we love Thee forever and forever enjoy Thy fires and holy kisses. He who loves Thee desperately with a flame beyond control, who loves Thee more than his own heart, a thousand joys are his, a thousand smiles, a thousand chaste kisses, a thousand sports, shiploads of delights come to him, harvests of sweets, torrents of charms. Live my light, live and consume me ever more throughly with Thy chaste fires."

Yet the reverend poet has nothing but abuse for the passion whose language and imagery he employs so freely. Always and under all circumstances it is base and foul. A prefatory note by the printer to the second and enlarged edition informs us that the book has been reprinted in response to " the almost daily demand of the gravest men and the youth of Flanders." When every allowance is made for a blurb, the fact that a second edition was called for proves that the volume had found many admirers, and hardly for the sake alone of its attractive illustrations. Nevertheless it is not easy to believe that young students were turned from earthly passion to devotion by denouncing the former while decking out the latter in its clothes. Once more the implication of symbolism has been missed. An opposition has been introduced between the stages of love's hierarchical ascent and the organic bond between the lower and the higher has been severed. Hoyer would have been well advised to have enlarged his reading of the classics and put Catullus aside for Plato. The Symposium would have taught him a truer view of human love and its relation to Divine than he could learn by confronting Catullus' passion ior Lesbia with St. Augustine's Confessions. And though there were, of course, exceptions, this advice might have been addressed not to Fr. Hoyer alone, but to the baroque religion of which he was a typical representative.

Nor was it only in its content that the baroque religion-culture was imperfectly organic. The same judgment must be passed upon its social and political aspects. It was essentially an aristocratic religion-culture. The masses, whether in town or country, had little share in the culture.[1] The religion, it is true, was theirs also. But their knowledge of it was in the main lamentably slight. Their religion was too often superficial and superstitious.

Rome was the capital of the baroque culture as of the Catholic religion. But the Roman populace was brutal and ignorant, finding its amusement in a race of half-naked cripples and quick to use the stiletto. Only on the virgin soil of Paraguay were the Jesuits able to construct a truly Christian society which cared for the religious and the secular welfare of all its citizens. And their opinion of European Catholics was significantly shown by their refusal to allow European traders to communicate with their natives. A society whose members were presumably unfit to enter a genuinely Christian society was not truly Christian itself. Christendom possessed a Christian religion-culture. And that was much, very much. But it was not a Christian society, which is much more. As Dr. Macleod has aptly put it,[2] " Christendom is not the description of an ideal state, but of an accepted ideal." The mass conversion of the Roman Empire had forced the Church to tolerate a society mainly composed of superficial Christians but in which she could work freely and by securing a universal Catholic allegiance could put a genuine Christianity within every man's reach. But the ignorant Catholicism of the masses in such a society could exist only under the protection of a Catholic state. Once heresy had found entrance or the more radical revolt of secular rationalism and the state had withdrawn its protection of the Church or even become hostile to the Catholic religion, these ignorant Catholics would fall from their faith like autumn leaves at the first storm of winter. And this has, in fact, occurred throughout modern Europe.

Meanwhile the new nationalist state exacted a high price for the patronage it extended to the Catholic religion, a

---

[1] They enjoyed, however, and presumably appreciated, if they did not understand, the architecture and decoration of their churches. And in Rome at least the gardens of cardinals, princes and noblemen were thrown open to them.   [2] *We Shall Rebuild*, p. 94.

patronage which the lack of a realised spiritual solidarity among Catholics rendered as indispensable as the analogous development of ecclesiastical authority. The French state was openly Gallican. His Most Catholic Majesty of Spain saw himself as the divinely appointed protector of the Church, and as such entitled to interfere in her affairs, to control the Inquisition and to appoint to every see and abbacy in his empire. A nephew of Philip II, a lay Cardinal, enjoyed unordained for many years the dignity and revenues of the Primatial See of Spain, until at last he·married his cousin and became Regent of the Spanish Netherlands. If in the Thirty Years' War Papal sympathies were divided, it is not surprising. A defeat of the Protestants would have given the Hapsburgs such overwhelming power that the Pope would have been in serious danger of sinking to the servile condition of the Patriarch of Constantinople under Byzantine Caesaropapism. These Hapsburg monarchs, Spanish and Austrian, were, however, devout Catholics, and maintained their dominions in the Catholic faith. But the day would come when the Austrian Joseph and his brother Leopold would be affected by the Enlightenment and harass the Church with their bureaucratic " Liberalism." And at the best of times it was very difficult for the Papacy to oppose these Catholic Erastians. For it could not count on the support of an instructed and devout Catholic population more loyal to Christ than to Caesar. Clement XII could not prevent a Spanish army invading and pillaging his neutral territory and impressing his subjects.[1] So weak in fact did the Pope become in face of the Catholic sovereigns, that Clement XIV sacrificed to their autocracy the body which for two centuries and a half had served the Papacy so loyally and had been the backbone of the Counter-reformation, the Society of Jesus. That shameful and ungrateful surrender was the beginning of the end, the end of Catholic Christendom and its religion-culture. Baroque religion was buried in the Jesuits' grave and would not rise again with them.

Scarcely had the Catholic religion mastered the enlargement of humanist and classical material, brought by the Renaissance, when the horizontal movement was reinforced

[1] Pastor *History of the Popes* (E.T.), vol. xxxiv, p. 368.

by the rapid growth of mathematico-physical science. The golden age of the baroque culture, the seventeenth century, was also the century in which the foundations were laid of the science which has revolutionised man's knowledge of the world and enabled him for good and for ill to transform his earthly environment. The philosophy inaugurated by Descartes saw nothing in the subhuman world save mechanism. It sought to rescue man's spiritual and intellectual life by divorcing the human mind from the world of matter and therefore from the body and severing it from them by an impassable gulf. On either side of the gulf mind and matter, thus forcibly torn asunder, strove for the mastery. Scientists began to entertain the prospect of explaining the entire universe, including man, by mathematico-physical laws. And idealist philosophy attempted in various ways to prove that the material world was wholly or in part a mental construction. In the field of metaphysics idealism prevailed over materialism. Science, however, pushed metaphysics into the background. The sceptre was passing into the hand of science, and a science that, as it became more clearly aware of its nature, tended to admit no valid source of knowledge save sensible data, and quantities abstracted from them. But its triumphs and even more its promises were dazzling. At last human reason, advancing from knowledge to knowledge, from power to power, could decipher the secrets of nature and control her forces at man's will. Forgetful of the depths and complexities of the human soul and the sin that warps it, reason in its pride believed it could control men's passions as surely as it could control the forces of inanimate nature. A new and a rational order would replace the existing social and political order with its irrationality and inequity. But this new order of reason could be inaugurated only when man had been emancipated from the irrational superstitions of religion, of its nature the ally of tyranny and privilege.

The achievements of science and the education of the critical reason had brought the European schoolboy to the verge of manhood. He was now the university undergraduate, clever and self-confident, daring and avid of novelty, dogmatic and sceptical, negatively credulous. Typical of this negative credulity was the refusal of a French scientific academy towards the close of the eighteenth century to receive a report on a fall of meteorites, because stones *cannot* fall from the sky.[1] But of one thing our undergraduate was assured, that the traditional faith and the traditional philosophy, the traditional knowledge and the traditional culture, the traditional order and the traditional way of living were obsolete and patently false. They did not even merit careful enquiry into their testimonials and their worth. To examine the evidence on their behalf was time wasted. They must be discarded en bloc and without discrimination.

We cannot condemn out of hand this rationalist enlightenment. Science was in truth bringing to man vast accessions of knowledge and power. The horizontal movement of the human mind was opening horizons never before visible. Any future religion-culture would be obliged to incorporate the new knowledge. The vertical movement of the spirit must face the task of ruling and employing a horizontal movement where scope was wholly unprecedented.

Moreover, the Catholic doctrine of a natural law governing men's conduct and providing a norm to which every human institution must conform, justified the Enlightment in its attack on irrationalities and inequities which contradicted this rational law. And the criticism, however hostile, of a scientific rationalism must in the long run purify a religion it is powerless to destroy. For it frees it from a host of legends and superstitions and a fundamentalism which obscures its abiding religious content of revealed truth. The critical work of the Maurists and the Bollandists sufficiently proves that scientific criticism is not incompatible with Catholic faith.

In the concrete, however, no reconciliation or synthesis was possible. The rationalists denounced religion or, at least, Christianity. Historical circumstances had, as we have seen, bound the Church closely to the system of government whose abuses and inequities were denounced by the Enlightenment. And the uncompromising hostility of the latter made the ecclesiastical authorities cling the closer to what seemed the sole bulwark against the common foe. Catholic spirituality was now too weak to attempt the gigantic task of grappling with the new material, humanist and scientific,

---

[1] This negative credulity is far from extinct. Many scientists and scientific bodies refused reports of Dr. Rhine's experiments in telepathy, because extrasensory perception is impossible. Stones *cannot* fall from the sky.

and moulding it by the form of Christian faith. Instead of harmony between the vertical and the ever-widening horizontal movements of the mind, there was open war between them. The representatives of each were, speaking generally, blind to the value and significance of the other.

The substitution by Rousseau and the later romantics of an emotional for a rationalist immanentism did not mend matters. The latter movement was as exclusively naturalistic and humanist as the former, equally hostile to a genuinely transcendental and supernatural religion. It was Blake the immanental mystic who deified man, rather than the rationalist Voltaire who, moreover, professed a transcendental deism. And if the earlier idealists retained, with Kant, a genuine theism, idealism ended by seeking reality in an immanent reason which had reached maturity in the mind of man.

Since the latter part of the seventeenth century Paris had replaced Rome as the intellectual capital of Europe. And even in Pascal's lifetime freethinkers, " Libertines," as they were termed, were so abundant in the Paris salons that he thought it necessary to devote his genius to the defence of Christianity. In the eighteenth century they ruled the intellectual world, Deists at best, but often frank atheists. In the England of George II Bishop Butler complained that it was commonly taken for granted that Christianity is incredible.

True, the assault was not unopposed. Even in the eighteenth century the Church produced great saints and new religious orders. England witnessed the Wesleyan movement and the Evangelical revival which followed it. But it was not halted. The more powerful currents of the age were flowing horizontally not vertically. In his own esteem man was coming into his earthly kingdom. Because of their nature the sciences are susceptible of an indefinite progress, the same progress was expected everywhere. Neither religion nor philosophy is susceptible of such progress. The former therefore was pronounced obsolete, the latter rejected or the method of the natural sciences unnaturally forced upon it.

Already on the horizon might be discerned the lineaments of the commercial and mechanical civilisation, if civilisation it can be termed, which applied science would erect on the ruins of the old religion-culture, in its visible embodiment, the manufacturing city, formless and squalid. Its birth awaited only the industrial revolution effected towards the close of the eighteenth century by the invention of power-driven machinery. An illustration in Otto Venne's *Emblemata Divini Amoris* is ominously prophetic of its still remote advent. It portrays Augustine's two cities, the diabolic city built by human pride and self-love, the heavenly city of God built by humble charity. The latter, Jerusalem, is depicted as a city whose central feature is a baroque church. It is built on a hilltop. For it is built by the vertical movement of the soul to God. Above it the sun is shining undimmed with the brilliance of noon, the Divine Wisdom that is the light of the heavenly city. At the foot of the hill a cherub holds aloft a cross and tramples on the globe. The city of an evil humanism sprawls over the plain covering far more space, extending, indeed, on either side out of the picture. For it is the product of the horizontal movement. Its central object is not a church but a huge blast-furnace belching flame and the smoke which covers the sky with an artificial night. It is a foresight of the city to be erected by the industrial revolution, Manchester or Birmingham. In front of its gate stands a cupid embracing the globe.

An unknown hand that has added English verses to my copy has written underneath these appropriate lines :

> The Pride of man embracing earthly things
> Built Babylon the seat of Asian kings
> Now levelled in the dust and quite forgot.
> We scorn those transient glories : fix our eye
> Upon a city which is placed on high
> The new Jerusalem, the Christian's lot.

I am not confusing the baroque religion-culture or any other with the heavenly Jerusalem. Nevertheless it is in these religion-cultures that the latter descends, though but in part, to earth. " I saw the new Jerusalem descending from God *out* of heaven."

Beside Venne's prophecy I keep a picture of its fulfilment, an envelope bearing two Czechoslovakian stamps. The stamp on the right shows a typical and charming baroque church crowning a mountain whose sides are clothed with forest. To its left is a stamp depicting a manufacturing city filled with smoking chimneys.

These pictures sum up the history of Europe during the last two centuries. Baroque culture has yielded to a civilisation progressively losing the culture which has survived from the past. Behind this cultural collapse has been the defeat of the religion which had given life to the vanishing culture. Man has ceased to look upwards to " the city whose maker and builder is God," and has been intent only on erecting the earthly Babel whose summit he has fondly dreamed will shortly reach the sky of a self-deified humanity. For the stellar spaces are no longer visible. Beneath the smoke of a false and nebulous philosophy to the glare of an artificial light which forgets the sun, man has built up and spread over the entire globe his earthly city of an exclusive horizontalism that has taken visible shape in the urban agglomerations miscalled cities. In his proud confidence he has not foreseen that the curse of Babel, the division of tongues, would ruin his work, that the place left vacant by God and his supernatural kingdom would be filled by national or class idols whose strife would bring down his city in ruin. To-day it is being literally " levelled in the dust " by the latest and most powerful misapplication of science.[1]

Contemporaneously with the industrial revolution which subverted the economic substructure of the traditional religion-culture, its political framework was demolished by the French Revolution and the wars which ensued. The fabric of the baroque culture, already lifeless, collapsed in ruin. And the enemies of the Church believed that they were assisting at her death-bed.

[1] In itself machinery is good, and if it is employed in accordance with a reason enlightened by religious faith and in due subordination to the ends of a genuine religion-culture could be a most valuable servant freeing man from the bondage of work truly servile. But it has been allowed to rule instead of serving man. It has been employed in the service of greed and pride and has therefore enslaved its inventor.

WINTER : THE MODERN WORLD

THE modern period is the winter of Christianity, indeed of religion generally. When the baroque religion-culture crashed in the Revolution Christendom fell. No other phase of the Catholic religion-culture took its place. There were survivals, even partial revivals, of the older Catholic order, revivals fostered on occasion by rulers for political reasons. But nowhere has there been an organic religion-culture extending throughout an entire nation. The intelligentsia have been increasingly hostile to Christianity and finally even to theism. The right wing, it is true, of the romantic revival which reacted against eighteenth-century rationalism and the Revolution was Christian, and, in Catholic countries, Catholic. But the strength of the movement lay with its left wing which was not Christian but represented a more or less explicit immanentism whose deity was a world-soul whose supreme manifestation is man. In English literature, for example, Wordsworth's best work was inspired by a nature mysticism of pantheistic colour. The work of his Anglican orthodoxy was of little value. And Blake, though his creed was a brand of Gnosticism peculiar to himself, deified man and did not believe in a transcendent God. German idealism was markedly immanentist as in its greatest representative Hegel.

Romanticism, that is to say, was the cult of a Pantheist indefinity. And pantheist indefinity aped theist infinity. We cannot always distinguish them at first sight. The Dark Night of Wagner's *Tristan und Isolde*, a hymn to the indefinite, bears a delusive resemblance to the Dark Night of St. John of the Cross, a hymn to the Infinite.

Many Romantics, for example, the English poets Blake, Shelley, and Keats, were bitterly hostile to the traditional religion. Though individual Romantics were Christian, even Catholic, Romanticism as a movement had broken with the religion of the European past and therefore with the organic religion-culture it had inspired. Æsthetic appreciation and an imaginative and historical sympathy cannot replace religious conviction. And Romanticism denied reason, the foundation upon which religious faith must build. Like its rationalist foe, though less blatantly, Romanticism rejected the religious, and therefore the cultural, tradition of Europe.

When the sun has set, the light lingers and often invests the clouds with brilliant colours. So when the sun of the Christian religion-culture had sunk below the European horizon, the light of the departed luminary glowed in its sky and produced a pageant of bright and various hues. Romanticism was the light of Christendom surviving its sunset. The colours were more brilliant and more diversified than the sunlight had been. But this afterglow was neither steady nor enduring. The splendours soon faded and night fell.

Moreover, the Romantics were alien, indeed hostile, to the power that would shape and rule the new age, namely, industrial capitalism served by applied science. Goethe, it is true, was keenly interested in science and his Faust found salvation in a work of engineering. But he was not a typical Romantic.[1] Romanticism was but one element of his comprehensive genius. That is to say, Romanticism had no vital relation to the forces which were fashioning the future Europe and the cosmopolitan civilisation it would spread over the globe.

As the century advanced Romanticism succumbed to the victorious advance of a positivism often brutally materialist. The transformation begun by Feuerbach and completed by Marx of Hegel's dialectical idealism into a dialectical materialism is representative of the process.

We look back to Victorian England as a Christian, if narrowly Protestant, country. Its Christianity, however, did not extend below the lower middle class. Only in the country did it embrace the labourers. " The middle classes," wrote the Census of 1851, " have augmented rather than diminished that devotional sentiment and strictness of attention to religious services by which, for several centuries, they have so eminently been distinguished. With the upper classes, too, the subject of religion has obtained of late a marked degree of notice, and a regular church attendance is now ranked amongst the recognised proprieties of life."

[1] Nor was Beethoven a Romantic. His place in music is analogous to Michelangelo's in the visual arts. Like him, this master of music was in the noblest and most comprehensibly human sense a classical artist, looking back on baroque art as the classical Michelangelo looked forward to it.

The comic touch of patronage is significant. The worship of God is regarded as something the upper classes patronise to adorn their position, a " recognised propriety." There is nothing here of the genuine religious attitude, the creature's humble service of His Creator. Such a " religion " could not endure. " But," the report continues, " while the labouring myriads of our country have been multiplying with our multiplied material prosperity, it cannot . . . be stated that a corresponding increase has occurred in the attendance of this class in our religious edifices. In our cities and large towns it is observable how absolutely insignificant a portion of the congregation is composed of artisans. . . . Perhaps in youth they . . . receive the elements of a religious education ; but no sooner do they mix in the active world of labour, than, subjected to the constant action of opposing influences, they soon become as utter strangers to religious ordinances as the people in a heathen country." [1] That is to say, the urban proletariate, already the majority of the nation, had lost contact with Christianity or religion of any kind.

As the nineteenth century advanced, the countries of Western Europe became increasingly urbanised and industrialised. Their proletariates were as irreligious as the British. And unlike the latter they were not merely indifferent but actively hostile to religion.

Consider the great thinkers of Europe from the Revolution onwards, the philosophers, scientists, poets, historians, economists, artists. Only a minority have professed any form of " orthodox " Christianity.

After death the body survives, under favourable conditions, for a considerable period. And the dead mollusc leaves its shell behind it. So it has been with the corpse of Christendom. Throughout the nineteenth century and to a considerable extent down to the present cataclysm, traditional institutions, social and political, of Christian Europe, more in one country than in another, but many in all, have survived the decease of the spirit that built them up. Much also of Christian morality and of the classical culture. It is only in recent years that Christian ethics have been publicly attacked and

[1] Quoted from J. L. and B. Hammond, *The Age of the Chartists*, p. 217, by Cyril Hudson, and M. B. Reckitt, *The Church and the World*, Vol. III, pp. 58-9.

have been rejected by influential leaders of thought with
the approval of large masses of the people.   And only the novel
totalitarian dictatorships have denounced the fundamental laws
of justice and charity, as they have been hitherto accepted,
if most imperfectly practised, by Christendom and the
civilisation which immediately followed its demise.   And it
is only of recent years that a classical education has become
the specialised education of a diminishing minority of students.
Conservative countries such as Britain, Scandinavia, and Spain
have even retained the state establishment of a Christian
Church.   But no European nation has been a society of
convinced Christian believers.   As the years have passed even
the external profession of Christianity has been progressively
discarded or nullified.   A century ago the Tractarians in
England, the defenders of Catholicism abroad, knew that
Christendom, the organic religion-culture of Europe, was dead.
They knew that whatever the statistics of denominational
allegiance might affirm, Christians were faced with the triumphant advance of an antichristian secularism gathering force
with every decade and effecting a rapid conquest of Western
civilisation.   Until the Revolution, the Christian religion-
culture, though it had long been sickly and senile, was still
a living organism.   Since the Revolution it has been dead.
And its corpse has been decomposing ever since.

Under these conditions there could be no question of a
Catholic culture or of a Catholic art expressing a collective
vision of Catholic truth.   Without the support of such collective insight the insight of even the most gifted individual
artist, whether in letters or some art in the stricter sense, was
obscured, or crippled in its execution.   It could achieve far
less and its sphere of influence was comparatively small.

Catholic art degenerated for the most part into a commercialised production of lifeless sentimentalities.   " Catholic
repository next door to Woolworth's " ; the notice put up in
a certain church porch informed us with a truth beyond its
intention.

In England the artistic offspring of the Romantic movement, the Gothic revival which had already begun in the
eighteenth century, gathered strength during the first half
of the nineteenth.   Pugin, a Catholic inspired by passionate
devotion to an idealised medievalism and in revolt against

THE CHOIR, LIVERPOOL CATHEDRAL:
ARCHITECT, SIR GILES GILBERT SCOTT

The Anglican Cathedral at Liverpool was designed by a Catholic youth of twenty. When finished, it will be 619 feet long with an area of 101,000 square feet, being the largest church in Britain, unless the Catholic Cathedral in Liverpool is completed earlier.

THE WINTER OF CATHOLIC ART:

CHRIST AND SAINT VERONICA, BY A. CARLI, THE LUXEMBOURG, PARIS

*Has the sculptor invested the sacred incident with its full divine significance? Should the almost cruel pathos which
pervades the figure of Christ be the dominant note? Typical of bad 19th-century Catholic Art.*

the squalor and secularism of contemporary building, struggled to revive the vanished glory of Gothic architecture. But the financial resources at his disposal were utterly insufficient. And, what was more fatal, he lacked executive craftsmen who possessed as a matter of course a collective vision of the significant form which had informed the Gothic religion-culture and the inherited technique which had embodied it. Therefore his work is disappointing and looks better in his designs than in their execution. It is true that this tour de force, continued over several generations by a group of Gothic enthusiasts, has revived a far more adequate knowledge of the medieval technique. This has enabled such architects as Sir Giles Gilbert Scott in England and Ralph Adams Cram in America, to erect Gothic buildings which are not mere copies of medieval Gothic but original variations upon its theme, buildings, moreover, equal in quality to much medieval Gothic and more satisfactory than some of it. Such is Sir Giles' nave at Downside, as I have already said, superior to the nave of Wells Cathedral and his Anglican cathedral at Liverpool. But this revived Gothic is nevertheless a tour de force, confined to an unrepresentative minority. And the vast majority of modern Gothic churches are completely without merit.

Another section of English Catholics in that " Second Spring," which alas has proved a St. Martin's Summer, turned towards the baroque culture. The Oratory was their centre. And the London Oratory is on the whole a satisfactory example of modern baroque though the exterior is too formally classical. There was bitter hostility between these two schools. Pugin on the one hand, Faber on the other, treated his preference as little less than a matter of religious principle. Had the antagonists perceived that Gothic and baroque were two phases of the same culture and inspired by the same spirit, and that, moreover, the Gothic as opposed to the classical, they might have exchanged the unnecessary and barren strife for a fruitful collaboration. Pugin might have employed his genius in erecting churches of a Gothic baroque in which Wren's work was continued and rendered Catholic. He might have built an Oratory which would have exemplified that domed Gothic of which I have long dreamed but which until the recent erection of a cathedral at Haarlem, has never been built. This, however, was hardly

11

to be expected in an England whose popular critic, Ruskin, was exalting Gothic to the skies and denouncing baroque as the revival of classical paganism..

The Continent does not seem to have produced better Christian art than England. Nothing could be imagined more tawdry than the decorations of the average continental church. And for the shrine of Lourdes Catholic France could produce nothing better than an example of Gothic inferior to Pugin's most unsuccessful work.

In an age devoid of an organic culture, because it lacked a religion to fashion it, art and literature were uprooted from the social soil. They lost contact with the people and could not appeal to any collective insight either to understand their message or to assist their work by subordinate labour. They were forced to depend solely on the private abilities and insights of individuals supported at best by sectional groups, often by small coteries.

As the gulf between the artist and the people widened, art became more dilettante and esoteric until it finally reached the unintelligibility of a purely private idiom. Painting bearing no kind of resemblance to what it purports to depict, books written in such private languages as are employed by Joyce and Gertrude Stein and on occasion by the Sitwells, have been the climax of this esotericism. To-day collective pseudo-religions have arisen inspiring pseudo-cultures which are but disciplined barbarisms and finding expression in an art and literature which, if once more popular, have no more worth than the ideologies they express. The best modern architecture is an architecture of naked utility and unadorned engineering, honest and powerful but bleak and devoid of charm.

If such have been, and are, the art and literature of the modern world, little could be expected from the art and literature of a depressed and often oppressed minority, expressing, moreover, what appeared, even at times to the temptation of sensitive Catholics, a lost cause and an impossible loyalty. Catholics have been fighting desperately a rearguard action against the superior forces of an advancing secularism. Their foes, on the other hand, have pressed forward with the confidence that the present is with them and the future their own. They stand for progress, for the new

world, the Christians, above all these most intransigent
Christians, the Catholics, for reaction and the vanished world
of the past. This alone is a justification and guarantee of
their victory. For progress is truth and future happiness,
reaction falsehood, the misery of the past. For a time Protestant Christians sought to combine traditionalism in religion
with confidence in secular progress. They desired the
Victorian combination of a Puritan Sunday and a pagan
week. But the latter prevailed over the former and Liberal
Protestantism proved a surrender to secular humanism.
Catholics, on the contrary, I mean of course Catholics fully
conscious of their religion, were thoroughgoing conservatives,
straight line regressives as opposed to the straight line progressives. In face of the intolerant continental Liberalism
which attempted to use the state for the educational destruction
of Catholicism and from time to time actively persecuted
the religious orders, the Popes and the Episcopate under
their command clung desperately to whatever yet remained
of the ancien régime. They were blind to the impossibility
of keeping Italy in Catholic obedience by the Austrian bayonets
of Metternich. Neither did they perceive how little reliance
could be placed on the belated conversion of aristocracies who
looked to the Church for protection from revolutionary con-
fiscation or guillotine.

On the other hand, the few Catholics who wished to come
to terms with the Liberal state, men such as Lammenais,
Lacordaire and Rosmini, failed to perceive that continental
Liberalism would make no terms with the Church except
those offered by the wolf to the lamb. Its leaders were
determined to destroy her influence over the European peoples.
No one seems to have advocated the only policy that had any
hope of success, the formation of Catholics everywhere into
a bloc opposed equally to both parties, the absolutists and
the anticlerical Liberals, and advocating a genuinely Liberal
and Christian policy, such as that put forward in recent times
by the Popolari in Italy and by the Spanish followers of
Gil Robles.

Catholic support of political reaction went hand in hand
until the accession of Leo XIII, with an attitude of rigid
traditionalism in regard to the many questions lying beyond
the sphere of defined dogma, and in which varying degrees

of human fallibility are involved. It was in fact impossible
to work out immediate answers to the host of novel problems
arising from a novel situation, social and economic problems,
problems of Biblical criticism and problems raised by scientific
discovery, for example, the bearing upon religion of Darwinian
evolution.

Under these conditions the reply was everywhere a non
possumus. The errors of modern thought were condemned
but nothing was done to show how Catholic doctrine satisfied
what was true in it or met the new problems raised. The
nineteenth century was the Maccabean epoch of Catholic
history. Catholics were engaged in the desperate attempt to
hold back the advancing hordes of secularism, forces of overwhelming strength, as the Maccabees had held back the forces
of Hellenism which threatened to destroy the Jewish religion.

The Maccabees could not finally overcome Hellenism. It
returned upon them supported by the arms of Rome. Such
men as Philo perceived that what was true and valuable in it
must be incorporated by Judaism and employed in the service
of its revealed truth. And this was accomplished by the
Christian fulfilment of Judaism. Such thinkers as Newman
saw that a merely negative attitude to modern secular thought
was not enough and that a sympathetic criticism must disengage
from it the truth it contained. For this he was held suspect.
And in fairness it must be said that the task whose necessity
he saw could not at that time have been successfully accomplished. Experience alone and the advance of knowledge
could show what in modern speculation and practice is true
and valuable. Time was required, for example, to distinguish
between the scientific fact of transformist evolution and a false
and irreligious philosophical misinterpretation of it. Only
when the negative credulity which to this day holds captive
rationalist critics of scripture has been abandoned, will it be
possible to work out a sober Biblical criticism avoiding the
opposite credulities and accepting frankly the obvious fact that
lack of evidence makes it impossible to answer many questions
concerning the date and authorship of Biblical writings.

Meanwhile, the Catholic, like the Jewish, Maccabees, held
fast the citadel of religious truth. Both wars, however, gave
birth to the evils inevitably attendant upon such conflicts for
ultimate values, bitter intolerance on both sides, and among

the defenders of religion self-satisfied and arrogant Pharisees and idolaters of the external law. The heroic resistance of the Maccabees under God's providence saved His revelation and prepared the way for Christ. But it also produced the enemies of Christ as they are depicted in the Gospel. In a subtler form the same is true of the Catholic Maccabean era. For evidence of these evils we have only to read the life of Newman.

Under these conditions of desperate and bitter warfare an organic Catholic culture and its art were impossible. The life of the Church was concentrated upon the struggle for her existence. That, like her Jewish predecessor, she could not be slain did not make the struggle less intense, the situation less grave. For it was through an heroic and a losing battle that God would in fact preserve her life.

Nevertheless, the final solution could not be the complete victory of the progressives or the regressives. Mankind does not advance in a straight line. Nor does it simply fall back or remain stationary. Through action and reaction born of the interacting factors, permanence and change, humanity advances on a spiral path,[1] and in particular the spiral is determined by the interaction between the vertical and the horizontal movements of the human mind, between transcendentalism and immanentism, theocentrism and humanism. Criticising the philosophy of Marx I have pointed out elsewhere that the dialectical progress of thought must advance through the thesis dialectical idealism (Hegel) and its antithesis dialectical materialism (Marx) to the synthesis dialectical ideal realism. Here I would maintain that the historical dialectic operating over a wider extent of history and on more comprehensive lines also requires an advance through the thesis of transcendentalism, the vertical movement, as it extends from the Christian era to the Renaissance and beyond it to the downfall of baroque through the antithesis of immanentism, the horizontal movement extending from the Renaissance to the present day and still predominant, to a synthesis of transcendentalism and immanentism, the religion-culture of the future.

This synthesis, it may be replied, has already been effected by the medieval culture and its baroque continuation. Certainly. My essay has attempted to show this. But the

---

[1] See Wilson, *Birth of Language*.

synthesis was necessarily incomplete and it was not fully organic. Even its baroque presentation did not sufficiently realise the immanental and humanist factor. The ideal synthesis, as it is depicted for thought in the Summa and for imagination on the roof of the Sixtine chapel, remained largely an unfulfilled ideal. This also I have sought to make clear.

The ideal could not in fact be realised until the horizontal and immanentist movement had been developed to the utmost, had unfolded its possibilities, been made aware of its inherent limitations and provided the material of a more comprehensive and more organic synthesis.

The old Catholic religion-culture of Europe is dead and is being carried out to burial. It cannot be raised from the tomb. Its world year is over, has ended with midwinter. For its matter the inheritance of classical culture no longer exists. It has been destroyed, overwhelmed by a vast influx of new knowledge, by the scientific mass civilisation of the modern world.

The union of form and matter which composes a religion-culture is as mortal as that which composes a living organism, plant or animal, even the embodied life of man. Those of us who prize the religion-culture which has perished are assured that its values will survive imperishably. But they will survive in a wider context and in novel and strange forms. The inheritance of the Eastern cultures must be incorporated and the scientific achievement and knowledge of modern man. And before this is accomplished we are likely to pass through a long period of uncultured mass civilisation, beneath some form or other of totalitarian despotism.

The form of the Catholic religion-culture now dead is immortal. For it is God's revealed truth which, therefore, cannot become obsolete. Nor are we to expect a further revelation of truth beyond that already given by Truth Incarnate. Nevertheless, the same form embodied in the matter of a new culture will not present altogether the same appearance. The development of dogma proves that the possibilities and implications of revealed truth are realised gradually and progressively. And this development has been largely conditioned by the cultural and social material to which this deposit of truth has been applied by the human thought which the Holy Spirit has employed to interpret revelation. So it will be in future also. The form and the matter of a religion-culture are so closely united in a single organism that the form of one matter cannot be in every respect identical with the form of another. Catholic truth differently embodied will present a different aspect, though the later aspect once displayed will be seen to have been implied in the earlier.

Can we in any respect forecast this future development ? Though we cannot see the detailed features of the future synthesis we can, I believe, discern its general character. It must incorporate and subordinate the horizontal movement, the immanentism represented by modern scientific civilisation and the social institutions it is in process of fashioning. For this the immanental aspect of the Christian religion, God's presence and work in nature and man, must be brought into greater prominence than in the past. This immanental operation, however, is, as we have seen, appropriated to the Holy Ghost. We are therefore to look for a dispensation of the Holy Spirit such as was promised by Our Lord to Lucie Christine. She relates in her Journal : " I saw, by a divine illumination, that, just as the Holy Ghost is the term of the Divine processions, so also He must be the term of the Divine manifestations. . . . In the latter days the Holy Ghost will make His heat and light more strongly felt in the hearts of the faithful. . . . I also thought I understood how the cult of the Sacred Heart of Jesus which offers us Divine Love in the heart of the Man-God, prepares souls for that diffusion of the eternal and personal love of God which will in one supreme effort include the whole world in its all powerful embrace. . . . I understood that time had thus to be divided into epochs corresponding to the Three Persons of the Adorable Trinity." [1] We should observe that Lucie Christine saw in the cult of the Sacred Heart a preparation for this age of the Spirit. At that time the original and theocentric meaning of the devotion as a cult of the Interior of Jesus as the supreme Priest and Adorer, had been lost sight of. So understood the devotion to the Sacred Heart is an even more fitting introduction to an age of adoring love, an age of interior prayer, when the souls of believers will be one with the Interior of Jesus in Its worship of the Triune Godhead, and the Spirit

[1] *Spiritual Journal of Lucie Christine*, English translation, p. 144.

that fashioned His Interior and dwelt in it as in His holiest shrine, will make known His presence and operation in Christ's members by the contemplative adoration He will inspire.

In this dispensation of the Spirit His work as the " soul " of the Church, continuing, as it does, His work as the " soul " of nature, will be understood more widely and more clearly and accomplished more perfectly in the Church than ever before. Catholic truth will be grasped from within, not only by a contemplative minority but generally by the members of the Church. Doctrines will no longer be accepted solely on authority and stored unused in the mind. They will be vitally assimilated and practically lived. That is to say, contemplation will be spread widely throughout the Church and with it mystical experience.

The power latent in the Christian religion will be released by a living understanding of Catholic truth. It will drive the machine of modern scientific civilisation, at present incapable of functioning, as it ought to function, if it is to serve human happiness which is and can be found only in the service of God, a machine vastly more complicated than the simple apparatus which Catholicism had to drive when the Roman Empire became Catholic. Contemplative prayer alone can achieve this understanding and release this latent power.

" Would God all the Lord's people were prophets," Moses exclaimed. In this third kingdom of the Spirit all the Lord's people will be contemplatives. Only thus will they be able to vanquish the assaults of a sceptical reasoning and the power of the naturalist and humanist energeticism which in one form or another has arisen on the ruins of a confident rationalism. Joachim of Flora,[1] who caught a premature vision of the Third Kingdom, envisaged it as a kingdom of monks and nuns. This would, of course, be the end of the world. He should rather have seen it as a kingdom of contemplatives, contemplatives of every status and honourable mode of life.

Another Catholic devotion developed during the Baroque period is preparing this order of contemplative prayer. It is the devotion to St. Joseph, the Saint of the hidden life. St. Theresa, whose ecstatic mysticism contributed so largely to

[1] He was not a formal heretic. On the contrary, his cultus has been sanctioned.

create the spiritual background of the baroque religion-culture, fostered devotion to St. Joseph as the patron and exemplar of the contemplative life. He has been officially declared the protector of the Universal Church. He is not, like St. Peter, her protector *in foro externo*, if one may so put it, but inasmuch as the Church is the body composed of all who are united with the Head by the charity whose flower is mystical union. It is in this " Inwardness," to borrow a term from Kierkegaard, that her strength lies. And it is as the Patron of that " inwardness " that St. Joseph protects her.

We may therefore look to him to assist at this rebirth of Christ's mystical body, as he assisted at the birth of His physical, and to cherish it by obtaining a wide diffusion by the Holy Spirit of that contemplative charity without which action is barren. Since St. Joseph is patron of contemplative prayer and as such of the Church of which contemplative prayer is the life-blood, we may trust that devotion to him practised with this aim will hasten the advent of the Kingdom of the Spirit, the kingdom of contemplatives, and with it the inauguration of another cycle of religion-culture, fulfilling that which has passed away.

When a powerful state was the sole defence of religion and culture against the anarchy of warring chiefs, and the masses were incapable of a truly individual conversion, the Church of necessity supported the Catholic state, and for the greater good of Christendom her rulers often turned a blind eye to acts of oppression committed by monarchs who were after all the indispensable guardians of Christian civilisation. To-day the position has changed completely. The strong national state, far from being a bulwark against anarchy, has become itself the source of an international anarchy which threatens to destroy civilisation. And even if the present epoch of war is followed by an international order strong enough to preserve peace, it will be some totalitarian regime of whatever complexion, at best no genuine friend, at worst the declared foe of Christianity. For the sovereign claim of genuine religion is incompatible with the self-deification of the totalitarian state as man's highest end.

Under these conditions religion must be revived and upheld by the free co-operation of men and women who hold it with a strong and intelligent conviction because they see its truth from within and who draw from the profound source of a supernatural life power to resist the force of a natural vitalism patronised by the state. Such, however, will be the contemplatives of whom I have just spoken and that life, the Love life of God Himself, " shed abroad " in their hearts by the Holy Ghost dwelling within them. Not by concordat, still less by establishment, will the Church of God vanquish a rebellious humanism, but by the refusal of men and women led and strengthened by the Spirit to co-operate with a godless state which refuses their right to the free exercise of their religion and free obedience to its precepts.

The religion that inspired the baroque culture and art was, as we have seen, a contemplative religion led by mystics. That mystical religion of an élite, foreshadowed, I believe, the mystical religion spread throughout Christ's entire body for which I look as the future kingdom of the Spirit. We should expect the autumn of one religion-culture to prophesy and prepare the spring of the next. The flower-buds of evergreen trees that will open in spring are formed the previous autumn.

" If winter comes can spring be far behind ? " The quotation is hackneyed but true nevertheless. The spring Shelley foresaw was the spring of a purely natural and humanist culture, of pantheistic faith, and the wind that stirred his song was, he thought, but the immanent life of the universe, a world-soul. But the spring for which he longed and which he depicted in his humanist Apocalypse, *Prometheus Unbound*, will in truth be the advent of a supernatural kingdom of God in redeemed humanity, an advent to which the future religion-culture will be a stage closer than the religion-culture that has perished. And the wind which inspired his noblest music was, though he knew it not, the Spirit whose coming in power will effect this further and more perfect establishment of God's Kingdom.

Already in the winter there are signs of the approaching spring. Catholic action is associating the laity with the Apostolic work of the Church. The organisations of Catholic workers are bringing the Catholic religion as a living faith to the urban proletariate, hitherto the nursery of every antichristian movement. For we must not expect the revival of religion to begin with the peasants. Though rather from a tenacious conservatism than enlightened conviction they kept their traditional religion longer than the uprooted workers of the city, they will be equally tenacious of the irreligion or pseudo-religion that is taking possession of them. The peasants, the Pagani, clung to heathenism so long that they gave their name to it. The last recorded instance of the pagan worship of classical antiquity was the worship of Apollo by the rustics of Monte Casino which St. Benedict's drastic action brought to a close. It was the dispossessed and rootless urban workers and the petty bourgeoisie, the classes which are likely to dominate the mass civilisation of the immediate future, who had welcomed Christianity. So, I believe it will be again.

Beyond these more active movements is the liturgical movement. It is not the ritualism of ecclesiastical dilettantes but a revival of the corporate worship which expresses and fosters the solidarity of Catholics and whose absence in Gothic and still more in baroque religion was so deplorable. Where it spreads it will effect that union of convinced believers which alone can defeat the foes of religion. If it proceeds on the right lines it will spread a knowledge and interior understanding of the spiritual and intellectual truth enshrined in the liturgical texts. It should create a conscious communion of praise that will reply to human self-deification by practising and teaching the humble worship of HIM " who is " by men " who are not."

All this must produce a revival of contemplative prayer, which should lead to genuine and intelligent worship and without which no exterior Catholic action can be fruitful. Of its nature hidden, its extent and growth cannot be determined. But I am confident that, as the Spirit works among Christians He will increase the number and the holiness of contemplative souls. Moreover, I look to this interior communion in the praise of God and in contemplative prayer to bring about in God's time and manner the reunion of Christians. For the Christian bodies at present are like islands visibly sundered by stretches of sea but united below the surface by the submerged land whence they rise. That land is the invisible communion of souls in grace. If that communion is better realised by the growth of grace and the deepening of the spiritual life through interior prayer, charity between those aware of this invisible communion must increase correspondingly and the desire for external communion be fostered. Moreover, an interior and spiritual understanding of doctrine will, I am convinced, do much to remove misconceptions of Catholic dogma and practices and to show that they are organically linked with truth already held by the non-catholic.

As we have seen, the concluding phase of the Catholic religion-culture, the baroque culture, was an age of extreme individualism, checked only by the development of the legal and juridical aspects of the Church.   This individualism was continued and even carried further in the nineteenth century. In the Catholic Church the baroque combination of religious individualism with a strong ecclesiastical government survived. In the Protestant Churches individualism was unrestrained. And in secular politics, above all in England and the United States, individualism reduced to a minimum the authority and interference of the state.   Anarchy was prevented by a survival of old traditions and even more by the existence of a powerful public opinion and code of conventions.   So far as the authority of the state is concerned this individualism was justified.   For authority based on the compulsion of physical force should be, as far as possible, restricted.   It should, however, have been replaced by a powerful but free solidarity based on common convictions freely held.   And since the demise of Christendom, this has been wanting.

To-day the pendulum has swung far in the opposite direction.   Individualism has yielded to what may be termed in a wide sense " socialism."   National Socialism, Fascism, and Russian Communism swamp the individual in the mass of a nation or a class.   A national or class solidarity of servile complexion has reduced to a minimum the individual's freedom of action and expression, has repressed his individuality, his consciousness of personal value and rights.   This solidarity is a biological solidarity, not rational, still less spiritual and above reason.   It is the solidarity of the hive or the herd. Therefore it enslaves reason.   The kingdom of the Spirit, as all the signs, not least the liturgical movement, suggest, will realise, as never before, the spiritual solidarity of souls in supernatural union with God, the solidarity of Christ's mystical body.   Above individualism and socialism is the communion of saints. Since this solidarity is spiritual and supernatural it will not sacrifice reason or the individual. On the contrary, it requires the free obedience of his rational will. It is thus a synthesis of individualism and socialism combining and harmonising both. And it is contemplation that will discover and produce this solidarity in the depths of spirit, in its union with God, One in all souls, in His One supernatural life, His One Spirit communicated to all. The Communion of saints is, of course, not new and Christianity has known it from the beginning. But the power of the Spirit, operative through contemplative prayer and charity, will realise it more widely and more perfectly than it has been realised in the past. This solidarity in the Spirit will be the ιoundation and substance, consciously apprehended and vitally understood, of prayer and of action.

The movements mentioned just now, encouraging though they are, cannot at present fashion an organic religion-culture. For they are confined, as yet, to a minority even of Catholics. Therefore, also, they cannot achieve a new Catholic art. But the spiritual impulse which has given birth to them has not altogether lacked artistic expression. A Catholic art has made its appearance which is not content to reproduce the past, however skilfully, or even make variations upon its work. It employs a new and a contemporary·idiom. It is tentative and uncertain, liable to fail badly. And the idiom it employs is too often the bare and stark idiom of a mass civilisation.

In his interesting book on the architecture and furnishings of modern churches,[1] the late Dom Roulin has depicted several churches which resemble anything but a place of Catholic worship. At Aix-la-Chapelle there is a church which is a factory without smoke issuing from its chimney tower and provided with an altar.[2] There is another ecclesiastical factory at Bale though it is less stark than the former.[3] Prague has given us a church so bare that it might be the hall attached to an institution, to house occasional meetings.[4] At Cork there is a church like a gymnasium,[5] at Seraing a garage, as Dom Roulin truly calls it,[6] and at Amlwch a church which he justly compares to a hangar.[7] St. Charles' Church at Lucerne is an auditorium.[8]

---

[1] *Nos Eglises.* [2] *Ibid.,* 107. [3] *Ibid.,* 365.
[4] *Ibid.,* 108. [5] *Ibid.,* 167. [6] *Ibid.,* 229.
[7] *Ibid.,* 318. [8] *Novocento Sacro,* 7a.

Less ugly, but distinctly bizarre, is the church of St. Jeanne D'Arc, recently erected at Nice, which, moreover, has distinctly the air of a mosque.[1]

But there are other churches which are both beautiful and original, continuing traditions of Gothic or Romanesque in new material such as reinforced concrete and adapted to modern conditions. Such is the beautiful Lutheran church of Engelbrekts at Stockholm. It makes a most effective use of the elliptic arch, and though based on Gothic, achieves a distinct novelty of style and is adorned with fine symbolic carvings.[2] A concrete church at Seattle,[3] also based on Gothic, has refashioned it to suit the new material. It makes impressive use of vertical lines. At Villemomble near Paris [4] and at Moreuil [5] imposing concrete spires are original adaptations of Gothic. The former has an indefinable suggestion of the Wren spire, though it has no actual feature in common with it. The Church of St. Thomas at Chicago [6] has a fine façade framed by classical pilasters. And the Church of St. Pierre du Chailet [7] at Paris, has a magnificent portal of Romanesque type decorated by carved scenes from the Apostle's life.

The Church of St. Louis at Frankenthal [8] and the church at Hauerstein [9] are successful modernisations of Romanesque. Both have fine reredoses set off by the economy of ornament.

The Italian Church of San Felice da Cantalice [10] represents an aspiration from the bare factory style towards a genuine architecture of simple dignity whose inspiration is not alien to that of the early Byzantine and Romanesque churches. The Church of Cristo Re at Rome [11] is interesting. The exterior is stark, of the factory style. But seen from within the central dome is distinctly baroque in feeling, so that the interior of the church is a piquant combination of the baroque and modern styles. The church certainly fulfils Fokker's criterion of baroque. For it makes an effective use of mass and space. The gigantic Christ in the apse seems to me justified by its effectiveness. The King dominates His palace.

There is evidently a widespread renewal of Catholic art adapting ancient styles, chiefly Romanesque and Gothic, to

[1] *Nos Eglises*, 320-99.
[2] *Ibid.*, 109-10.
[3] *Ibid.*, 143, 164.
[4] *Ibid.*, 139.
[5] *Ibid.*, 139, 175.
[6] *Ibid.*, 149.
[7] *Novocento Sacro*, 44-5.
[8] *Ibid.*, 49.
[9] *Nos Eglises*, 257.
[10] *Novocento Sacro*, 13-14.
[11] *Ibid.*, 24-26.

new material, needs and technique.   It thus corresponds to the intellectual and, even more, the spiritual movement to which it gives artistic expression.   That movement is an attempt to apply the old, the enduring truth of the Christian revelation to the new theoretical and practical material, to the sciences and their uses, to a new social and economic order and by this application to bring out new implications of its content, achieving a deeper understanding of it.   And it will thus guard against the danger of explaining that truth away to suit passing philosophical or supposedly scientific phases of thought. Such a movement surely is the preparation and initiation of the Kingdom of the Spirit, an order opposed alike to modernism and to fundamentalism, to anarchy and to legalism.

It is perhaps significant that of all this contemporary Catholic art nothing strikes us as truly artistic, save that which continues and reinterprets a traditional style.   So assuredly will it be with the religion of the future.   It will be genuine religion, religion as it has been known in the past, not the mere religiosity of humanism wearing the clothes of religion.

The childhood of medieval man penetrating so deeply the spiritual and the intellectual depths of theology and philosophy clothed its intuitions of this central truth in the naïve garb imposed by an unscientific and uncritical view of the world and of human history.   Rebellious adolescence has impatiently rejected together with this unscientific surface the profound truth within it.   It will be for man's future maturity to reaffirm the religious and philosophical truth held by the simple and pure vision of the medieval child while disengaging it from the unscientific setting and uncritical presentation of intellectual childhood, and placing it in the setting provided by the scientific and critical knowledge of the adult intelligence.   The medieval child was wise in the centre, ignorant and stupid on the surface of truth.   The modern adolescent is ignorant and stupid in the centre, learned on the surface.   The future adult will be wise in the centre, learned and intelligent on the surface.   The abiding and immutable truth of metaphysics and revealed religion must be reclad in new garments woven by a scientific and historical knowledge incomparably vaster than was ever before possessed by man.

Modernism essayed the task but failed. For instead of harmonising the discoveries of scientific and historical research with the truths of philosophy and religion it distorted and largely rejected the latter to make them conform with unsound philosophies of subjectivism and immanence and with the usurpations of scientists in a territory beyond their jurisdiction.

And the modernists, reacting against the positive credulities of fundamentalism, rushed headlong into excesses of negative credulity. They accepted as the proved result of Biblical criticism what was too often enforcement upon the evidence or lack of it, of *a priori* canons imposed by a negative creed or philosophy assumed from the outset. Where modernism failed a sounder procedure must succeed. And applied science must be redeemed from the service of Mammon and Mars to the service of Christ.

The more perfect balance between immanentism, God in creatures, and transcendence, God in Himself above creatures, that will distinguish the synthesis and the religion-culture of the Spirit will observe better than it has been observed hitherto the rule of Christian appraisement and morality formulated at the outset of this essay—a maximum of detachment, a maximum of appreciation. For the detachment corresponds to the Divine transcendence and the vertical movement to transcendent Deity, the appreciation to the Divine immanence and the horizontal movement to creatures and thereby to God in creatures. Detached from all things save God, appreciating all things for His Presence in them and in the measure of His Presence and communication, the soul in the Kingdom of the Spirit will rule and enjoy creatures in the right way by an entire surrender to their Creator. Pagan religion and its culture were immanental, the horizontal movement with little transcendence, a worship of vital forces. Christianity hitherto has pre-eminently represented transcendence, the vertical movement with a relatively inadequate appreciation of immanence, of the horizontal movement. This was inevitable, in fact salutary, if the *distinctively* religious movement and factor, the vertical movement and the transcendence it seeks, were to attain their rightful supremacy.

After the thesis the antithesis. Modern secularism, often miscalled neopaganism, is more exclusively immanental and horizontal than the paganism defeated by Christianity. We await the synthesis, the harmony and balance of both movements, the horizontal and the vertical, of immanence and transcendence. It has been adumbrated already by the highest achievements of the Catholic past, by the philosophy of St. Thomas and the art of Michelangelo, and was realised by baroque culture to a larger extent, though so imperfectly, than by any previous religion-culture in human history. For the advent of this genuinely new order which, nevertheless, like every new order that deserves the name, will complete and fulfil the old, we must hope and pray. It will come.

For centuries the shrine of Our Lady of Walsingham has been an historical memory. Now once again pilgrims visit her image erected in a medieval chapel, where, it is said, they took off their shoes to walk barefoot the remaining mile to the shrine and to which, there is some reason to think, a hermitage was attached. The shrine has been spared the tawdry ornament and commercialised vulgarity which made Huysmans conclude that the devil, the lord of ugliness, had been permitted to take possession of the architecture and ornaments of Lourdes. The road to the chapel is a quiet country lane shaded with trees, and lined on one side by a hedgerow. On the other a stream flows down beneath the trees, the water symbol of the Holy Spirit, " the waters of Shiloah that go softly," the " flow of the river making glad the city of God." Within the chapel, an attractive example of Decorated architecture, near an altar of medieval fashion, is seated Our Lady's image. It is too small for its canopy and is not superficially beautiful. " Non est species neque decor," there is no comeliness or charm in that expressionless face with heavy eyelids. But let us look carefully, and allow the image, as every work of art should be allowed, to speak to us in its own language. We become aware of an inner beauty more impressive than outward grace. That expressionless countenance expresses what is beyond expression. It is the countenance of one whose spirit dwells in a region beyond emotion and thought, the centre of which mystical writers speak. Mary is beyond joy and sorrow. For her spirit is in God, and she knows as He knows, receiving His knowledge. No longer the Mother of Sorrows nor yet of the human joy of the crib, she understands the secret counsel

12

of God to whose accomplishment Calvary and Bethlehem alike ministered. Therefore her peace, the central peace of God, is beyond the changes of earthly experience. And the inscrutability of that illegible countenance is the inscrutability of the Divine Will made known to her.

Troubled by a serious difficulty in regard to God's government of the world, I spoke of it once to a priest versed in the ways of the interior life. Just then his telephone bell rang. " While I answer it, worship the inscrutable will of God." He returned, " Well, Father, what answer can you give ? " " Have you done as I asked ? " " Yes, Father." " That *is* your answer." It is the answer given by Our Lady of Walsingham to those who bring their troubles and difficulties to her shrine. If we will let her, she will unite us to the inscrutable Will into which she has entered. Our Lady of Walsingham is the Queen of Contemplatives. She will introduce us into the silence of her adoration, the silence of God. And the silence is full of power, pregnant with the spiritual forces which can create a new and a supernatural world. Our contemporaries worship power, the natural energy that drives machines, and on a higher level is the life-force of animate things. Before the new world they desire can be born they must learn the lesson Our Lady of Contemplation would teach us, that the power which alone can bring that new world to birth is supernatural, the power of God, the power that is also rest and silence, the power of contemplative prayer. In that sense rather than in impressive statistics of conversions will the saying prove true that when England goes to Walsingham, England will return to the Church. When the world goes thus to Walsingham, it will return to the Church. Nay, it will become the Church.

It is good that interior prayer rather than visible miracles has been the special grace given at Walsingham and that beside Our Lady's shrine is the newly erected chapel of the Holy Ghost. If we are looking for the kingdom of the Holy Ghost, the reign of contemplatives and the birth of a new religion-culture of their fashioning, we shall do well to pray for it in spirit, if we cannot in body, at the shrine of Walsingham, the shrine of Our Lady of Contemplation.

The mystery honoured at Walsingham is and always has been the Incarnation of the Word, the conception of Christ's physical body in Mary's womb. The contemplation expressed

by her second image and taught by the Spirit is the womb in
which Christ's mystical body will be born again to a new and
a vaster life from the death of historic Christendom.

In this dark contemplation beyond feeling and thought
the spirit of man is touched and made fruitful by the Spirit
of God. From these Divine depths the kingdom of the
Spirit, the manifestation of the corporate Christ and the
sanctification of the entire world of nature and of art will be
born. " Ex utero ante luciferum genui te." " From the womb
before the star of dawn have I begotten Thee." Over these
dim waters the Creative Spirit is brooding, fashioning the
embryo of His new world. The aspiration of mankind to-day
is looking for this new world, though mistakenly from man's
unaided endeavour. It will be satisfied by the new world
wrought by the Holy Ghost.

" But this surely is Dawnism, the Dawnism which is the
delusive faith of the Liberal Progressive and the Communist ? "
Yes, it is Dawnism. But it is not theirs. They expect the
dawn from human knowledge and effort. Their opponents say
it will never come. I expect it from the grace of God. They
proclaim that man is at last entering into his kingdom. Their
adversaries know the kingdom is God's not man's. But
forgetting the Lord's prayer and St. John's prophetic vision
they confine the kingdom to heaven. I believe the kingdom
of God will descend to man on earth and be the kingdom of
God in man, the kingdom of a deified humanity. It has
descended already in Christ and in the Saints who have followed
Him. It will descend in His entire body. And as in the
Saints, so in all believers it will be the charity of contemplative
prayer, the reign of the Spirit in contemplative souls and in
their corresponding action and achievement.

In an article in the *Tablet*, 10th May 1941, Mr. Hollis
writes, " It is hardly an exaggeration to say . . . that human
history has been but the story of man throwing off one tyranny
only to find he has put himself under a new tyranny in its
place, exchanged kings for feudal barons, territorial magnates
for capitalists, capitalists for commissars." Certainly. But
what if commissars were replaced by contemplatives ? The
exchange will, I believe, be effected by the reign of the Spirit.
The rulers, the " commissars," will not necessarily be contemplatives, though history knows of saintly kings. But

they will be powerless to oppress the contemplatives, the freemen of the Spirit.

Already Christianity has given man an interior freedom previously unknown. It has only to be extended, and realised externally. In the same article Mr. Hollis shows the value, indeed the necessity, of conservatism, of a traditional order universally accepted. But this order, the order of the traditional religion-culture of Europe has been destroyed. It is as impossible to re-erect it as to put Humpty Dumpty together again after his fall. It must be succeeded by a new order, conservative in as much as it conserves the religious truth and abiding values of the old, but revolutionary in their application to new conditions and new knowledge. And such, I believe, will be the kingdom of the Holy Ghost.

Meanwhile, the world is delivered as a prey to the unleashed forces of animal vitality restrained by no rule of reason or faith, the fitting Nemesis of human pride seeking self-sufficiency. Whatever is rotten, however venerable its antiquity, must perish in the storm. But prayer can take refuge in the sanctuary of Walsingham and there in union with Mary's adoring contemplation ask that the inscrutable will of God, by ways known to Him and to her, may prepare an Epiphany of His Spirit that will defeat these merely natural and human forces. And Catholic art can learn here to express indirectly in the more austere idiom suited to our age and technique what cannot be expressed directly, not like baroque art ecstatic emotion, but the silence of union with God in the depths of spirit. Catholic thought can learn to view Catholic truth inwardly as the organic unfolding of Living Truth incarnate and the fulfilment of all the religious and, by implication, of all the metaphysical truth anywhere disclosed to the human mind. From this centre of vision we can look beyond the thesis of a too exclusively vertical movement, the preoccupation with God and the soul to the neglect of nature and man's secular interests and the antithesis of an exclusive horizontal movement, a pure immanentism and secular humanism, to the synthesis of a vertical movement which takes full account of the horizontal, an adoration of transcendent Godhead which does justice to His immanence in creatures, an organic Christian humanism embracing all human knowledge and art, all natural or otherwise valuable human groups, all human interests. In short, we can look for the new religion-culture, the Kingdom of the Holy Spirit.

So shall man's rebellious adolescence grow to a maturity that will combine the spiritual vision of childhood with the experience and critical reasoning of the adult, the adult grown " to the full age of Christ." For his maturity will be a return to childhood, a spiritual childhood. To advance from adolescence to maturity is to become a child once more. Maturity will not be the childhood of inexperience and scientific ignorance. But to illuminate and explain the adult's knowledge it will possess the simple, direct and keen vision of the child. In a moment of unwonted insight Bertrand Russell caught a glimpse of this truth when he said that man can be saved from the destructiveness of the critical reason only by advancing beyond it to spirit.

It was for this surely that St. Theresa of Lisieux was commissioned to teach her way of spiritual childhood and that God has made it known by inspiring devotion to the teacher throughout the Catholic world. It is children in heart [1] and in the heart's profound wisdom, adults in knowledge and in critical intelligence who shall enter the kingdom of the Spirit.

The contemplation of Our Lady, type and exemplar of the contemplative Church, sees horizontally the ends of becoming, the issues of history. Vertically it scans the depths, or shall we say the heights, of Being, its unmoved transcendence of the process in which It is immanent. Thus her contemplation anticipates the final synthesis of the historical dialectic, the perfect harmony of the horizontal and the vertical movements, of becoming and being, the synthesis, to which the synthesis to be effected by the future religion-culture of the Spirit will be a closer approximation. In this contemplation the Church, after the fashion possible in mortal flesh, will share, more abundantly, I believe, hereafter than hitherto. Contemplation bears the fruit of the past, the bud of the future. It must be understood in the breadth as well as in the height. In the latter it is religion, in the former culture, in both praise. It is the praise of the Divine Glory, Its manifestation, Its service and Its worship.

---

[1] By heart I mean, not feeling, but the central spirit deeper than reasoning, Claudel's *anima*, Pascal's *coeur*.

" Beauty ever ancient yet ever new," as Augustine greeted Thee of old, may we, when this night of tyranny and war or the fear of them, is passed, behold Thy splendour brighter even than it was seen by our fathers. And may it be embodied in a culture and an art fairer than theirs. So shall the Kingdom of the Spirit fulfil the Kingdom of the Son.

In this study of the Catholic religion-culture I have traced three movements still in process. The first of these is the growth of the European mind, from childhood through the schoolboy and the youth to adult maturity. Apparently this movement is rectilinear. But it bends back upon itself. Childhood returns in maturity.

The second is the dialectical movement from the thesis, transcendence, through the antithesis, immanence, to the synthesis, transcendence in and beyond immanence, from the human point of view from the vertical movement, the thesis, through the horizontal, the antithesis, to the vertical-horizontal, the synthesis.

The third is a circular movement, the cycle of the seasons, from the autumn and winter of the classical religion-culture through the spring, summer, autumn and winter of the Catholic religion-culture, to another spring when the age of the Spirit will open.

The interaction of these three movements produces the spiral progress characteristic of human history, as viewed by dialectical ideal realism. Dialectical ideal realism is a synthetic philosophy. It continues the Platonic Aristotelian philosophy employed by the Church and resolves in a higher synthesis the thesis, dialectical idealism, and its antithesis, dialectical materialism. It is a synthesis also of intellectualism and voluntarism, of formalism and energeticism and of transcendence and immanence. It views history synthetically, as it is the product of real and ideal factors : of thought and desire, of knowledge progressively gathered and cumulative practical achievement ; of agents operative in many spheres and on many levels, geographical, economic, social, political, military, racial, national, cultural, scientific, philosophic and religious ; the action and reaction of contrasted, though not contradictory, views of reality and their corresponding attitudes ; instinct, reason and spirit, that is to say the animal, mental, and spiritual lives ; nature and supernature ; appreciation of creatures and detachment from them ; contemplation and action directed to creatures and in and beyond them to God ; man's acquisition of knowledge and God's revelation to man ; human endeavour and the Divine Gift ; the realisation of human possibilities and the Advent of God's Kingdom from above ; man's preparation of a body and the Incarnation therein of the Word.   To display somewhat of this synthesis and thereby of the Catholic vision, has been the purpose of this essay.   It is a prospect of hope, in the Word made Flesh, of spring, when " the rains " of winter are " over and gone," of dawn, when the night is spent, and on the human horizon once more the Divine Sun shall rise.

PRINTED IN GREAT BRITAIN AT
THE UNIVERSITY PRESS
ABERDEEN